# Improving Job Attendance

# Improving
# Job
# Attendance

*John V. Schappi*

The Bureau of National Affairs, Inc., Washington, D.C.

**Library of Congress Cataloging-in-Publication Data**

Schappi, John V.
    Improving job attendance.

    Includes index.
    1. Absenteeism (Labor)—United States.    2. Hours
of labor, Flexible—United States.    3. Job satisfaction—
United States.    I. Title.
HD5115.2.U5S33    1988        658.3'14      87-27638
ISBN 0-87179-535-3

Printed in the United States of America
International Standard Book Number: 0-87179-535-3

# Preface

Restoring America's competitiveness has become today's rallying cry for business and union leaders as well as politicians because it is becoming as vital to the success and survival of individual enterprise as it is to the nation.

The concern to restore competitiveness has escalated as a result of several trends that peaked in the mid-1980s. The balance of trade for U.S.-manufactured products, which as recently as 1981 showed a surplus, ran a deficit of over $100 billion in 1985. By 1986 the United States became the world's largest debtor nation as foreign investment poured in to finance the budget deficit and surging imports.

The causes of these major shifts were years in the making, but they were obscured by the illusion of ever-increasing prosperity. Americans were able to maintain this myth because of a number of changes that had been developing for some time: the growth in two wage-earner families, reductions in the size of families, delays in marriage, and the subsidy of foreign investment.

But in the mid-1980s, we had nearly used up these options for keeping our standard of living rising. Today, more than two-thirds of young families already rely on two wage-earners, the birth rate is no longer falling, and we cannot depend on the rest of the world to lend us money forever.

Some government and business leaders believe the solution lies in enacting protective trade laws and other restrictions. But many increasingly have come to recognize the wisdom of the Pogo comic strip character: "We have met the enemy, and he is us." Since the old options for raising prosperity are no longer available, the best solution is to get U.S. productivity growing again.

Raising productivity takes time and involves complex issues that may seem beyond the reach of the individual manager or union leader. However, since a major first step in improving productivity is to reduce absenteeism, managers' individual efforts can have a demonstrable impact.

Absenteeism disrupts operations and clearly reduces the productivity of the absent worker. It also can be an insidious drain on the productivity of others, since an organization with high absenteeism usually also has low morale and relatively poor performance by those who do report for work. The rate of physical absenteeism usually parallels the extent of on-the-job absenteeism. Fortunately, improving one typically improves the other.

Few of the problems that drain productivity are as clearly identifiable and correctable as absenteeism. Yet monitoring and improving attendance gets relatively little attention. Business management libraries are overflowing with how-to books on improving performance, but there is a dearth of books on how to improve job attendance. This book attempts to fill that gap.

The paucity of literature on the subject does not reflect a lack of concern among managers. The Bureau of National Affairs, Inc. (BNA), my employer for more than 30 years, periodically surveys employers on their attitudes and policies regarding employee discipline. These surveys invariably show that absenteeism and other attendance-related infractions are by far the major ongoing disciplinary problem. In the most recent survey, reported in January 1985, 6 in 10 employers ranked such infractions as their most serious disciplinary issue.* An earlier 1973 survey found that attendance was considered the biggest difficulty by nearly four out of five employers.†

In the labor arbitration cases coming into BNA, attendance is one of the most prevalent topics. Many of these cases wrestle with the difficulties of applying traditional discipline-for-misconduct concepts to attendance problems that may or may not involve deliberate wrongdoing.

Many employers today are looking for alternatives to the traditional discipline-for-misconduct concept. For example, audiences

---

* The Bureau of National Affairs, Inc., "Employee Discipline and Discharge," *Personnel Policies Forum*, Survey No. 139, January 1985 (Washington, D.C.: BNA, 1985): 1.

† The Bureau of National Affairs, Inc., "Employee Conduct and Discipline," *Personnel Policies Forum*, Survey No. 102, August 1973 (Washington, D.C.: BNA, 1973): 7.

at BNA's annual employee relations briefing sessions clearly snapped to attention at a mention of the no-fault absenteeism policy in the settlement between Xerox Corporation and the Amalgamated Clothing and Textile Workers Union that subjected employees to automatic termination for more than four "occasions" of absence in any 12-month period. BNA's employee relations publications also have reported on experiments with "positive discipline" as a new incentive for employees to change their job behavior.

But many managers today find that even no-fault and positive discipline policies emphasize the negative approach by using discipline to control absenteeism. The focus in many organizations now is shifting to the broader issue of improving attendance, with discipline considered only as a last resort.

Employers increasingly are recognizing that punitive approaches have failed to provide real remedies and are attempting to redress the underlying cause of attendance problems. The prevalence of two-career couples in the workplace has led employers to adopt a variety of experiments to deal with work/home conflicts— employer-sponsored day care, flextime scheduling and parental and adoption leave, among others. Since sickness and injury are the leading causes of absenteeism, employers are trying to address the underlying problems through wellness programs, job safety policies, and disability management techniques.

This book attempts to pull together the wide variety of approaches that organizations are using today to improve employee attendance. The intent has been to display the broad range of policies and practices that are being tried with varying degrees of success, with an emphasis on those that have been tested and found effective. The diversity of approaches that will be discussed should convince readers that no single magic formula will produce sudden, dramatic results. The result should be that managers will come away with ideas for techniques and programs that, given the particular organizational environment and culture, might be worth trying to see if they produce results.

Part 1 starts at the beginning, with recommendations for the basic steps in developing an overall policy for improving attendance and handling each of the main types of leaves of absence. Next, it examines other essential components of an attendance policy—a system for keeping accurate and detailed records of absences and the reasons for their occurrence, policies for requiring employees to notify management of absences, and procedures for protecting against sick-leave abuse by asking for verification or documentation.

It concludes with a review of federal and state legal constraints on job attendance policies, including laws that deal with religious observances, handicapped employees, and maternity leaves, and long- and short-term leaves for military duty.

Part 2 covers attempts to alleviate some of the underlying causes of poor attendance—the rise of dual-career families, single-parent workers, and employees with responsibilities for elderly parents—through programs for child and dependent care, alternative work schedules, and parental leave. Part 2 also reviews corporate wellness programs that are directed at the potentially controllable causes of most illness-related absenteeism, such as smoking, hypertension, high cholesterol, obesity, and stress. It concludes with a discussion of job safety programs that are designed to reduce on-the-job accidents and disability-management programs that assist the rehabilitation of the employee who has been absent due to illness or injury.

Part 3 deals with "corrective measures"—nondisciplinary policies and techniques designed to foster good attendance patterns and habits, emphasizing the role of the first-line supervisor. It also covers (1) techniques for rewarding good attendance and imposing penalties other than discipline for poor attendance; (2) procedures for dealing with absenteeism caused by drug and alcohol abuse; and (3) programs for assisting employees with other personal problems that affect job attendance.

Part 4 addresses the disciplinary measures aimed at absenteeism, using as a source the valuable guidelines found in the labor arbitration awards published by BNA over the past 40 years. Although arising out of union contract disputes, these awards provide guidelines of general applicability, since, particularly in dealing with the subject of absenteeism, arbitrators apply basic concepts of what is fair and reasonable.

In reviewing traditional discipline guidelines, Part 4 covers some of the most common disciplinary problems and issues—misrepresentation and abuse of sick leave, excessive absenteeism of chronically ill employees, attendance problems resulting from alcoholism and drug abuse, absences caused by confinement in jails or mental institutions, and other special attendance problems. The alternatives to traditional discipline approaches—no-fault discipline and positive discipline—are discussed in the concluding chapter of this part.

This book provides an overview of the melange of issues raised by the broad title "Improving Job Attendance." One of the major factors influencing job attendance is the degree of job satisfaction. Since this issue would require a separate book, it is only touched upon here.

Most of the chapters contain "Guidelines" summarizing suggested pointers for relevant policies and practices. These are only suggestions, not rigid rules.

Where applicable, "Resource Center" sections list sources for additional information and assistance in setting up specific programs. Also included are sample policy statements and forms that can be adapted to implement job attendance programs. Liberally sprinkled throughout are examples of actual policies and programs used by organizations, private and public, union and nonunion.

*John V. Schappi*

*Washington, D.C.*
*November 1987*

# Introduction

American management often is criticized for a tendency to seek quick fixes for complex problems that are not amenable to easy solutions. The rush into drug testing as *the* answer to the problem of substance abuse is only one of the most recent examples of this tendency.

To realize a substantial improvement in employee attendance, management must invest time, effort, and money. A comprehensive strategy rather than a piecemeal approach that relies on one or two methods will produce the best results. Thought must be given to how specific attendance improvement techniques fit in with other personnel practices and with the corporate culture.

Techniques used in the past or newly introduced should be reviewed and analyzed carefully to see if they actually have an impact on attendance. Even though the advent of computerized record-keeping has made this easier to do, it often is neglected.

For example: A company that had required a written doctor's excuse from its hourly workers upon return from sick leave experimented with suspending the requirement at several locations and found that the absenteeism rate changed little. It therefore eliminated the requirement, saving substantial money and aggravation. But another company might experience the opposite result. The point is that organizations should constantly review and verify, rather than blindly adopt techniques that may have worked in the past or in other settings.

## ATTENDANCE INFLUENCES

Recent research has identified some of the key dynamics to absenteeism, thus opening up possibilities for testing innovative strategies for attendance improvement. One review of over 100 empirical studies of absenteeism concluded that the factors influencing attendance could be categorized under two headings—(1) the ability to come to work, and (2) the motivation to attend work.*

### Ability to Attend

Most absences—some estimates range from a half to two-thirds—result from the employees' inability to come to work due to sickness, although much of this may be due to psychological factors, including job-related stress, or substance abuse problems. Such illness-related absences can be prevented or at least reduced through wellness programs, disability management, and substance abuse and employee assistance programs. Disruptions caused by family problems and transportation constraints can be minimized by efforts directed toward reconciling family/work needs.

### Motivation to Attend

Attendance motivation is influenced by job satisfaction and by various internal and external pressures. Job satisfaction factors that play a part in attendance motivation are varied. A common assumption is that job enrichment reduces absenteeism, but this has not been clearly demonstrated. But evidence does support the theory that higher level or more challenging jobs produce better satisfied employees who are less likely to be absent.

Increased job satisfaction and lower absenteeism have been correlated with smaller work groups, at least for blue-collar workers. Attendance motivation also appears to be influenced by the extent to which an employee's values and expectations are met. Research is divided on whether a direct relationship exists between

---

* R.M. Steers and S.R. Rhodes, "Major Influences on Employee Attendance: A Process Model," *Journal of Applied Psychology* (August 1978).

job attendance and other factors of job satisfaction such as co-worker relations and opportunities for advancement.

Among the major external pressures motivating an individual to show up for work are economic and labor market conditions. Empirical studies confirm an inverse relationship between changes in the local unemployment rate and absenteeism rates.

The individual's personal work ethic and the norms of the work group toward job attendance are two similar pressures—one internal, the other external—that impact on attendance. The first-line supervisor clearly can influence attitudes of both the individual and the group, which is why a major chapter is devoted to a discussion of the role of the supervisor.

Perhaps the greatest debate in the reports on empirical studies is whether incentive/reward systems have a positive effect on job attendance. Several studies suggest that sick leave itself may adversely affect absenteeism by rewarding nonattendance. But bonuses and rewards for good attendance, particularly when developed with employee input, have been shown to improve attendance at least in the short run.

## ATTENDANCE IMPROVEMENT POLICIES

Attendance improvement policies can center on disciplinary approaches and/or motivational measures. In the 1981 BNA survey of its *Personnel Policies Forum* members, the largest group—more than one-third—cited disciplinary rules as the most effective method in curbing absenteeism. But nearly as many cited counseling employees as the key. Ten percent found that having a consistently administered and well-established policy made the most difference, while another 10 percent stressed the supervisor's role as the key element.*

Another 1981 survey asked personnel managers to rank 34 absenteeism control methods according to their perceptions of which ones worked the best.† The three top-rated approaches were (1) a

---

* The Bureau of National Affairs, Inc., "Job Absence and Turnover Control," *Personnel Policies Forum*, Survey No. 132, October 1981 (Washington, D.C.: BNA, 1981).
† D. Scott and S.E. Markham, "Absenteeism Control Methods: A Survey of Practices and Results," *Personnel Administrator* (June 1982).

consistently applied attendance policy, (2) termination for excessive absenteeism, and (3) a progressive discipline system for excessive absenteeism. Despite these ratings, other answers suggested that relatively few organizations had a clearly written attendance policy and that termination and discipline for absenteeism were not consistently administered or based on accurate data.

This survey also found that some of the most frequently used control methods were not considered very effective. In this category were requirements for a written doctor's excuse, discussion of attendance requirements during formal employee orientation, and using peer pressure by requiring co-workers to fill in for absent employees.

Another finding was that attendance reward programs, which are highly praised in management literature, were used infrequently, even though they were rated as fairly effective techniques.

In recent years, many organizations have been replacing traditional discipline with no-fault absenteeism and positive discipline policies. This stems partly from the philosophical and practical difficulties in applying traditional discipline, which uses progressively stiffer penalties to correct misconduct, to absenteeism that may or may not result from factors within the employee's control. But the move away from traditional discipline also has its roots in a belief that other measures show better results in improving attendance.

Increasingly managers are designing multifaceted policies that rely simultaneously on sanctions of some sort, on positive reinforcements, and on programs that address some of the underlying causes for poor attendance. But the first step in deciding upon any attendance improvement strategies is to measure and understand the extent and nature of absenteeism within the organization.

This requires collecting data that separates sickness, injury, and other unavoidable absences from casual and avoidable absences. The data also should be broken down by department and section to identify where the problem is the most severe. Simply collecting attendance data will help reduce absenteeism, but periodically reviewing and analyzing the data will have an even greater effect.

Measuring and controlling absenteeism should be the joint responsibility of personnel staff members and line managers. Personnel managers are responsible for making line management aware of the importance of job attendance to the organization and for giving them the necessary policy tools. The line managers then are responsible for directly addressing the issue.

A recurring theme in literature and studies dealing with job attendance is that organizations must clearly state and communicate their absenteeism policies. Too often, employees are not aware whether attendance is important or what management's policies are. Orientation and training of both employees and supervisors have proved effective in improving attendance.

The numerous creative programs discussed in this book show that employee attendance can be improved. What management needs is to recognize the importance of such programs and to commit itself to continual experimentation and analysis to determine which programs produce the best results for their particular organization.

Only by abandoning the idea that high levels of absenteeism are an irreversible fact of business life can we reduce its excessive drag on American productivity.

# Contents

# List of Exhibits

# List of Sample Policies

# Part 1

# Policy Considerations

# 1

# Creating a Policy and Monitoring Compliance

Despite widespread concern over high absenteeism rates, many organizations do not have a formal policy or procedure for encouraging job attendance. In many cases, perhaps, this is due to the organization's culture or tradition regarding absenteeism. If management's attitude is lax and job absences are accepted as the norm, the organization's culture may have to be changed before attendance can be improved.

## CREATING A POLICY

Establishing an easily understood attendance policy is an essential first step. The policy should be developed under the aegis of top management and should be clearly explained and universally communicated so that both employees and supervisors understand its provisions, standards, procedures, and guidelines. It should be made part of the employee handbook, posted conspicuously, and reviewed and updated periodically. Basic steps in creating an effective policy include the following:

1. *Determine the extent and nature of absenteeism.* Absenteeism patterns vary by industry, geographical location, and the age, sex, and pay classifications of employees. They can also differ among departments within the organization and fluctuate from day to day. Some departments may be particularly plagued by a frequent offender, the employee with numerous one-day absences often on a Friday or Monday, while long-term absenteeism

3

may be the main problem in other units. To achieve best results, management needs a clear picture of the organization's absenteeism pattern before deciding upon an attendance improvement policy.

2. *Determine the approach to encouraging job attendance.* A variety of approaches are discussed throughout this book, to serve as a guide to selecting the best combination of policies for particular corporate environments and cultures. The approaches, which are not mutually exclusive, include the following:

- Preventive measures look at the most common underlying causes for poor job attendance and attempt to find ways to alleviate the problems. Efforts here might address conflicts between family responsibilities and work obligations, job safety factors, or unhealthy employee lifestyles. See Part 2.

- Corrective measures focus directly on job attendance issues. Since supervisors play a key role in this approach, they may be trained on how to stress the importance of good attendance and how to counsel absence-prone employees. Other corrective efforts include using rewards for good attendance or nondisciplinary penalties for poor attendance. Partly corrective and partly preventive are programs to deal with drug and alcohol abuse and to assist employees with other personal problems that interfere with job attendance. See Part 3.

- Disciplinary measures—the oldest and most common technique for dealing with job absenteeism—impose increasingly stiff penalties on the chronic absentee. But traditional discipline presumes deliberate—and therefore punishable—employee misconduct. Since many absenteeism cases do not involve willful misconduct, employers have experimented with other disciplinary techniques, such as no-fault discipline and so-called positive discipline. See Part 4.

3. *Define "absence" and "tardiness."* This sounds simple, but surveys have shown that the definition of a recordable absence can vary considerably among employers. One commonly used definition of absence is unscheduled time off from work. Other accepted definitions and formulas are discussed below under "Defining and Counting Absences."

Employers frequently distinguish between "excused" and "unexcused" absences by counting only the latter when determining a worker's absence rate. This approach generally excuses such absences as a management-approved vacation, leave, or holiday, jury or military duty, a death in the family, job-related injuries or illness, hospital confinement, or an employer-authorized absence for bad weather or other emergencies. Policies and practices for handling particular types of leave are discussed in Chapter 2.

A definition of tardiness should identify a specific point—e.g., 10 minutes after a worker's scheduled starting time—at which late penalties will be charged. Similar provisions might cover early departures and unauthorized extensions of lunch and rest breaks.

4. *Determine what constitutes excessive absenteeism.* Employers vary in their approaches to identifying the point at which a worker's absences will be considered excessive. Some employers' absenteeism policies precisely define "excessive." For example, more than three absences in a month or 12 in a 12-month period may be considered excessive. Others define excessive absences as those in which employees exceed their sick and annual leave allotments. Some employers prefer to avoid a rigid definition and instead make determinations on a case-by-case basis, figuring, for example, that an employee with a record of 10 scattered Monday absences is more disruptive than an employee who is absent for a three-week illness.

Once the policy is developed and approved by top management, it is important to communicate it to all levels of the company. See the sample policy statement in Exhibit 1.1.

## MONITORING COMPLIANCE

The next step in developing an overall policy is to keep accurate and detailed records of absences and the reasons for them. Management needs such records at its fingertips to compute absence rates and thus determine the extent of the problem in the organization.

Furthermore, accurate absenteeism records and rates can pinpoint where the most critical problems lie by comparing departments, by identifying which employees are most frequently absent and why, by ascertaining whether the organization can change the

## EXHIBIT 1.1

─────────────────────── **SAMPLE POLICY** ───────────────────────

**Subject:** Absenteeism and Tardiness

**Purpose:** To identify the proper procedures for reporting absences and ensure consistent and equitable treatment of absences, late arrivals, and early departures throughout the organization.

**Guidelines:**

1) All employees are expected to report to work as scheduled and to work their scheduled hours and required overtime. Employees will be charged with an absence occurrence when they fail to report for their scheduled work hours. Employees will be considered tardy and charged with a partial absence occurrence when they report to work more than six minutes past their scheduled starting time. Similarly, workers who leave early or extend authorized breaks past their official limits may be charged with a partial absence occurrence.

2) Absences for which employees will be charged with an occurrence include failures to report for such reasons as personal business, an illness or accident not involving hospitalization, or an emergency other than those, such as weather-related closings, officially recognized by the employer. Absences of several days duration will be treated as one occurrence. Absences that will not result in an occurrence charge include those involving jury or military duty, work-related injuries or illnesses, hospital confinement, and the use of authorized bereavement leave. The employer has the right to require workers to submit a doctor's note or undergo a physical examination to verify a claim of illness or injury.

3) Employees must notify their supervisor in advance when possible — and in no case later than 30 minutes after their starting time — of their inability to report for work as scheduled. If a supervisor cannot be reached, workers should inform the personnel office as soon as possible that they will not be able to show up for work. In providing this notification, employees should give a reason for their absence and an estimate of when they will return to work. Supervisors will maintain written records of employees' absences and tardiness, which will include the reasons given by employees for missing work.

4) Employees who are absent for three consecutive working days without notifying the employer are subject to termination as voluntary quits.

5) Once employees have accumulated a total of six occurrences in a 12-month period, their supervisor will discuss with them the reasons for their absences and the organization's need for regular attendance by all workers. The accumulation of two more occurrences within the 12-month period will result in an oral warning. The ninth occurrence will elicit a written warning; the 10th, a three-day suspension; and the 11th, a 10-day suspension. Employees who are charged with 12 occurrences within a 12-month period will be subject to discharge. Supervisors will provide counseling at each step of this progressive procedure, and will refer employees to outside sources of counseling and assistance for help in dealing with medical, physical, or personal difficulties related to their attendance problems.

6) Employees who have perfect attendance for a one-month period (four consecutive workweeks) are entitled to have one occurrence expunged from their records. Workers who have perfect attendance for a six-month period will be eligible for a $50 attendance bonus, while a 12-month perfect attendance record will earn employees an additional $100 bonus.

7) In dealing with attendance problems — especially those involving an illness or physical or mental incapacity to report for work — the employer will consider all the facts and circumstances of a particular case, including the employee's overall attendance and performance records, reasons for missing work, and prospects for future improvement and maintenance of an acceptable attendance record. The employer reserves the right to make exceptions to the disciplinary procedures outlined above in the interest of fairness.

8) This policy is effective immediately.

*Source:* Employment Guide, p. 40:23, copyright © 1986, The Bureau of National Affairs, Inc.

causes for absenteeism, and by measuring the effectiveness of supervisory efforts to improve job attendance.

Finally, one of the most important influences affecting absenteeism is the employees' knowledge that their employer keeps accurate job attendance records, monitors those records, and acts upon the data.

## Reporting & Recording Absences

In almost all companies, employees must notify either their immediate supervisor or the personnel department as early as possible when they are absent or are going to be absent. It generally is a good idea for the supervisor to ask employees to report the reason for the absence and to estimate how long they expect to be off work. This permits the supervisor to reschedule work and get a temporary replacement if necessary, thereby minimizing the disruption of the absence.

Records should be kept of the absence, the reason given for it, its date, and its duration. Although the immediate supervisor usually makes the initial recording, uniform standards should be established so that comparable records are kept throughout the organization.

The attendance policy also should specify if and when employees must obtain a doctor's certificate. For example, the policy could require a written verification from a doctor for any illness exceeding five days.

## Defining & Counting Absences

As noted earlier, an absence may be broadly defined as the failure of an employee to report to work when scheduled. The term usually encompasses time lost because of illness or injury as well as unscheduled time away from work for other reasons.

Unfortunately, absenteeism has no universally accepted definition. A widespread practice, however, is to count as absences only *unscheduled* time off the job, since these unanticipated absences are what disrupt productivity and efficiency.

For its quarterly survey of job absence rates among more than 1,000 organizations, The Bureau of National Affairs, Inc. defines an absence as any unscheduled time off from work, regardless of whether it is paid or excused.[1] The BNA definition also includes only the first four days of the unscheduled absence, since any work disruptions presumably would be resolved for longer absences.

In the survey, absenteeism rates are computed using a formula suggested by the Department of Labor:[2]

$$\frac{\text{number of worker days lost through job absence during month}}{\left(\begin{array}{c}\text{average number} \\ \text{of employees}\end{array}\right) \times \left(\begin{array}{c}\text{number of} \\ \text{workdays}\end{array}\right)} \times 100$$

Here, the "average number of employees" means the average of the numbers of active employees on the first and last payrolls of the month. "Numbers of workdays" excludes days that consist entirely or primarily of overtime work.

For example, Company "Z" employs 250 workers. During one month (24 working days), 200 worker days are lost through job absences. The absentee rate for employees is determined as follows:[3]

$$\text{absence rate} = \frac{200}{250 \times 24} \times 100 = 3.3 \text{ percent}$$

The all-company average absenteeism rate in the BNA survey was 1.9 percent for both 1984 and 1985. The survey found that the smaller the work force, the lower the absenteeism rate. Rates ranged from a low of 1.7 percent among employers with 250 or fewer workers to a high of 2.3 percent for those with 1,000 to 2,499 employees and 2.2 percent for those with more than 2,500 workers.

Another method of measuring absenteeism is the "occurrence index," which records each absence "occurrence" regardless of length. By focusing on patterns of absence, this measure helps identify where and with whom problems lie.

Other formulas used to compute absenteeism rates are as follows:[4]

Percentage of the work force absent during a specified period—

$$\frac{\textit{number of employees absent during period}}{\textit{number of employees on payroll during period}} \times 100$$

Average number of days absent per employee—

$$\frac{\textit{number of worker days of absence during period}}{\textit{number of employees on payroll during period}}$$

## Monitoring Attendance Records

Attendance records should be reviewed periodically to determine how individual employees or departments compare with the organization as a whole. The records also can serve to compare the organization with other employers in the area or industry.

Individual employee records can alert management to patterns, such as frequent Monday or Friday absences, hunting season absences, or baseball home-game absences. Comparison of records for different departments or job units can suggest possible reasons for above-normal absenteeism rates, such as boring, menial work or the supervisor's personality.

Most organizations today computerize information on absences and provide periodic printouts of the records by individual and work unit. The supervisor can save time in monitoring absenteeism records by using the computer to flag questionable patterns or total occurrences of absences.

Computerized records also can encourage supervisory follow-up on problem employees. The computer can generate follow-up notices concerning employees whose absence records have not improved after initially being flagged for questionable patterns. This follow-up notice could be sent both to the immediate supervisor and his or her superior.

Records can be designed to give exceptional treatment to absences that abut a holiday or weekend or to frequent short-term absences as distinguished from a single long-term absence.

See Appendix A for several samples of forms used by organizations to record attendance, absences, and tardiness and to monitor other aspects of an attendance improvement program.

# GUIDELINES

The computer has made it easier to collect attendance records and to flag questionable absence patterns for individuals within units; by sex, age, or other demographics; and to provide other helpful information for attempting to improve attendance. But the cold data needs interpretation and evaluation by the supervisor before determining whether or how to confront an employee.

Attendance records can serve as creative and appropriate tools for supervisors to use in their overall evaluation of employee performance. The computerized records also can provide valuable data for managing by exception. These suggestions should help management to keep tabs on absences:

- Keep accurate attendance records that list reasons, dates, and duration of each absence.

- Decide what formula to use in calculating absence rates and what constitutes an "absence" under that formula.

- Review attendance records regularly and compare individual employees to each other and departments to other departments.

- Keep an eye out for absence patterns: the Monday/Friday syndrome, frequent short-term absences, and the like.

## ENDNOTES

1. The Bureau of National Affairs, Inc., "Job Absence and Turnover Control," *Personnel Policies Forum*, Survey No. 132, October 1981 (Washington, D.C.: BNA, 1981).
2. M. G. Miner, "Job Absence and Turnover: A New Source of Data," Monthly Labor Review (Oct. 1977):26.
3. Ibid.
4. The Bureau of National Affairs, Inc., *BNA Policy and Practice Series, Personnel Management* (Washington, D.C.): 241:112.

# 2

# Defining Policies for Specific Types of Leave

Employees miss work for a wide variety of reasons. In establishing a job attendance policy, an employer should look at the main types of absences and consider how each should be handled. If employees feel that the firm's policies are fair, they will be less likely to set their own liberal leave policies.

Two questions usually need to be answered for each type of absence. Should the time off be paid or unpaid? Should it be excused or considered a potential cause for discipline? The answers to these questions should be clearly set forth in any written attendance policy. See Exhibit 2.1 for a sample attendance policy.

## SICK LEAVE

Most organizations offer sick leave, paid at the employee's regular rate, to workers who have completed their probation period. Employees typically earn or are credited with a specific amount of sick leave each pay period. The rate at which sick leave is accrued may vary on the basis of employees' seniority or job classification.

Generally, exempt employees are more apt to be granted sick leave than are production workers, who are more likely to be covered by short-term disability (sickness and accident) insurance. In a 1983 BNA survey, more than nine out of 10 companies had a paid sick-leave policy for their office and management

11

## *EXHIBIT 2.1*

---

**SAMPLE POLICY**

---

**Subject:**  Vacations and Holidays

**Purpose:**  To outline the rules for accruing and using vacation leave and to identify the paid holidays observed by the organization.

**Guidelines:**

1) All new employees will earn one day of paid vacation leave for each month worked through December during the first year they are hired. While new workers will earn vacation leave during their first three months of service, they normally will not be allowed to use the leave until after they complete their probationary period. However, supervisors have the discretion to approve probationary workers' requests to use their earned leave.

2) In the calendar year following the one in which they are hired, workers will begin earning paid vacation leave as follows: two weeks per year during the first five years of employment; three weeks after five years; four weeks after 15 years; and five weeks after 20 years.

3) Employees will be permitted to carry over unused amounts of earned vacation from one calendar year to the next, up to a maximum of the number of annual weeks they are eligible to earn.

4) In years that an employee is absent for more than 50 normally scheduled workdays, vacation leave will be prorated. Vacation credit will not accrue during a lengthy leave of absence (30 days or longer) or during a period of layoff.

5) Vacation pay will be computed on the basis of a worker's regular wage or salary for a comparable work period.

6) Terminating employees who comply with the advance notice requirements for resigning from a job will be paid for vacation leave they have earned but not used.

7) Workers should inform their immediate supervisors of their vacation scheduling requests. Supervisors will try to comply with workers' requests as long as the organization's production and staffing needs are met. In the event that a supervisor cannot grant requests for the same vacation time filed by two or more workers, employees will be granted vacation leave in the order of their seniority.

8) Employees who have completed their probation period will be entitled to six paid holidays each year. These holidays are New Year's Day, Memorial Day, Independence Day, Labor Day, Thanksgiving, and Christmas Day. To receive holiday pay, employees must be at work on the scheduled work days immediately before and after the holiday, unless previously excused by their supervisor.

9) The employer acknowledges its duty to make a reasonable accommodation to employees who wish time off to observe religious holidays. Requests for such time off will be granted where possible, based on the scheduling and staffing needs of affected departments. Employees wishing to take time off work for religious observances should inform their supervisors as early as possible.

10) Employees will be given paid time off to vote in local, state, and national elections. Employees who are registered to vote may take up to a maximum of three hours off to vote. Supervisors may ask employees who are given paid time off to vote to supply proof that they actually voted in the election.

*Source:* Employment Guide, p. 30:43, copyright © 1986, The Bureau of National Affairs, Inc.

personnel, compared with just over two out of three who had such a policy for production workers.[1]

The amount of sick leave granted by employers varies widely; most organizations allow workers between five and 12 paid sick days each year. The BNA survey found that the median days of sick leave credited to employees in the first full year of eligibility were five for plant/service workers, six for office clerical workers, and 10 for management and other exempt workers. (These medians were somewhat higher for nonbusiness establishments.) Among firms that credit employees with sick leave on a monthly basis, nonmanufacturing and nonbusiness firms provided a median of one day per month for all three categories of workers, while manufacturing firms provided medians ranging from one-half day for plant/service workers to four-fifths of a day for management/exempt personnel.[2]

Employers generally allow workers to carry over paid sick leave from year to year, although many place a limit on the amount that may be carried over. In some organizations, an unpaid waiting period is required before paid sick leave may be used; this requirement is more commonly imposed on production workers.[3]

Most employers require workers to provide prompt notice of illness in order to be eligible for sick leave. In many organizations, workers may have to provide proof of illness, such as a doctor's note. These verification requirements normally are triggered once an employee is absent for more than a specified number (typically three) of work days.[4] See Chapter 3 for further discussion of notice requirements.

Some employers (just over 10 percent in the BNA survey)[5] advance sick leave to workers who need more than they have earned, but extended absences due to illness usually are covered under short-term disability insurance plans or leave-of-absence policies.

Some organizations "buy back" unused sick leave from workers, either at the end of the year or at retirement, in an effort to control sick-leave abuse and ease scheduling problems caused by unexpected absences. These buy-back plans typically pay workers a formula-based cash bonus for unused leave, for example, 50 percent of the accrued leave amount. Similarly, a number of employers provide incentives to encourage workers not to use sick leave. These include cash bonuses and extra vacation or personal-leave days for employees who meet designated attendance goals. The use of rewards regarding sick leave is discussed in more detail in Chapter 10.

## Sick-Leave Substitutes

Several studies suggest that the typical sick-leave plan actually may increase sick-leave use—or abuse—by employees.[6] One study concluded that organizations with paid sick leave experience nearly twice the amount of absenteeism of organizations without such a program.[7]

Under the typical sick-leave plan, a certain number of employees, perhaps only 5 to 10 percent, treat the leave as an earned right that they must use or lose. Others occasionally use paid sick leave in situations where they would report for work if leave were not available—slight fatigue, minor ailments, inclement weather, child care difficulties, transportation problems, and other personal problems. A standing joke among some employees is the need to take an "R&R day" for "rest and rehabilitation."

Recognizing this potential for abuse, several organizations have experimented with substitutes for the traditional sick-leave plan.

### Sick-Leave Banks

Sick-leave banks permit employees to pool some of their paid sick-leave days into a common fund. Employees then can draw upon this fund when they exhaust the remaining days due to extended illnesses.

Under a typical plan, employees might earn 10 days of annual sick leave and elect to bank one day. Since all employees "own" the days in the sick-leave bank, considerable peer pressure mitigates against individual abuse. So that conscientious workers do not end up subsidizing profligate leave abusers, an employee committee generally authorizes withdrawals from the leave bank. Another way to police the system is to treat withdrawals as loans that employees must pay back before requesting another withdrawal.

Sick-leave banks are fairly common in the public sector, particularly among teachers, police, and firefighters. In recent years, these programs have begun to spread into the private sector.

*Well-Pay Plan*

Some organizations have experimented with well-pay programs that reward employees for perfect attendance. One such program had these features:[8]

- The former traditional sick-leave plan was discontinued, and accrued sick-leave credits were frozen.

- A well-pay plan was instituted under which employees with no monthly absences received bonuses of four hours' pay.

- Pay was docked for the first eight hours of an illness-related absence. Paid sick leave picked up after this one-day hiatus.

The cost of paid sick leave plus well-pay bonuses in the new plan's first year exceeded the annual cost of the paid sick leave under the old plan. However, the company figured the plan brought a net saving due to the increased productivity resulting from reduced absenteeism and easier work scheduling. A possible negative impact of the plan is that the one-day hiatus in paid sick leave may have encouraged employees to stretch one-day illnesses into two or more days of absences.

# MATERNITY, PATERNITY, AND ADOPTION LEAVE

Federal law bars employers from discriminating against workers on the basis of pregnancy. The impact of this law on maternity-leave policies is discussed in Chapter 4.

Many employers have a maternity-leave policy that allows workers to use a combination of paid and unpaid leave to cover absences related to pregnancy, childbirth, or adoption. While some employers set no maximum length on grants of unpaid maternity leave, many do specify a limit, such as three to six months.

According to the BNA survey,[9] paid sick leave could be used for maternity absences in about seven-tenths of the responding organizations. About two-fifths also permitted the use of annual or vacation leave.

About two-fifths of the employers surveyed by BNA had

policies permitting male employees to take time off from work for the birth of their children. Nearly half of these employers permitted fathers to use paid vacation or annual leave, while from one-third to two-fifths authorized using paid sick leave.[10]

About one-fourth of the participants had a policy providing leave to an employee for purposes of adopting a child. Most of these firms (77 percent) permitted workers to take time off without pay, usually in the form of unpaid personal leave.[11]

## MILITARY LEAVE

Federal law requires employers to grant workers military leave for both short- and long-term absences. For a discussion of the legal constraints on military leave, see Chapter 4.

Most employers have established a military-leave policy covering short-term absences for reserve duty. Although employers are not required to pay workers who are absent for such reasons, many do provide employees on reserve duty with some pay, which usually is computed as the difference between an employee's regular wages and military pay.

About half of the employers in the BNA survey calculated military-leave pay in this manner. In one-fourth to one-third of the firms, however, extra military-leave pay was not provided unless the employee first used annual or vacation leave for the training period.[12]

## JURY DUTY LEAVE

Generally, employer payments to workers on jury duty represent the difference between a worker's regular pay and the jury pay or expense payment made by the court. This was the practice of 77 percent of the respondents in the BNA survey for their plant/ service workers, of 64 percent for office/clerical staffs, and of 59 percent for management/exempt personnel. The remaining firms paid employees their regular wages in full, over and above any payments received from the court.[13]

Some organizations also extend jury-duty pay to trial witnesses. A few employers set an annual limit on the number of jury-duty days granted to workers.

## FUNERAL OR BEREAVEMENT LEAVE

This typically is a short-term, paid leave for workers who suffer a death in their immediate family. More than three-fourths of the employers surveyed by BNA set their funeral leave at three days.[14] Some employers require proof of funeral attendance.

Many employers establish definitions of "immediate family," which usually includes a spouse, children, parents, and siblings. More than nine-tenths of the firms in the BNA survey included these family members in the definition of "immediate family." Less frequently covered were parent-in-law (71 percent), grandparent (61 percent), grandchild (47 percent), and brother-in-law and sister-in-law (41 percent).[15]

In some organizations, employees are granted different amounts of leave for different relatives, e.g., five days bereavement leave in the event of the death of a spouse, child, or parent and three days for other relatives.

## PERSONAL LEAVE

Employers increasingly are providing a set amount of paid leave that employees can use at their discretion and normally with prior approval from their supervisor. This was the only time-off benefit that increased significantly in the 1983 BNA survey when compared with a 1975 survey. About half of the employers in the 1983 survey provided such leave, compared with about one-fourth in 1975.[16]

Most employers condition eligibility for personal leave on completion of probation. Personal leave usually is granted as a set number of days per year, rather than accrued over time. One or two days were the most common leave amounts specified in the 1983 BNA survey.[17]

Personal leave generally is not regarded as an earned right that can be carried over from one year to the next. "Use it or lose it" is the usual policy.

## UNPAID LEAVES OF ABSENCE

Employers frequently allow workers to take an extended unpaid leave of absence for personal or other reasons. Employees may request such leave for a variety of purposes, including recovery from physical problems, dealing with an illness in the family, and engaging in educational, political, or social-service activities or travel.

More than nine out of 10 participants in the BNA survey made some provision for unpaid leaves of absence. The most common reason for granting employees an unpaid leave of absence was physical health problems of an extended nature. At least 75 percent of the responding employers provided unpaid leaves for extended illnesses, and nearly as many permitted workers to take unpaid leaves for alcohol or drug abuse rehabilitation, mental health problems, and other personal or family problems.

Approximately half of the survey participants with unpaid-leave policies allowed unpaid educational leaves, and about two-fifths permitted employees to extend their vacations with unpaid leave. [18]

Employers usually reserve the right to decide the propriety of each leave request on a case-by-case basis. Approvals of leave-of-absence requests usually hinge on such factors as the length of leave requested, the organization's production and staffing needs, and the worker's skill and ability levels and performance record.

Employees usually are permitted to continue their insurance coverage while on unpaid leaves. The same or a comparable job generally is guaranteed to employees returning from unpaid leave.

Keep in mind that employee morale may suffer if workers think that leave requests are handled in an arbitrary or unfair fashion. Most employers who grant leaves of absence place a time limit on the length of leave allowed, which, in some cases, may range up to a year or longer.

---

## ALL-PURPOSE LEAVE

Some organizations have developed combined leave plans that lump together vacation leave, paid holidays, and the average number of sick-leave days formerly paid per employee. This combined paid-leave total then can be used by employees at their discretion. Since employees in effect administer their own leave program, those who take little if any sick leave are awarded with extra vacation leave. Employees who take an above-average number of sick days cut into their banks of vacation/holiday leave.

Under this program, a separate long-term disability leave plan may be added for employees who have prolonged illnesses.

Organizations with these plans report reduced absenteeism, better job scheduling, and improved employee morale.[19]

Two company policies that combine sick leave and other leave are described below.

### Flexible Time Off

**Hewlett-Packard Company** in January 1982 began offering a combined vacation and sick-leave package, dubbed "Flexible Time Off." Hewlett-Packard previously had granted vacations ranging from 10-25 days depending upon seniority and had allowed 10 days of annual sick leave. Unused sick leave could accrue from year-to-year with a cash payout—after 20 years of service—of up to 50 percent of its value.

Under the new plan, employees receive the same vacation benefits plus five days in lieu of the old sick leave. The number of days an employee can carry over at the end of a year also varies by seniority and is paid in full upon termination. Sick leave accumulated under the old plan was banked in a separate account that employees could use under the old sick-pay rules.

A company brochure explains that the policy change resulted from employee suggestions and perceived inequities in the old policy. Under the old program, only 20 percent of the employees accounted for 80 percent of the sick leave used. The new plan places the responsibility of managing total leave on the employee.

### Personal Days Off

**Control Data Corp.** (CDC) abolished vacation and paid sick leave in favor of a new Personal Days Off policy in 1985. Under this policy, employees basically retained their former vacation leave entitlements and picked up an additional four or five days in place of the average sick leave used annually. Leave days are vested, and employees are paid for any unused time upon termination. Previously, vacation leave, but not sick leave, could accrue.

In introducing Personal Days Off, the company also shortened the waiting period for short-term disability benefits from 23 days to five. These benefits also were increased to provide 65 percent of income, up from 60 percent. Employees are warned to save enough personal days to cover the five-day waiting period.

Any sick leave accumulated under the old plan was set aside for illnesses for injuries lasting longer than five consecutive working days. This leave must be used up before short-term disability benefits are paid.

In adopting the new plan, CDC hoped to reduce the casual use of sick leave, achieve more effective management of the leave program, and discredit the notion that employees "owned" their sick leave. Employees, for their part, hoped to gain more flexibility in managing their time off. Many employees also had resented the sick leave abuse by a minority of the employees.

After the first year's experience with the new plan, the company reported being very pleased. The new plan is not less costly in total leave payments, but it has rechannelled how the money is being spent. Employees are managing their short-term, intermittent absences better. As a result, fewer production disruptions due to short-notice one-day absences occur.

Employees who do not abuse their sick leave or who are blessed with good health appreciate their additional paid leave.

Discontent with the plan comes mostly from the small fraction of employees who cause the bulk of the lost time due to illness.

## ENDNOTES

1. The Bureau of National Affairs, Inc., "Policies on Leave from Work," *Personnel Policies Forum*, Survey No. 136, June 1983 (Washington, D.C.: BNA, 1983): 13.
2. Ibid., 14.
3. The 1983 BNA survey found that 22 percent of the responding firms imposed an unpaid waiting period for plant/service workers, compared with 12 percent for office/clerical staff and 6 percent for management/exempt employees. Ibid., 17.
4. In the 1983 BNA survey, only one out of eight firms required a doctor's certification in all instances of sick leave. But more than two-thirds required proof under some circumstances. Ibid., 17.
5. Ibid., 20.
6. B. H. Harvey, J. A. Schultze, and J. F. Rogers, "Rewarding Employees for Not Using Sick Leave," *Personnel Administrator* (May 1983): 55.
7. D. Willings, "The Absentee Worker," *Personnel and Training Management* (December 1968): 10.
8. B. H. Harvey, J. A. Schultze, and J. F. Rogers, note 6 above, at 56.
9. The Bureau of National Affairs, Inc., note 1 above, at 22.
10. Ibid., 26.
11. Ibid., 28.
12. Ibid., 8.
13. Ibid., 3.
14. Ibid., 5.
15. Ibid., 7.
16. Ibid., 1.
17. Ibid., 29.
18. Ibid., 34.
19. Note 6 above, at 55.

# 3

# Establishing Notification and Verification Procedures

Two major policy considerations are (1) whether and how to require employees to notify management of contemplated absences, and (2) whether and how to verify the reasons proferred by employees for their absences. In discussing these issues, this chapter makes extensive use of awards issued by labor arbitrators, since these often provide guidelines on accepted standards of fairness for company policies even if a union is not involved.

## NOTICE REQUIREMENTS

Company rules usually require that an absent employee both notify the employer and present a justifiable excuse. Notice alone, without valid excuse, usually does not fulfill the employee's obligation. Nor does a good excuse for the absence necessarily justify an absence without notice.

Management may prefer to enforce its notice rules by denying sick leave or other relevant leave rather than by using the standard discipline for employee misconduct. But discipline may be used when the employee's failure to follow established policies is particularly egregious.[1]

If absent employees are expected to give notice, failure to attempt to meet this requirement normally will justify discipline or denial of sick leave even if the reason for the absence is valid.[2] "An employee is obligated to report for work regularly and to seasonably notify his employer of circumstances which prevent him

22

from reporting as scheduled," Arbitrator Harry Dworkin observed.[3]

## Employer's Obligation

Management should make clear what it expects in the way of notification. Different rules obviously are required for anticipated absences as opposed to sudden illnesses or other unexpected events. The person to be notified and the time to do it should be spelled out.

Even when an employee fails to comply with notification requirements, the company may want to attempt to contact the absent employee to determine his or her whereabouts or to inquire about the state of his or her health before resorting to discipline. Common courtesy and good employee relations prompt such inquiries, particularly if this would be just as easy for the employer as sending a termination notice.[4]

## Employee's Obligation

Usually the employee has the burden of complying with reasonable notice requirements despite a valid reason for the absence.

Since a management representative usually is "just a phone call away," only an extremely rare situation would excuse an employee's failure to call in with notice of an absence. At times, an employee may claim to have been too traumatized by the cause of the absence to remember to call in. But arbitrators generally are reluctant to buy such arguments.

For example, an employee with a bad attendance record missed work on four successive days without calling in. He later explained that he had a touch of the flu on the first day, that he found a friend murdered in his home on the second day, and that he was so badly shaken by the murder that he never thought about calling in. An arbitrator said that given the employee's irresponsible attitude, he should not expect the employer to "take more interest in him than he is willing to take" in his job.[5]

Similarly, an employee claimed that he could not call in during a two-week absence because he was emotionally upset over persistent marital and financial difficulties. The arbitrator discounted the employee's claim that he did not know what to do other than to stay at home "thinking and drinking." Stressing the "substantial responsibilities on the part of any employee, including the responsibility to report to work when scheduled unless circumstances justify absence," the arbitrator decided that the employee "certainly was aware of these responsibilities, and his failure to meet them cannot be excused on the basis of ignorance or naiveté."[6]

Notifying the employer of a contemplated absence at the outset does not absolve the employee from keeping the employer posted if the absence will extend beyond the period initially contemplated. Notification requirements stem from the employer's need to schedule substitutes for missing employees, and this need lasts as long as the absence.

Thus, in one arbitration case, an employee was allowed one day's leave to aid her sister who had been in an accident in a distant city. She remained away for a week, however, in order to care for her sister's children. Although the situation justified the employee's absence, she still was required to notify the company of the need to extend the leave, the arbitrator ruled.[7]

If employees must give notice of their absences, failure to attempt to meet this requirement normally will justify discipline or, at least, denial of paid leave, regardless of the merits of the reason for the absence. But management should be careful to spell out what it expects from employees in the way of notification.

## GUIDELINES FOR NOTIFICATION

In developing a policy, management might want to consider these questions:

- For anticipated absences, such as a planned hospitalization or an out-of-town trip, how much advance notice should be required?
- For unexpected absences, such as a sudden illness, should the employee call in before the workday begins?
- Who should be notified? Can the employee simply get word to a co-worker or should the employee try contacting the supervisor or personnel office?
- If notice is provided and leave is authorized, what rules come into play if the employee needs to extend the leave?

- What are the penalties for not complying with notification rules? Denial of paid leave? Normal discipline? Loss of seniority?

## VERIFICATION ISSUES

To protect against sick-leave abuses, employers often attempt to distinguish between excused and unexcused absences. The employer asks for an explanation and then evaluates whether it justifies the employee's absence.

Problems can occur since the employee usually has sole possession of the relevant facts, and his or her explanation is necessarily self-serving. Consequently, employers need to determine how much documentation or verification the explanation requires.

### Doctor's Note

The most common requirement for documentation is a doctor's note. How far can an employer go in imposing such a requirement?

Requiring a doctor's note for every illness probably will be regarded as unreasonable. Yet there inevitably will be employees whose own statements or those of friends or relatives will not satisfy the employer, particularly if the employee has a history of casual absenteeism. Pertinent considerations include the nature of the illness, the employee's past experience with such illness, the availability or need of a doctor's service, the employee's attendance record, and other special circumstances.[8]

Management generally has a recognized right to require employees to verify claimed illness. In fact, some arbitrators have said that management not only has a right but also a duty to guard against fraudulent sick-pay claims and therefore may promulgate reasonable rules concerning documentation of illness.[9]

However, management should give reasonable notice of what it expects of employees. One arbitrator, for example, overruled a denial of sick leave even though the employee's explanation of his absence was "open to suspicion, if not outright disbelief." The umpire noted that the company had no rule or past practice governing medical proof and demanded verification long after the claimed illness.[10]

Requiring proof in questionable cases has been upheld even if proof had not been required in all cases.[11] On the other hand, blanket requirements of documentation for all absences have been overturned by arbitrators. Here are a few such decisions:

- Demanding medical proof in all cases was "decidedly unreasonable" because the employer was "questioning the veracity and honesty of all its employees and not merely those whose honesty and veracity it has the right to question." [12]

- Before requiring a doctor's note, management should consider each case individually, taking into account the employees' "previous record of absenteeism and the length of their illness." [13]

- A blanket rule requiring doctors' notes is unreasonably strict. A better solution would be to require doctors' slips only when the employer finds "that a pattern of absenteeism is being formed by an employee because of alleged illness."[14] Other arbitrators, however, have endorsed such a blanket policy as a reasonable curb to abuses.[15]

### Timing

If management is going to require a doctor's note or other proof, it probably should do so when the employee returns from the absence. Prompt delivery allows the employer time to make further inquiries of the doctor or the employee.[16] But the employee should have a reasonable time to comply with a medical certification requirement.[17]

### Questions of Fraud

Even a doctor's certificate may be questioned if the employer has reason to suspect the validity of the certificate. Deplorable as it may be, doctors' notes may be bought or forged. However, the employer has the burden of proving fraud conclusively.[18]

## Second Opinion

Management may want to get a second opinion from its own doctor, rather than rely on the employee's doctor's note. Even if it does not suspect fraud, the company may feel that the employee's family physician could be swayed more by compassion than by scientific objectivity. There is also a good chance that the family doctor has little knowledge of the facts of industrial life and of specific job requirements other than what the patient volunteers.

A company's doctor, on the other hand, can more accurately gauge the physical demands upon the employee by observing the work site, the equipment, and job requirements. Given that honest medical authorities sometimes disagree, the company retains the right to have its own physician determine the patient's physical condition.[19] If a dispute develops, an arbitrator will not necessarily give the company doctor's opinion greater weight than the family doctor's.[20]

When confronted with conflicting or ambiguous medical opinions, management has the right to determine if an employee is qualified to return to work without being "handcuffed" by the medical reports, an arbitrator ruled. Doctors lack familiarity with the workplace and the specific extent of the job's physical demands, whereas managers are both qualified and able to evaluate the job and the employee's ability to do it.[21] On the other hand, in a case where nothing in the record justified discounting a doctor's release, an arbitrator ruled that the employer had improperly discharged the worker.[22]

## Definition of "Doctor"

If a company requires a medical certificate when an employee returns from sick leave, the credentials of the medical person used by the employee may be questioned. Here are a few examples:

An employer with a policy requiring certification of sickness or injury absences by a "legally licensed physician" rejected a chiropractor's certification. Although the parties had excluded chiropractic services in the medical plan and other contexts, the arbitrator decided that this merely showed that when the parties intended to exclude chiropractic services they did so clearly. Therefore, he held that the company improperly rejected the chiropractor's certification.[23]

Another employer paid for an employee's examination by a private physician who advised that he was ready to return to work. The employee, however, saw a chiropractor who recommended several more days of bed rest, advice which the employee took.

Deciding that the employee was within his rights, the arbitrator declared that "a person who has physical problems is justified in seeking treatment from a licensed practitioner, and absence required by the treatment is 'illness'."[24]

But when an employer consistently had refused to pay claims for "healing services" rendered by persons "other than practicing physicians," an arbitrator held that an employee was not entitled to be paid for workdays missed while under a chiropodist's care.[25]

On the other hand, when an employer uniformly had accepted previous certificates of illness from a "naturopathic physician," an arbitrator held that management could not change its mind without giving prior notice and deny sick pay to a worker who had been treated by the same "drugless therapist."[26]

## Personal Business

Employees at times are reluctant to disclose their reasons—good or bad—for wanting to take time off from work. To avoid unpleasant situations, employers frequently accept personal business as a valid excuse for some absences. But at other times, management may be uncomfortable with the "personal business" escape hatch.

Thus, when a company decided to crack down on absenteeism because of suspected abuses, an arbitrator held that it could require employees to come up with something more than "personal business" to explain absences. In such cases, the arbitrator said that the company legitimately can inquire into the general nature of the business without invading the employee's privacy. Since it would be almost impossible to prescribe a set formula covering every situation, the arbitrator recommended separately diagnosing and treating each personal absence.[27]

At issue in such cases, another arbitrator pointed out, is the "employees' right to privacy with respect to their personal lives" versus management's right "to discourage unnecessary absenteeism" and to ensure that workers "will not be away in such numbers as to impede operations."[28]

This case-by-case approach generally is approved. For example, "personal reasons" were held acceptable since the employer ordinarily accepted that excuse, even though the disputed absence occurred on the day before a scheduled vacation.[29] On the other hand, an employee's suspension was held justified when his only explanation was that he had been "out of town."[30]

When another employee had a record of extensive absenteeism and failure to call in or explain his absences, an arbitrator upheld his discharge for refusing repeated requests to come up with something other than "personal business" to explain a week's absence. In view of his record, the company could require a more substantive explanation, the arbitrator ruled.[31]

## GUIDELINES FOR VERIFICATION

Since management has a legitimate concern in preventing abuse of sick leave claims, arbitrators generally agree that the employer may take the following steps:

- Formulate rules for the documentation of an illness.[32] But, as with all company rules, management's efforts to police "unexcused" absences must not be arbitrary, discriminatory, or unreasonable.[33]

- Prescribe forms for the employee and/or his doctor to fill out.[34] However, doctor's notes probably should not be required for every illness absence but rather should be limited to cases of suspected abuse.

- Require second opinions from the company's doctor in certain cases.

- Develop a system to police a sick benefits plan that requires proof from employees with high absenteeism rates.[35]

- Decide whether to require explanations and/or documentation for absences due to "personal business." Management generally has discretion to grant or deny leaves of absence for personal reasons provided it does not act in an arbitrary or unreasonable manner.

### ENDNOTES

1. Central Ill. Pub. Serv. Co., 44 LA 133 (Young, 1964); FMC Corp., 74 LA 1185 (Doering, 1980).
2. Lau Blower Co., 24 LA 52, 55 (Warns, 1955); Southwestern Ohio Steel, Inc., 58 LA 501, 505 (Stouffer, 1972).

3. American Airlines, Inc., 47 LA 266, 269 (Dworkin, 1966).
4. Cooper Indus., Inc., 78 LA 850 (Aisenberg, 1982) and cases cited therein.
5. FMC Corp., 74 LA 1185, 1187 (Doering, 1980).
6. Hayes-Albion Corp., 70 LA 696, 698 (Glendon, 1978).
7. Dixie Belle Mills, Inc., 43 LA 1070 (Dworet, 1964).
8. R. Block and R. Mittenthal, "Arbitration and the Absent Employee," in *Arbitration 1984*, Proceedings of the Thirty-Seventh Annual Meeting, National Academy of Arbitrators, ed. W. Gershenfeld (Washington, D.C.: BNA Books, 1985): 81.
9. Curtiss-Wright Corp., 36 LA 842 (Seitz, 1961); General Baking Co., 40 LA 386 (Corsi, 1963); Federal Servs., Inc., 41 LA 1063 (Williams, 1963); City of Detroit, 68 LA 848 (Roumell, 1977).
10. Bethlehem Steel Co., 42 LA 851 (Hill, 1964).
11. Marion Power Shovel Co., 43 LA 507 (Dworkin, 1965).
12. General Baking Co., 40 LA 386, 389 (Corsi, 1963); *see also* Spencer Foods, Inc., 55 LA 847, 849 (Doyle, 1970) and Block and Mittenthal, note 8 above, at 81.
13. Galloway Co., 49 LA 240, 245 (Gundermann, 1967).
14. Altec Corp., 71 LA 1064, 1066 (Hays, 1978).
15. Federal Servs., Inc., note 9 above.
16. Block and Mittenthal, note 8 above, at 82.
17. Tri-State Eng'g Co., 69 LA 980 (Brown, 1977).
18. Bi-State Dev. Agency, 67 LA 231 (Dugan, 1976); Hayes-Albion Corp., note 6 above.
19. Dayton Steel Foundry Co., 53 LA 537 (Seinsheimer, 1969).
20. Pittsburgh Plate Glass Co., 52 LA 985 (Duff, 1969).
21. National Standards Co., 85 LA 401 (Butler, 1985).
22. St. Regis Paper Co., 75 LA 737 (Andersen, 1980).
23. Consolidation Coal Co., 83 LA 927 (Duff, 1984).
24. Sears, Roebuck & Co., 72 LA 238, 240 (Blackmar, 1979).
25. Union Carbide Nuclear Co., 41 LA 122 (Schedler, 1963).
26. Shenango Valley Water Co., 51 LA 799 (Duff, 1968).
27. Fairbanks Morse, Inc., 47 LA 225 (Fisher, 1966).
28. Union Carbide Corp., 47 LA 531, 533 (Merrill, 1966).
29. General Elec. Co., 31 LA 386 (Sutermeister, 1958).
30. American Steel & Wire Co., 12 LA 47 (Seward, 1948).
31. Mead Corp., 51 LA 1121 (Griffin, 1968).
32. Federal Servs., Inc., 41 LA 1063 (Williams, 1963); Memphis Publishing Co., 48 LA 554 (Oppenheim, 1967).
33. National Airlines, Inc., 43 LA 1169 (Black, 1964).
34. Ohio Edison Co., 52 LA 593 (Marshall, 1969); Booth Newspapers, Inc., 41 LA 1133 (Ryder, 1963).
35. Socony Mobil Oil Co., 45 LA 1062 (Kadish, 1965).

# 4

# Observing Legal Constraints

In developing policies regarding attendance, management must take into consideration the potential impact of federal and state laws, particularly the laws specifying fair employment practices with respect to religious observances, handicapped employees, maternity leaves, and military duty leaves.

## RELIGIOUS LEAVE

Employees often request time off to meet their religious obligations, especially when they are scheduled to work on Sundays, Saturdays, or other Sabbath days on which their religious beliefs preclude work. Situations also arise when employees are absent due to religious holidays, church meetings, and similar occasions.

Management's attempt to deal with these absences is complicated by the ban on religious discrimination in Title VII of the federal Civil Rights Act of 1964 and by similar bans in many state fair employment practice (FEP) laws. Title VII requires that employers "reasonably accommodate" an employee's religious observance or practice unless doing so would cause "undue hardship" to the business. Most state FEP statutes contain similar language.

### Supreme Court's View

In the leading decision interpreting Title VII, the U.S. Supreme Court construed the terms "reasonably accommodate" and

31

"undue hardship" to give the employer considerable leeway. The Court set forth these guidelines:

*"Reasonable accommodation"* does not require the employer to take any steps that would violate an otherwise valid collective bargaining contract or the seniority rights of other employees.

*"Undue hardship"* occurs whenever the employer must incur more than minimal costs to accommodate an employee's religious practices.[1]

The Supreme Court also has specified that the duty to accommodate an employee's religious beliefs does not require an employer to accept the accommodation preferred by the employee. If the employer can show it has made a reasonable accommodation, it has met its duty; it need not further show that the alternative accommodation preferred by the employee would result in undue hardship.[2]

To establish religious discrimination, court rulings suggest, the initial burden is on the employee to show these facts:

- His or her religious beliefs and objections are bona fide.

- The employer had notice of the employee's religious beliefs.

- The conduct required by the employer contravenes the employee's religious beliefs.

- The employee has been threatened with or subjected to discriminatory treatment, such as discharge, for his or her inability to fulfill the disputed job duties.

Once the employee has met this initial burden of proof, the burden then shifts to the employer to demonstrate that it made good-faith efforts to accommodate the employee's religious beliefs, and, if unsuccessful in those efforts, that it could not reasonably accommodate the employee's beliefs without undue hardship.[3]

## Accommodation/Hardship Balance

Other courts have considered the following factors in determining whether employers have made reasonable efforts to accommodate their employees' religious practices:

*The nature of the job.* If the job is specialized or unique, the employer may discharge an employee whose religious practices conflict with the employer's needs.[4]

*The size of the employer's establishment.* A large company may be harder pressed to explain why it could not transfer the employee to a different operation.[5]

*The effects of transferring the employee to a different job.* If a transfer means a substantial reduction in pay, the employer may have to show that no other method of accommodation is possible.[6]

*The effects of accommodation upon the morale of other employees.* Some courts have approved this reason for failure to accommodate.[7]

*The employee's efforts in making an accommodation.* If an employee fails to communicate his or her needs or refuses to cooperate with the employer in trying to reach an accommodation, the employee may lose the right to reasonable accommodation.[8] Moreover, the employee must be willing to accept a reasonable compromise. For example, an employee's demand for a "guarantee" that she would never have to work on her Saturday Sabbath was found unreasonable and the employer's refusal to rehire her was not a Title VII violation.[9]

## Undue Hardship

Scheduling problems, the expenses of overtime pay, and the violation of seniority provisions of a collective bargaining agreement have been considered undue hardships.[10]

Arbitrators generally have followed the same liberal definition of undue hardship as the courts and have upheld discipline for the following religious-leave absences:

A member of the Jehovah's Witnesses took a two-week leave to attend Bible school after the employer refused to grant the leave because it coincided with the employer's busiest production schedule.[11]

An employee insisted, over the employer's objection, on leaving the plant for two hours every Wednesday for a Bible study meeting, and the employee's replacement was able to produce at only 71 percent of the employee's rate.[12]

## Types of Religious Practice

The term "religion" in the federal law has been given a broad reading by the courts. Thus, one court observed that if an employee's conduct is religiously motivated, the employer must tolerate it unless doing so would cause undue hardship to the business. "All forms and aspects of religion, however eccentric, are protected," the court said, "except those that cannot be, in practice and with honest effort, reconciled with a business-like operation."[13]

Protection of the Civil Rights Act has been held to allow an employee who was a minister to attend a monthly church meeting on a day other than the Sabbath.[14] Similarly, an arbitrator held that the Act, as interpreted by the courts, protected an employee/minister who took time off from his job to preach at a funeral.[15] But in another case, the discharge of an employee/minister for leaving his job to preach at a funeral was upheld by an appeals court since the absence had created an undue hardship on the employer.[16]

## Employees' Beliefs

An employee suing for religious discrimination must first establish that his or her beliefs are religious within the meaning of Title VII. The Equal Employment Opportunity Commission has taken the position, with court approval, that an employee's beliefs are protected as religious if they are as "deeply and sincerely held as more conventional religious convictions." It thus has been held that atheists are protected by Title VII.[17]

Although some courts have appeared not to be concerned about the employee's sincerity, a number have. One court, after determining that the employee sought to observe a religious holiday because of "convenience rather than conviction," dismissed the case.[18]

But the protection accorded an individual's religious beliefs does not preclude an employer from making "reasonable, limited inquiries to determine if an employee, in fact, holds a religious belief that requires abstention from work on a given day," an arbitrator held. In upholding such a policy adopted by the Social Security Administration (SSA), the arbitrator noted that the SSA was not attempting to judge whether a given religious belief was "legitimate" or "rational." The policy reflected a valid concern that many thousands of hours of religious leave were being taken under highly questionable circumstances.[19]

## RELIGIOUS-LEAVE GUIDELINES

The bans on religious discrimination in Title VII of the Civil Rights Act and in similar state statutes are the main inhibitors on management's freedom in dealing with employee requests for time off to meet religious obligations. Fortunately for management, the courts have given these laws a fairly narrow interpretation.

Management may be able to justify discipline of an employee whose religious beliefs have caused unacceptable absences under these circumstances:

- The employee's religious observances conflict with the specialized or unique nature of the employee's job.
- Transferring the employee to a more suitable job would violate the seniority rights of other employees.
- Accommodating the employee is onerous because of costs, scheduling problems, or lack of comparable posts.
- The employee has failed to accept reasonable compromises.
- The employee lacks a bona fide religious belief.

## MATERNITY LEAVE

Under the Pregnancy Discrimination Act of 1978, which amended Title VII of the Civil Rights Act, employer short-term disability plans must treat disability due to pregnancy and childbirth the same way they treat any other disability. Thus, employers must offer short-term disability benefits for maternity leave if they provide such benefits generally.

The key factor is the need for equal treatment of pregnant employees. A policy that affects pregnant employees, such as requiring a doctor's statement, must be applied to employees with other disabilities.

As with other disabilities, forced time off for pregnancy-related conditions must be related to inability to do the job. Leave for child care, after the employee is medically able to return to work, should be granted on the same basis as leave for other nonmedical purposes. For example, a company that limited pregnancy leave to three months while placing no time limit on unpaid leave for other medical disabilities, was held to have violated the pregnancy disability amendments.[20]

## MATERNITY-LEAVE GUIDELINES

Any policy applied to a pregnant employee should be subjected to the question: Is the same policy applied to employees with other medical disabilities? Policies such as the following should be subjected to this test:

- Short-term benefits provided for disabilities.
- Requirements for doctor's certificates.
- Time limits on unpaid leave.
- Requirements for mandatory leave unrelated to the ability to work.

## HANDICAPPED EMPLOYEES' LEAVE

The employer who attempts to deal with the attendance problems of handicapped employees should be aware of the federal and state laws protecting such employees against discrimination. Employees protected by these laws are not just those who are clearly physically handicapped. The protection may extend, for example, to employees suffering from tuberculosis or other contagious diseases[21] and to alcoholics and drug addicts. It also may extend to actions taken by an employer based on the mistaken perception that an employee has a handicap.

## Discrimination Laws

Under federal law, the Rehabilitation Act of 1973 prohibits discrimination against handicapped employees. It applies to federal contractors (Section 503) and recipients of federal financial assistance (Section 504). In addition, a majority of states now include handicapped workers under their fair employment practice laws.

The federal Rehabilitation Act has been interpreted to include alcoholics and drug addicts within the term "handicapped person." In 1978, Congress amended the statutory definition of "handicapped" to exclude alcoholics and drug abusers whose current condition precludes safe and efficient job performance. Interpretations of the law as applied to these persons provide guidelines for dealing with other employees whose handicaps interfere with their attendance or other job performance standards.

Thus, under federal regulations, an employer may hold an alcoholic or addict to the same performance standards as other employees or job applicants. In evaluating any employee, an employer may consider past personnel records; absenteeism; disruptive, abusive, or dangerous behavior; violations of rules; and generally unsatisfactory work performance. The only requirement is that these standards be applied in a nondiscriminatory manner.[22]

## Reasonable Accommodation

The federal law requires covered employers to make "reasonable accommodation" for an employee's handicap. In applying this requirement to cases involving alcoholics or drug abusers, a distinction is made between current abusers and "recovered" individuals.[23] Thus, a court ruled that absenteeism caused by alcoholism prior to treatment should be considered as different from post-treatment absenteeism. The court found that a federal agency had failed to forgive an alcoholic for drinking-related absences that occurred prior to treatment. Under the Rehabilitation Act, the court said that employers must provide "reasonable accommodation" by forgiving an alcoholic's misconduct prior to undergoing treatment.[24]

In another interpretation of "reasonable accommodation," a court held that an alcoholic federal employee who was fired for excessive absenteeism should have been offered leave without pay to obtain treatment prior to his discharge. Although the employee previously had failed to complete a rehabilitation program, the court said that management should have given him a last chance by requiring him to undergo successful detoxification or face suspension or other serious disciplinary action.

Not every employee whose absenteeism continues after failing to complete a treatment program is entitled to further medical leaves, the court noted. But, it ruled, if evidence shows that such a leave would be beneficial, the "reasonable accommodation duty requires the agency to evaluate whether such a leave or an alternative arrangement" would amount to an "undue hardship."[25]

## GUIDELINES FOR ACCOMMODATING HANDICAPPED EMPLOYEES

Provided reasonable accommodation is made for an employee's handicap, an employer may hold the handicapped employee to the same performance standards as other employees. In dealing with a handicapped employee's absenteeism, employers should keep these points in mind:

- A distinction probably should be made between absenteeism that may have been due to the onset of the handicap and absenteeism that occurs after the employee's recovery or rehabilitation and after the employer's efforts to provide reasonable accommodation for the handicap. The prior handicap-related absenteeism may have to be forgiven, but the rehabilitated and accommodated employee may be held to the usual attendance standards.

- A reasonable accommodation for the employee's handicap may include offering leave without pay to obtain treatment or rehabilitation, provided this does not present an undue hardship for the employer.

- An employer can require reasonable documentation of the employee's claim of a handicap that requires accommodation from the employer. A physical examination by a doctor selected by the company or other independent evidence may be required.

# MILITARY LEAVE

Federal law—the Vietnam Era Veterans' Readjustment Act—requires employers to grant workers military leave for both short- and long-term absences. Generally, workers are eligible for such leave if they must take time off to comply with military reserve service or training obligations, or if they are noncareer veterans who are seeking to return to their former positions or employer after active duty.

Under the law, employers must reinstate these individuals and generally provide them with the same employment rights and privileges to which employees returning from furloughs or leaves of absence are entitled. Any fringe benefits earned on the basis of length of service must also be awarded such employees.

Veterans qualify for reemployment rights if they have served less than four years, are honorably discharged, and notify their employers within 90 days of discharge of their intention to return. Reservists who complete an initial training period of at least three months must inform their employers within 31 days of discharge of their plans to return to the job. Reservists on other than initial training duty must inform their employers of their training obligations and report for the next regularly scheduled work period after training ends, with a reasonable time allowed for travel.

Upon reinstatement, workers are entitled to the pay rate they would have received had they not been absent and to an opportunity to regain former proficiencies. They also are protected from discharge "without cause" for one year from the date of their reinstatement.

An employer is not required to accommodate reserve and guard obligations by scheduling work around periods of duty, according to the U.S. Supreme Court. It upheld an employer's refusal to rearrange the work schedule of a weekend reservist who, one week each month, could not put in his full 40-hour week because his job rotation called for weekend work. The law was intended to protect employee-reservists against discrimination, not to confer special benefits.[26]

## MILITARY-LEAVE GUIDELINES

Reservists and guardsmen, upon request, must be granted leaves of absence to cover time off from the job for periods of training subsequent to initial active training duty. Such leave must be given regardless of the time involved or whether the employee volunteered for the duty. In addition:

- A request for leave does not have to be submitted in advance or in any particular form. Nor must the employee separately request leave for each training period in a regularly scheduled series. The employer, however, should be given sufficient notice so that work schedules may be adjusted to accommodate the needs of both the business and reservists.

- The leave of absence includes both the training period and the travel time required to return from the training site. Leave time must be extended for delays in returning caused by factors beyond the employee's control and for periods of hospitalization incidental to the training, up to a maximum of one year following scheduled release from duty.

- Reporting-back time is set as the "start of the next regularly scheduled shift after expiration of the last calendar day necessary" to travel home from training, or after the worker has had reasonable time to rest. Failure to comply with this provision subjects the worker to the employer's normal disciplinary measures for unexcused or unscheduled absences or tardiness.

---

## ENDNOTES

1. Trans World Airlines v. Hardison, 432 U.S. 63, 14 FEP 1697 (1977).
2. Ansonia Bd. of Educ. v. Philbrook, 42 FEP 359 (1986).
3. Postal Workers v. Postmaster Gen., 35 FEP 1484 (N.D. Cal. 1984); Burns v. Southern Pac. Transp. Co., 589 F.2d 403, 17 FEP 1648 (9th Cir. 1978).
4. Weitkenaut v. Goodyear Tire & Rubber Co., 381 F. Supp. 1284, 10 FEP 513 (D. Vt. 1974); Olds v. Tennessee Paper Mills, 11 FEP 350 (E.D. Tenn. 1974); Roberts v. Hermitage Cotton Mills, 8 FEP 315 (D.S.C. 1973), *aff'd*, 8 FEP 319 (4th Cir. 1974).
5. Claybaugh v. Pacific Nw. Bell Tel. Co., 5 FEP 719 (D. Or. 1973); Drum v. Ware, 7 FEP 269 (W.D.N.C. 1974).
6. Ward v. Allegheny Ludlum Steel Corp., 11 FEP 594 (W.D. Pa. 1975).
7. Cummins v. Parker Seal Co., 429 U.S. 65, 13 FEP 1178 (1976); Johnson v. United States Postal Serv., 8 FEP 371 (5th Cir. 1974); Reid v. Memphis Publishing Co., 11 FEP 129 (6th Cir. 1975).
8. Chrysler Corp. v. Mann, 15 FEP 788 (8th Cir. 1977), *cert. denied*, 16 FEP 501 (1978).

9. Jordan v. North Carolina Nat'l Bank, 15 FEP 1322 (4th Cir. 1977).

10. Trans World Airlines v. Hardison, note 1 above; Johnson v. United States Postal Serv., note 7 above; Reid v. Memphis Publishing Co., note 7 above.

11. J. Schoeneman, Inc., 69 LA 325 (Oppenheimer, 1977).

12. Norris Indus., 68 LA 171 (Rehmus, 1977).

13. Cooper v. General Dynamics, 533 F.2d 163, 167–168, 12 FEP 1549, 1553–4 (5th Cir. 1976).

14. Weitkenaut v. Goodyear Tire & Rubber Co., note 4 above.

15. Alabama By-Products Corp., 79 LA 1320 (Clarke, 1982).

16. Howard v. Haverty Furniture Cos., 615 F.2d 203, 22 FEP 766 (5th Cir. 1980).

17. EEOC Dec. No. 71–779, 3 FEP 172; Young v. Southwestern Savs. & Loan Ass'n, 10 FEP 522 (5th Cir. 1975).

18. Hansard v. Johns Manville, 5 FEP 707 (E.D. Tex. 1973).

19. Social Sec. Admin., 79 LA 449 (Mittelman, 1982).

20. Maddox v. Grandview Care Center, Inc., 37 FEP 1263 (11th Cir. 1986).

21. Arline v. School Bd. of Nassau County, 39 FEP 9 (11th Cir. 1985).

22. 42 *Federal Register* 22686 (1977).

23. Viewing alcoholism as a lifelong chronic illness that can be abated only through abstinence, members of Alcoholics Anonymous prefer the term "recovering" alcoholic.

24. Walker v. Weinberger, 36 FEP 1527 (D.D.C. 1985).

25. Whitlock v. Donovan, 36 FEP 425 (D.D.C. 1984).

26. Monroe v. Standard Oil Co., 107 LRRM 2633 (1981).

# Part 2

# Preventive Measures

# 5

# Reconciling Family/Work Needs

Employers rank family responsibilities as one of the leading causes of job absences.[1] Moreover, work/family conflicts may have a hidden impact not shown on attendance records, since employees often will cite another reason rather than acknowledge that these problems caused their absences.

These conflicts are not limited to child-care difficulties. With the "graying" of our population, care for elderly family members is an increasing cause of job attendance problems.

## CHANGING DEMOGRAPHICS

Employers today are looking at a strikingly different work force from the one that existed a generation ago. Less than 10 percent of today's population live in families headed by a male breadwinner and a mother who stays at home.

Female participation in the labor force has grown from 38 percent in 1970 to just about 50 percent in 1985. Much of this growth has come from women with children. By 1990, two-thirds of new entrants will be women; by the year 2000, women will be participating to the same extent as men.[2]

Nearly 60 percent of married mothers with children age five or younger now are employed, compared with 37 percent in 1970.[3] The number of single-parent households is expected to rise by 48 percent—between 6 million and 8.9 million—from 1980 to 1990.[4]

Projections show that by 1990, 60 percent of all families will be dual-career families. Two out of three mothers with children under age 13 will work, and 55 percent of these mothers will have

45

at least one child under the age of 6.[5] Despite these statistics, "We still act as though workers have no families," Labor Secretary William Brock commented in 1985. "Secure parents who aren't worried about their kids are better workers,"[6] he observed.

## Impact on Job Attendance

Working parents miss about one week of work each year because of child-care problems, according to a survey of 1,243 working parents conducted by Child Care Systems, Inc., a child-care information and referral services firm.[7] The study found that such problems as sick children, ill child-care providers, school holidays, and transportation disruptions cause working parents to miss an average of 5.4 workdays annually. To receive compensation, the study found, employees most often report these missed days to their employers as vacation days (34 percent), sick days (30 percent), or personal days (25 percent).

In addition to requiring full-day absences from work, child-care problems cause the typical working parent to lose slightly more than eight work hours per year because of early departures from or late arrivals to the job, the study reported. Nearly one-third (30 percent) of the employees with children said they leave work early or arrive late at least twice a month.

## Effect on Productivity

Besides the direct impact on job attendance, child-care problems have other serious consequences on employee productivity. The study also found that more than one-fourth (27 percent) of the employees indicated that during work hours they call, or are called, at least once a week on matters about their children, receive calls from their children, or arrange for child-care adjustments.

Selecting appropriate arrangements for child care takes an average of 8.8 hours each time changes are made. The hours are spent placing phone calls, visiting prospective providers, and discussing arrangements with friends—activities that typically occur during the workday. Just about half of the employees make new child-care arrangements at least once during a 12-month period, and 72 percent said that they spend at least one week trying to find child care.

Finally, nearly two out of five working parents who took part in the survey reported that they have considered leaving their jobs because of problems related to child care.

## CHILD-CARE ARRANGEMENTS

Child care usually takes one of these forms:

1. In-home care, which uses someone other than the parent to provide care at the child's home,
2. Family care, which provides child care in another adult's home, or
3. Child-care centers, which provide group care at a facility.

Child care in the parents' home or in another adult's home are the most prevalent types of arrangements. Nearly four out of five working mothers surveyed in 1982 by the Census Bureau used in-home child care and family care for their preschoolers. Only one-fifth of the mothers used child-care centers.[8]

The cost of this care is the fourth largest budget expense item in most American households, behind food, housing, and taxes. Away-from-home care for one child can range from $1,500 to $10,000 a year, with most parents paying $3,000.[9]

## EMPLOYER-SUPPORTED PROGRAMS

Given these trends, it is not surprising that employer-supported child care has grown rapidly in the United States, with the number of employers who subsidize child care quadrupling between 1982 and 1985. But by 1985, only 2,500 out of 6 million employers offered some type of child-care service, according to a Conference Board survey. Relatively few of these 2,500 firms run day-care centers themselves. The study estimated that only 150 companies and 400 hospitals currently sponsor day-care centers at or near their facilities.[10]

This relative dearth of job-site centers appears to accord with

employee preferences. A study of employee attitudes found that
75 percent of working parents prefer child-care arrangements nearer
to their homes than to work, and also prefer family care and home
care to center-based care.[11]

## Financial Aid

The fastest growing form of employer assistance, according to
the Conference Board survey, is direct financial aid. The four most
widely used approaches are described below.

### Vouchers

Some employers help foot child-care costs by adding money
to employee paychecks or supporting programs selected by the
parents. All of the firms with voucher plans set ceilings on voucher
payments, based either on family income or on actual costs. Many
companies limit voucher eligibility to relatively low-income groups
or to children below a certain age.

The following examples illustrate several different company
policies to help employees offset the cost of child care.

### Child-Care Center Subsidies

**Polaroid Corp.**, Cambridge, Mass., pays a direct subsidy
to cover a percentage of an employee's day-care bill; the percentage varies according to a sliding scale based on income.
In 1986, employees with family incomes of $30,000 or less
were eligible, and more than 100 employees participated. Employees must use licensed day-care centers or homes.

Polaroid opted for the voucher system, rather than an on-
site center, because its work force was spread out among a
number of locations.

### Sick Child Care

**Minnesota Mining and Manufacturing Co.** (3M) has a
program, operated in cooperation with Children's Hospital,
St. Paul, Minn., under which a trained health care worker is
sent to care for a sick child of a 3M employee who otherwise

would have to leave the child home alone or miss work. The service does not apply, however, if medical services are needed. The company pays a portion of the hourly fee on a sliding scale based on a family's ability to pay.

### Discounts with Local Child-Care Centers

About 300 of the employers surveyed provide discounts. Most of them obtained a flat 10-percent discount from the child-care center, and about half of these employers also paid another 10 percent of the fees, reducing the overall child-care costs by 20 percent. The following example typifies such arrangements.

**Endless Vacation Systems, Inc.**, Indianapolis, Ind., has a contract with Kinder-Care Learning Centers, Inc., a major day-care chain, under which Endless Vacation's employees get a 20-percent discount, half from the company and half from Kinder-Care, on child care at a nearby center. The company says the center has reduced absenteeism and turnover.

### Flexible Spending Accounts

Under these plans, which were offered by some 800 employers in 1985, employees can draw from funds set aside by the company to cover optional benefits over and above the firm's basic benefit package. Virtually all of these plans are funded by reducing the employee's salary, but they can yield substantial tax savings to the employee. For example, a $50,000-a-year employee with $3,000 in child-care expenses could pay income taxes based on a $47,000 salary and spend the $3,000 on child care out of pretax dollars. However, it should be noted that these plans have met serious objections from the Internal Revenue Service. Any plan in which employee benefits are to be nontaxable should be checked carefully against current IRS requirements.

### Comprehensive Cafeteria or Flexible Benefit Plans

Offered by 150 major corporations in 1985, these plans allow employees to choose child care from a large menu of benefits that supplement the basic "core" benefits. The programs are financed by creating employee credits through employer contributions and a portion of employees' salaries.

Since employees who do not need or want child-care benefits can opt for other benefits of equal value, these cafeteria plans avoid the complaints that may occur when an employer funds child-care services for a small fraction of the work force. This advantage also pertains to the flexible spending account programs since they too offer benefits other than child care.

In a 1985 survey conducted by Louis Harris & Associates, 15 percent of the employers offered flexible benefit arrangements, and an additional 19 percent expected to introduce such plans within two years.[12]

Below is an example of a cafeteria benefit plan that provides child-care assistance as one of the elective benefits.

### Cafeteria Benefit Plans

**Comerica, Inc.,** Detroit, Mich., a large bank holding company, adopted in 1982 a flexible reimbursement plan that includes child-care reimbursement as an option. About 200 employees, representing between 3 and 4 percent of the work force, have elected this option.

Each employee receives a standard benefit plan, including medical, life, and disability insurance. An employee can "purchase" additional benefits with either "benefit credits" or "salary credits." The benefit credits are earned if the employee declines some or all of the standard benefits. The salary credits are available when the employee elects to purchase benefits out of pretax income. Supplemental benefits include extra vacation, dependent life insurance, a capital accumulation plan, disability benefits, and child-care reimbursement.

The child-care reimbursement benefit may be used only for children under 15 years of age. The care may be provided inside or outside the home, but not by a dependent of the employee. If employees select a facility that cares for more than six children at one time, it must have a state license. The child-care service must be necessary to enable the employee to work.

Since 95 percent of Comerica's 5,500 employees have elected benefits different from the standard package, the company has concluded that its old benefit package was not doing the job. Participation of the employees, 75 percent of whom are female, in the child-care plan is less than anticipated. Part of the reason, management speculates, may be its requirement for statements from the employees on child-care expenditures. "If they're paying Aunt Matilda, she may not be declaring their payment as income, and they don't want to get her in trouble," a company spokesman commented.

## Child-Care Centers

Employer-sponsored centers can be on-site or off-site; and in either case, they can be administered by the company or by an outside service. The employer sponsorship usually involves a co-payment, with the employer subsidizing some of the cost but with employees who use the centers paying a fee.

On-site centers appear to be the exception rather than the rule, except among hospitals. On-site child care has become a relatively popular benefit for hospitals because of their need to attract and retain skilled nurses who must work irregular hours and the availability of the hospitals' support services to the child-care center.

Following are examples of a corporate on-site center and a near-site center.

### *On-Site Centers*

**Stride-Rite Corp.** maintains one child-care center at its corporate headquarters in Cambridge, Mass., and another at its warehousing facility in Roxbury, Mass. Both centers are available to employees and the community, which includes many poor and single-parent families. The children receive all necessary support services such as medical, dental, and psychiatric care, as well as reading and writing readiness, arts appreciation, painting and dance, and creative play programs.

Parents begin and end their workday with their children, often have lunch with them, and participate in center decision making. Fees are based on a percentage of the parents' income; remaining costs are borne by the company. Public funding enables children from low-income families to attend.

Stride-Rite estimated that it would spend $150,000 on child care in 1985, but that this cost would be more than offset by the improved caliber of job applicants as well as better attendance and morale.

Since 1975, Stride-Rite has helped about 50 public and private employers establish day-care centers. The firm offers monthly seminars and has a full-time staff to help employers develop day-care budgets and curricula.

**Hoffmann-LaRoche, Inc.** opened its child-care center in 1980 one block from its Nutley, N.J., headquarters. The center serves 165 children, providing full-time care for preschoolers, a kindergarten that meets public and private school standards, and part-time care for those of school age. Other services include a full-time summer program, emergency care, a drop-in program for preschoolers who need ongoing but intermittent full-time care, part-time care for children in shared-custody arrangements, emergency care for times when "the babysitter suddenly quits," a parent-child consultation service on child development, and an employee information network to help workers locate child care in their home communities.

The staff includes a director, three certified teachers, three teacher assistants, two teacher interns, and a cook. The center teaches reading, math, science, creative arts, music, drama, safety, health, and nutrition. The company subsidizes one third of the child-care costs—or $7 out of an estimated $21 daily expense per child in 1985.

Hoffmann-LaRoche considers its support for child care an investment that has paid handsome dividends. "If employees have not resolved their child-care problems, they are not free to devote their best professional efforts to the job," Leonard Silvermann, the firm's vice president for human resources, told a 1985 child-care seminar. More than two-fifths of the employees who took advantage of the child-care center reported reduced job absences.

When an employer chooses to subsidize community day-care centers rather than run its own on-site center, its employees may receive preferential admission and/or reduced rates in exchange for the employer's financial support. This route saves the employer the administrative headaches and potential legal liabilities involved in running an on-site center.[13]

## Information and Referral Services

Providing child-care information and referral services is a relatively inexpensive method of helping working parents, and it has become one of child care's "growth industries." Most companies that furnish such services contract with an existing referral agency in the community; others opt for an in-house "hot line."[14]

Apart from the cost factor, employers are attracted to these services since they do not raise the same issues of equity of benefits that the more expensive child-care options do. But employers often find that they need to add a recruitment component to find additional providers, particularly for infant and sick child care.[15]

The following examples show several company's programs to help direct their employees to child-care resources.

### *Information/Referral Programs*

**International Business Machines (IBM)** has established a nationwide resource and reference network of more than 200 community-based agencies and individuals delivering services to worker families. The referral service directs IBM employees to a trained child-care expert who knows the local resources and can help parents clarify their needs.

IBM prepays the cost of the referral service, and the IBM parent pays the child-care fees. The service will contribute to local community efforts to plan for and increase the availability of quality child-care services.

The service's parent education efforts cover licensing standards, how to interview a provider and conduct a site visit, and what to do if there are problems with the provider. A child-care handbook has been developed to help parents in their evaluation and decision-making process.

**Minnesota Mining and Manufacturing Corp.**, St. Paul, Minn., has established an information and referral service operated by a full-time child-care coordinator. Through seminars and other vehicles, the coordinator helps parents make decisions about child-care situations.

**An office park on-site resource center** is subsidized by several small companies in the Prospect Hill Executive Office Park, Waltham, Mass. The center includes a library, a child-care referral system, lunchtime seminars for parents, and an after-school call-in system for employees' children.

**Community Coordinated Child Care (4C),** a community resource for information and referral on child care, is subsidized by a consortium of about a dozen companies in Holland, Mich. Each company pays an annual fee based on the number of employees. The services provided by 4C include matching referrals to the type of care requested, parent counseling, educational programs for day-care providers, and on-site inspection of day-care facilities.

## MATERNITY LEAVE

The use of paid sick leave for maternity purposes is permitted for office and managerial employees by 75 percent of the companies covered in a 1983 BNA survey and for plant employees by 63 percent of the companies.[16]

In discussing maternity leave, a distinction needs to be made between two types of leave. The first covers the period of physical disability associated with the pregnancy, birth, and post-natal recovery; this leave is basically the same as regular sick leave or disability leave. The other type of maternity leave allows the parent to spend time at home with the newborn child; this leave usually is unpaid and is similar to unpaid leaves of absence for personal reasons.

More than nine out of 10 companies surveyed by BNA provided unpaid maternity leave. The most common length was six months, although more than one-fourth of the employers said they have no maximum limit.

The survey indicated that maternity leave policies were in a state of flux. About one-fourth of the companies had made major policy changes in order to meet requirements of the federal law; many others were contemplating changes once the Equal Employment Opportunity Commission and the courts elaborated on the ground rules. The requirements of the federal law regulating maternity leave are discussed in Chapter 4, "Legal Constraints."

## PATERNITY LEAVE

Far fewer firms provide child-care support for male workers than for female employees. According to the 1983 BNA survey, about two out of five employers give male employees time off for the births of their children. Of these firms, nearly half allow the father to use annual leave, while less than two out of five allow the use of sick leave; the rest allow unpaid leave.[17]

Organizations with paternity leave plans report that it is rarely used. Many men apparently fear the time off might harm their promotional opportunities or their images as career-oriented employees. Nevertheless, most organizations that provide the leave conclude that it is "a nice thing to have on the books."

The following examples describe several forms of parental leave available to employees.

### Maternity/Paternity Leave

**Foley, Hoag & Eliot,** a Boston law firm, provides eight weeks of paid leave for any attorney unable to work because of pregnancy, childbirth, or other conditions related to pregnancy. Beyond the eighth week, the firm continues to pay an attorney's full salary if her physician certifies she is unable to work. The firm also provides unpaid parenting leave to male or female attorneys.

**Bank Street College of Education,** New York City, permits up to three months of paid leave for workers who are the primary caregivers for new children and other children in the family. Employees who adopt children younger than 36 months old are eligible for the same amount of leave. In addition to the paid leave, unpaid leave of six months to a year is available, depending on an employee's particular work situation.

## ADOPTION LEAVE

Adoption leave is far less common than maternity and paternity leave. One out of four firms responding to the 1983 BNA survey reported leave policies for employees who are adopting children. More than three-fourths of these firms allow the use of unpaid leave, while most of the rest permit the adoptive parents to use accumulated personal leave.[18]

The general lack of adoption leave has become a controversial issue. Proponents note that most adoption agencies require working parents to take time off to care for the new child. An arbitrator held that a collective bargaining contract's maternity leave clause should apply to all employees who become mothers, including adoptive mothers. Providing such leave aims primarily at facilitating mother-child relationships, not medical recovery from childbirth, the arbitrator concluded.[19]

## ALTERNATIVE WORK SCHEDULES

Nontraditional work schedules have become the most popular means of accommodating working parents. The most commonly used types are described below.

### Flextime

This program allows employees to select their own work hours, provided each employee works a specified number of hours each day and is present during "core hours" fixed by the employer. The following examples show the range of scheduling options these programs provide.

> **General Motors of Canada** has used flextime for certain office staff and salaried plant employees since early 1975. Under the program, the standard workweek is 40 hours, and employees are required to work at least five but no more than 12 hours a day.
>
> The permissible workday extends from 7:45 a.m. to 4:30

p.m., with the core period from 9 a.m. to 2:30 p.m. Within that core period, workers select a lunch break of at least a half-hour between 11:30 and 1:00.

According to company studies, the program has improved employee morale and reduced lost hours due to tardiness and absenteeism for personal business, overtime costs, and turn-over.

**Hewlett-Packard Co.**, Palo Alto, Calif., uses flextime in its manufacturing operation, even though flextime is usually considered unsuitable for production workers. The 8-hour day can run as early as 6:30 a.m. to 3:00 p.m. or as late as 8:30 a.m. to 5:00 p.m. Flextime is successful, the company says, because of its "single station," rather than assembly-line, production system. In those units that require cooperative work, the group chooses a uniform schedule.

**International Business Machines** allows a modified flex-time for most of its employees that permits starting and quit-ting times to vary by a half-hour from the standard daily working hours. Management finds that this makes it easier for most employees to handle doctor and dentist appointments and other personal errands outside working hours.

**SmithKline Beckman Corp.** offers a flexible work sched-ule to a majority of its employees. With approval from their supervisors, employees can start their seven-hour workday any time between 7:30 a.m. and 9:15 a.m. and leave any time between 3:00 p.m. and 6:00 p.m., with two restrictions: They must be on the job a minimum of five and one-half hours during the company's core workday of 9:15 a.m. to 3:00 p.m., and they must work a five-day week. Reductions in absentee-ism and tardiness are cited by management as among the major benefits of the flextime program.

## Compressed Work Schedules

This plan alters the traditional five-day, 40-hour week, most commonly by compressing the workweek into four 10-hour days.

An obstacle to this option for many employers in the past had been the federal laws requiring firms with government contracts to pay overtime after eight hours' work in any one day. These laws now have been amended so that, beginning in 1986, overtime compensation is required only after 40 hours per week. Removal of this legal hurdle may encourage more employers to consider this option. Below is an example of one plan whose operation has proven a success over the years.

### Compressed Workweek

**Uniformed Services Automobile Association** has used a compressed workweek of a four-day, 38-hour schedule since 1971. About 80 percent of the employees work Monday through Thursday, with the rest covering Tuesday through Friday. When a holiday occurs, all employees work the remainder of the week. Overtime is paid at a straight rate through 40 hours, after which time and one-half is paid.

Employees say they like the schedule because of reduced commuting and child-care costs, as well as the three-day weekend. Management praises the system for reducing turnover, sick leave usage, and employee errors on the job, while increasing productivity and improving service to clients.

## Job-Sharing

This program allows two employees to hold down one job, with each working a part-time schedule. One problem with this option is its higher cost. Two half-time workers usually cost more than one full-time worker since some labor costs are fixed per employee regardless of the number of hours worked.

A job-sharing manual suggests that this arrangement works best where (1) a job can be split into separate, but related, assignments; (2) a supervisor can provide continuity to the total job and still evaluate the sharers individually; and (3) the sharers are compatible and dedicated.[20] These specifications may explain why this option has had limited application.

## Half-Day Vacations

One survey found that about nine out of 10 working parents favored policies allowing use of vacation time in half-day segments to handle family responsibilities. This low-cost option may save considerable costs through avoiding use of sick leave instead.[21]

## Working at Home

This option becomes more viable as new technology permits electronically hooking up home workers with the office. Today the practice is found largely in informal special arrangements between supervisors and individual workers. By the 1990s, as many as 10 million workers may have home work stations.

Obviously, new, more task-oriented methods of monitoring will need to be developed as this option spreads. The work-at-home option initially may be limited to dependable employees whose work can easily be performed at home—researchers, writers, data processers, computer programmers, and the like. Usually both the employer and the employee benefit by a mix of hours at home and in the office.[22]

## Pros and Cons

According to a 1984 BNA survey, about one in three employers offered flexible hours to at least some segments of the work force. These arrangements were more common among large companies and nonbusiness organizations.[23]

A 1985 study for the American Management Association found that more than one-third of the 1,618 surveyed organizations used flexible schedules.[24] About the same number had "permanent" part-time jobs, under which part-time workers received full-time employee benefits. Less frequently used options were work-at-home arrangements and job-sharing programs.

"Progressive" employers that use innovative and alternative work arrangements "gained clear financial rewards," the study concluded. Such firms consistently outperformed "nonprogressive" companies that used fewer alternative arrangements.

In a report based on an 18-month study, the Work in America Institute predicted that by 1990 more than 50 percent of the U.S.

work force will be on alternative work schedules.[25] For employers, the institute noted, alternative work programs can help alleviate such problems as lateness, absenteeism, turnover, high labor costs, excessive overtime payments, and underutilization of equipment. Such arrangements also can enhance job satisfaction and organizational climate.

The single most important obstacle to flexible scheduling, the institute found, is the "autocratic tradition of supervision," which views rigid work schedules as essential to efficiency. Unions also have been somewhat resistant to alternative work schedules, largely out of fear that employers might use them to evade overtime compensation.

In one of the most extensive surveys of experience with flexible work schedules, the Office of Personnel Management polled 325,000 federal employees enrolled in 1,554 alternative work schedule experiments conducted in 20 different federal agencies over a three-year period. An interim 1981 report found that 93 percent of the employees surveyed, and an even higher percentage of single parents, rated as "very to somewhat important" the ability to set their own work schedules. About half of those surveyed reported that their use of short-term leave decreased somewhat or greatly.[26]

# ELDERLY DEPENDENT CARE

While much attention in recent years has focused on the child-care problems of working parents, a significant number of employees find that caring for elderly relatives or friends causes a similar drain on time and energy. This will become a greater problem given demographic projections of substantial increases in the proportion of elderly people in the population. Some have predicted that "eldercare aid" will become the pioneering employee benefit of the 1990s.

In a 1985 survey, The Travelers Corporation found that 20 percent of employees in its home office provided some form of care for an older person, with 8 percent devoting 35 hours or more a week to the task.[27] Many of these employees were in their 30s and

40s, members of a "sandwich generation" raising younger children as well as caring for older persons.

Nearly one-half of the employees said they use outside sources to provide some or all of the care. The kinds of help utilized include homemaking, nursing, meal deliveries, counseling, adult day care, and telephone monitoring. Four out of five employees said they would like more information about community resources, such as home care, and nearly as many wanted information on insurance coverage, specific illnesses, and support groups.

The typical person receiving care was 77 years old and usually was the mother of the caregiver. More than half lived in their own home or apartment, but 20 percent lived with the caregiver and 15 percent lived in nursing homes.

People caring for aging relatives are three times more likely than the person being cared for to experience depression, and four times more likely to feel anger, according to a University of Michigan School of Nursing study.[28] Similarly, a study by Duke University's Center on Aging notes that 33 percent of those caring for relatives with Alzheimer's disease use prescription drugs for tension, depression, and sleep disorders (compared with 10 percent of the general population), and 22 percent use alcohol to relax or sleep.[29]

Nearly two-thirds of the firms surveyed by the New York Business Group on Health cite workers' eldercare responsibilities as a reason for declining work performance.[30]

The following are experimental methods some employers have used to ease employees' eldercare burdens:

*Distributing information.* Some employers have compiled information for their workers, set up information centers, or sponsored special seminars and "caregiver fairs" to put workers in touch with outside experts.

*Providing financial assistance.* Some firms help cover the cost of visiting nurse or respite care programs. Others aid workers by establishing a dependent care assistance plan as a benefit option, often as part of a flexible benefit plan.

*Introducing flexible schedules.* Since time off during normal working hours often is critical for employees with eldercare responsibilities, flexible schedules and leave policies can help employees meet these responsibilities.

*Exercising business clout.* Employers can join coalitions advocating improvements in government policy toward caring for the elderly.

## GUIDELINES

Employers previously have been reluctant to assist employees with family/work conflicts largely because of cost and equity concerns. They feared, for example, that subsidizing a child-care center would benefit only a small fraction of the work force and cause resentment among other employees.

But today job attendance difficulties and other drains on productivity from family/work conflicts are recognized as not exclusively the problems of women, minorities, or the poor. Also, some of the arrangements that can help resolve these conflicts, such as flexible work schedules and cafeteria benefit plans, offer benefits to all employees and thereby defuse the equity concern.

*Flexible Work Schedules.* Of all of the options for dealing with family/work conflicts, flexible work arrangements probably receive the most employee support, since this benefit appeals to employees generally regardless of dependent-care responsibilities. Yet employers have been slow to adopt these arrangements, although the pace has picked up significantly in recent years. A major source of resistance is the fear of tradition-bound supervisors of losing control.

Careful planning is necessary before implementing a flexible work schedule, whether across the board or only within a specific department. Before implementing such an arrangement, management should take the following steps:

- Solicit input from all organizational levels. Ideally, a committee of employee representatives, first-line supervisors, and higher-level management should investigate the need for and feasibility of a new work schedule. Subsequently, the committee can help promote the program.

- Define underlying objectives. A list of goals will help in setting up the program and can serve as a yardstick to gauge its success. Common objectives include avoiding rush-hour congestion, expanding hours of service, making better use of facilities and equipment, allocating job responsibilities more effectively, and improving job attendance and morale by providing employees with more time for leisure or family responsibilities.

- Determine operational requirements. The first step is to identify customer needs, client services, or output levels and then evaluate whether these can be achieved under the proposed schedule, given departmental needs and staffing levels. Attention also should focus on workload distribution, supervisory responsibilities, and such special services as maintenance and security.

- Analyze subjective factors. It is important to assess the new schedule's probable impact on employees in terms of such things as transportation and child-care arrangements, as well as more intangible concerns, such as workplace camaraderie.

- Test the new schedule. A test run can not only assess the program's impact in a controlled manner, but also work out kinks. The pilot test should last at least a few months.

- Conduct information sessions. All employees and supervisors should be briefed on the program before it is formally implemented. Small orientation sessions are ideal forums for outlining the new work schedule, discussing its ground rules, and answering questions.

*Day-Care Centers.* Most employers do not favor totally subsidized on-site day-care centers. Even working parents prefer sites closer to home or at least away from work. Hospitals, however, are a major exception in providing on-site day-care centers.

Employees generally do favor their employer providing financial assistance for child care, particularly if it is part of an equitable cafeteria plan that includes dependent-care assistance as one of an array of supplemental benefits. Careful needs assessment and planning must take place before offering such assistance. Many of the planning steps noted above for implementing a flexible work schedule also apply here.

*Information/Referral Services.* Cost and equity objections pose less of a hurdle for information and referral services and educational programs. The cost of such services is relatively low, and most employees can benefit from information and education on dependent care, particularly if the service covers care of elderly relatives as well as children.

*Supervisor Training and Education.* One of the least expensive, and perhaps most effective, means of helping employees deal with family/work conflicts is to educate supervisors about the problems, available resources, and ways to be responsive and flexible in handling these problems.

## RESOURCE CENTER

### General

American Red Cross
17th & D Sts., N.W.
Washington, D.C. 20006
202-737-8300

The Red Cross offers workshops, some of which can be given at the worksite, on preparation for parenthood, child rearing, stress management, and first aid. Contact your local chapter or National Headquarters.

Business and Professional Women's Federation (BPW)
2012 Massachusetts Ave., N.W.
Washington, D.C. 20036
202-293-1200

BPW provides information on child care, pensions, flextime, job sharing, and parental leave.

Catalyst
250 Park Ave. South
New York, N.Y. 10003
212-777-8900

This organization, originally established to develop career options for women, works with individuals and corporations on a broad range of work/family issues. It has an extensive library on career and family issues accessible through a computer database service. It has produced special reports and worked with corporations on such issues as maternity/paternity leave policies, relocation, child care, flexible benefits, and education for family and career planning.

Children at Work, Inc., A Division of Adolf Rose Associates
65 Bleecker St.
New York, N.Y. 10012
212-777-4900

This national consulting firm helps employers understand and respond to the needs of working parents and employees with aging parents.

Coalition of Labor Union Women (CLUW)
2000 P St. N.W., Room 615
Washington, D.C. 20036
202-296-3408

In 1978, CLUW established the Center for Education & Research, Inc., as a separate nonprofit entity to provide the necessary tools for union and CLUW members to be effective advocates for women in the workplace and within the labor movement.

Family Resource Coalition
230 North Michigan Ave., Suite 1625
Chicago, Ill. 60601
312-726-4750

This is a national nonprofit organization that focuses on developing community-based family support programs that include programs for employers and employees. Its services include a clearinghouse, technical assistance, networking, and public education.

Women's Bureau
U.S. Department of Labor
200 Constitution Ave., N.W.
Washington, D.C. 20210
202-523-6611

The Women's Bureau has published a number of reports, pamphlets, and surveys of its own, and it also maintains information on resources available from others.

Work and Family Information Center
The Conference Board
845 Third Ave.
New York, N.Y. 10022
212-759-0900

This is a national clearinghouse for information on personnel policies and practices relating to work/family conflicts, innovative employer/government/community partnerships, legislative/regulatory actions, and trends in work/family characteristics.


## Child Care


Child Care, Inc.
125 West 109th St.
New York, N.Y. 10025
212-864-3310

This nonprofit organization conducts a program showing employers how to offer employees full access to child-care information.


Children at Work, Inc.
569 Lexington Ave.
New York, N.Y. 10022
212-758-7428

This organization provides special reports, needs assessments, workshops, and assistance in developing, designing, and managing on-site or consortium child care.


National Employer Supported Child Care Project (NESCCP)
330 S. Oak Knoll, Room 26
Pasadena, Cal. 91101
213-796-4341

In connection with a national study of employer-supported child-care services, NESCCP has published a how-to manual for employers that includes information on how to implement eight major program options and to conduct a needs assessment.

Work/Family Directions
Wheelock College
200 The Riverway
Boston, Mass. 02215
617-734-0001

Work/Family Directions operates a child-care project for sick children. It also provides resource and referral services to major corporations and consultation on options for employer-supported child
care.

## Alternative Work Patterns

New Ways to Work
149 Ninth St.
San Francisco, Cal. 94103
415-552-1000

This is a clearinghouse for information on reduced work time options, such as job sharing and work sharing. It has issued a number
of publications on the subject.

National Council for Alternative Work Patterns
1925 K St., N.W., Suite 308A
Washington, D.C. 20006
202-466-4467

Information on and assistance in setting up new ways of scheduling
work may be obtained from the National Council for Alternative
Work Patterns, Inc., a nonprofit organization. As a resource clearinghouse, the council publishes the *Alternative Work Schedule
Directory*, which contains summary descriptions of the flextime,
compressed workweek, permanent part-time work, and job-sharing
practices of some 300 public and private organizations.

### ENDNOTES

1. The Bureau of National Affairs, Inc. "Job Absence and Turnover Control,"
   *Personnel Policies Forum*, Survey No. 132, October 1981 (Washington, D.C.:
   BNA, 1981): 5.
2. U.S. Department of Labor, Bureau of Labor Statistics, *Labor Force Statistics*

*Derived from the Current Population Survey: A Databook, Volume 1*, Bulletin 2096 (Washington, D.C.: Government Printing Office, 1982): 722.

3. H. Hayge, "Working Mothers Reach Record Number in 1984," *Monthly Labor Review* (December 1984): 31.

4. U.S. Congress, House Select Committee on Children, Youth, and Families, *Families and Child Care: Improving the Options*, 98th Cong., 2nd Sess., 1984, v.

5. J.P. Fernandez, *Child Care and Corporate Productivity* (Lexington, Mass.: Lexington Books, 1986): 181.

6. The Bureau of National Affairs, Inc., "Work & Family: A Changing Dynamic," BNA Special Report (Washington, D.C.: BNA, 1986): 20.

7. Child Care Systems, Inc., *Workplace Impact of Working Parents* (Lansdale, Pa.: Child Care Systems, Inc., 1985): 5.

8. U.S. Bureau of the Census, Current Population Reports, *Child Care Arrangements of Working Mothers: June 1982*, series P-23, No. 129 (Washington, D.C.: Government Printing Office, 1983): 5.

9. D. Friedman, "Corporate Financial Assistance for Children," Research Bulletin No. 177 (New York, N.Y.: Conference Board, 1985): 7.

10. Ibid., 25.

11. *Workplace Impact of Working Parents*, note 7 above, at 2.

12. Equitable Life Assurance Society, *Survey of Corporate Initiatives and Employee Attitudes on Flexible Benefits*, (New York, N.Y.: Equitable Life Assurance Society, 1986): 3.

13. Employee Benefit Research Institute, "Child Care Programs and Developments," *Issue Brief*, May 1984, No. 42 (Washington, D.C.: Employee Benefit Research Institute, 1984).

14. Ibid.

15. The Bureau of National Affairs, Inc., note 6 above, at 32.

16. The Bureau of National Affairs, Inc., "Policies on Leave from Work," *Personnel Policies Forum*, Survey No. 136, June 1983 (Washington, D.C.: BNA, 1983): 21.

17. Ibid., 26.

18. Ibid., 28.

19. Ambridge Borough, 81 LA 915 (Stoltenberg, 1983).

20. B. Olmsted and S. Smith, *The Job Sharing Handbook* (New York: Penguin Books, 1983): 13.

21. J.P. Fernandez, note 5 above, at 148.

22. Ibid., 148–149.

23. The Bureau of National Affairs, Inc., "Productivity Improvement Programs," *Personnel Policies Forum*, Survey No. 138, September 1984 (Washington, D.C.: BNA, 1984): 23.

24. American Management Association, *The Changing American Workplace: Work Alternatives in the '80s* (New York, N.Y.: AMA, 1985): 5.

25. Work in America Institute, Inc., *New Work Schedules for a Changing Society* (Scarsdale, N.Y.: Work in America Institute, 1981): 7.

26. Office of Personnel Management, *Interim Report on the Alternative Work Schedules Experimental Program* (Washington, D.C.: Government Printing Office, 1981): 9.

27. The Bureau of National Affairs, Inc., note 6 above, at 63.

28. The Conference Board, "Eldercare: The Employee Benefit of the 1990s," (New York, N.Y.: The Conference Board, 1986): 12.
29. Ibid., 13.
30. The Bureau of National Affairs, Inc., *Employee Relations Weekly* (April 7, 1986): 4:425.

# 6

# Encouraging Employee Wellness

Most illness-related job absences in the workplace result from such potentially controllable problems as alcoholism, smoking, high cholesterol, hypertension, and obesity. Most of the nation's $400 billion health-care bill goes to treat these ailments.

The workplace is the prime location from which to promote health care and disease prevention. Yet wellness programs, while becoming something of a fad in the mid-1980s, are approached gingerly by much of the business community, primarily because of the following reasons:

- Uncertainty over costs and benefits.

- Unfamiliarity with the techniques and philosophy behind health promotion.

- Lack of hard data on the benefits of particular wellness strategies.

- Increased health insurance costs for certain preventive measures.

## COST EFFECTIVENESS

Data on cost savings from wellness programs are difficult to quantify and, in many cases, either do not exist or would be too expensive to obtain. Most of these programs have been in place only a short time, and it will take time to document their possible impact on illness, hospitalization, and mortality rates. Health-promotion advocates concede that it may take five years to get a payback in lower health-care expenses from a wellness program. But employees will show improved attitudes toward work within a year, they argue.

A frequently heard criticism of wellness programs is that they "preach to the converted." Another criticism is that they are dominated by better-educated, high-paid employees rather than blue-collar workers. Both criticisms probably have greatest validity when directed at exercise and physical fitness programs. However, any wellness program must make special outreach efforts to assure widespread participation from all levels of the organization.

Wellness programs have the potential to involve a much greater proportion of the work force than a traditional employee assistance program (EAP). An estimated 75 percent of the typical work force may have one or more of the risk factors, such as overweight, hypertension, high cholesterol, and smoking, that a comprehensive wellness program could address. An EAP, on the other hand, usually targets the 10 to 15 percent of the work force that may have substance-abuse problems or serious emotional illnesses, and only 10 percent of these afflicted employees usually will make use of the EAP.

The most cost-effective wellness programs are in the following areas:

1. Smoking cessation. This type of program can show the quickest results. An individual's risks associated with smoking go down to nearly zero within two to three years after cessation. Good quality smoking cessation programs can be delivered at a cost of $100 per participant, while the cost of smoking to business has been estimated at $600 annually for each smoker.

2. Hypertension control. High blood pressure is a hidden disease that makes it difficult to show immediate results. It takes an estimated eight to nine years of blood pressure screening and monitoring to show a measurable decrease in the rate of heart attacks and strokes in the work force.

3. Weight reduction. This area ties in with efforts listed above. Weight reduction is usually a major measure for controlling an individual's blood pressure. And stopping smoking typically will lead to weight gain unless the individual works on weight control.

4. Cholesterol testing and nutrition. This also relates to the preceding areas. As with blood pressure screening, a cholesterol check, by itself, is relatively easy and inexpensive. A new finger-prick technique gives employees quick blood test results within 90 seconds.

Not included in this list are alcohol and drug abuse programs and other employee assistance programs for mental illness, financial difficulties, and personal, not physical, problems. These programs are discussed in Chapter 11, "Dealing With Alcohol/Drug Abuse," and Chapter 12, "Assisting Employees With Problems."

## PROGRAM ALTERNATIVES

An employer can spend anywhere from a little to a lot on a wellness program, depending on the organization's size, resources, objectives, and employees' needs. The following alternatives are suggested by the Wisconsin Association of Manufacturers and Commerce:[1]

*Level one: Minimum cost and administration.* Typical offerings include smoking cessation, hypertension control, and weight/diet control. These programs usually require minimal time and expense to set up and run because of readily available local resources, such as the American Heart Association, the American Cancer Society, the Red Cross, and the YMCA. Programs of this nature generally are informal and require only one person to serve as a coordinator-administrator. They should include monitoring and support systems to help employees break the smoking habit; on-site screening to check blood pressures levels; and regular "weigh-ins" and educational materials for employees who want to lose weight.

*Level two: Medium cost and administration.* These more formal programs, emphasizing health awareness along with the smoking cessation and diet control tips of level-one programs, require a heavier investment of time and money. Possible components include exercise and fitness classes, using hired instructors, and health fitness assessments conducted by an outside firm. Other topics under these medium-cost programs could cover stress management, alcohol- and drug-abuse control through an employee assistance program, and personal safety training to reduce accidents on and off the job.

*Level three: Comprehensive health management.* These are the most expensive wellness programs. Mainly offered by major companies, they require major capital outlays for equipment and full-time employees.

The following examples describe four different types of comprehensive health programs used to encourage employee wellness.

### Comprehensive Plans

**Johnson & Johnson**, New Brunswick, N.J., offers a "Live for Life" program to more than 25,000 company employees at 45 locations. Initial individual health risk appraisals and evaluations are provided at no cost on company time. The actual lifestyle change modules are done on the employee's own time. The health risk appraisal consists of two questionnaires covering nutrition; health knowledge; self-care habits, such as seat-belt use or gynecological check-ups; stress management practices; attitudes toward the company; and drug/alcohol use. A 10-minute physical test is then given.

This is followed by a three-hour, one-on-one counseling session, much of which is devoted to health education. The information and employee reports are completely confidential. "If you do absolutely nothing else, start with blood pressure screening," recommends a Johnson & Johnson spokesperson. This is a low-cost program that can save a great deal of money.

Under Johnson & Johnson's program, if an employee's initial screening reveals elevated blood pressure, a second screening is done 10 days later. If the pressure is still high, the employee is encouraged to enter the blood-pressure control program, which includes referral to a doctor, regular blood-pressure testing at the worksite, and educational sessions every three months for as long as the worker is with the company. The goal is to bring 80 percent of the people who are hypertensive under control—either through medication, lifestyle changes, or a combination of both—within a year.

The lifestyle change modules are offered in smoking cessation, weight control, stress management, nutrition, exercise, and high blood pressure control. These programs use a variety of formats, including groups, individual consultation, self-help kits, and telephone support. Shorter educational and promotional programs cover such themes as breast self-examination, biofeedback, nutrition, blood pressure, and carbon monoxide analysis for smokers.

All the lifestyle change modules operate on three levels: informational, motivational, and behavioral. The nutrition program, for example, includes nutrition demonstrations in the cafeteria, films, behavior change classes, bulletin board postings, listing calorie counts along with food prices in the company cafeteria, and working with the cafeteria vendor to lower fat and cholesterol content in recipes.

Initial reports from a two-year epidemiological study are highly encouraging, Johnson & Johnson reports. The program's impact on hypertension and smoking habits has been particularly substantial. Cost-benefit analysis shows savings in illness-care costs in particular, but other anticipated benefits include lower absenteeism, turnover, and accident rates.

**Campbell Soup Co.**, Camden, N.J., started an Institute for Health and Fitness, a nonprofit division, in 1982 at its headquarters and has gradually expanded it to plant sites around the country. The institute promotes a "Turnaround Lifestyle System" to encourage positive behavioral changes.

Turnaround offers a fitness regime, motivational programs to encourage sustained participation, behavior management classes, and lifestyle programs. The fitness regime begins with a medical screening including personal and medical history; blood tests; a health risk assessment; and tests for body fat percentages, flexibility, muscular strength, and cardiovascular efficiency. The test results are discussed in a group counseling session. Each participant receives exercise prescriptions and is taught proper exercise techniques. Participants are retested after three months and six months. A 10,000-square-foot fitness center was developed at the Camden facility.

Lifestyle programs include stress management, low-back care, relaxation techniques, self-defense, nutrition awareness, smoking cessation, and dance classes.

A Turnaround Workshop includes a workbook and leader's kit for use at conferences, seminars, and meetings. The workshop emphasizes behavior modification, sound nutrition, and regular exercise. Exercise and other fitness activity classes are offered before and after work and at lunchtime. Most classes meet for an hour a week for six weeks. The program also seeks to penetrate the worksite culture by such activities as:

- Exercise breaks conducted in conference rooms at regular break times.

- Monthly lectures on such topics as goal setting, first aid, nutrition, and fitness.

- Fitness walking groups at break times.

- A monthly awards luncheon to recognize employees who have improved their health and fitness.

- A monthly newsletter with health information, program announcements, and recognition of individual achievements.

**Control Data Corp.**, Minneapolis, Minn., offers the StayWell Program, an employee health benefit program that is available to full-time permanent employees, regular part-timers, spouses, and retirees. The program, which is free to all eligible employees, includes:

1. A mandatory, one-hour orientation program offered on company time for all eligible employees.

2. A health risk profile questionnaire that includes height, weight, blood pressure, and a blood sample. Employees are encouraged to complete the assessment on company time.

3. Interpretation sessions, during which results of the health assessment are explained and specific lifestyle changes are recommended. These interpretation sessions are on company time.

4. Lifestyle change courses on how to relax, be fit, eat right, quit smoking, lose weight, and prevent high blood pressure. These courses are available at the job site for employees to pursue on their own time. Each course is offered in three ways: (1) computer-based courses, averaging eight lessons of 30 to 45 minutes each, in which the employee uses a terminal and a workbook to advance at an individual pace and in privacy; (2) group courses in which eligible employees and a classroom instructor meet weekly in six to nine sessions lasting an hour or a half hour; (3) self-study courses, consisting of five to eight lessons averaging 45 minutes each, which employees can complete at times and locations most convenient to them and then send back to the StayWell office. All courses are taken on the employee's own time.

5. Action teams consisting of employees and spouses who get together on their own time to pursue health-related endeavors including fitness or exercise programs and efforts to improve both home and work environments.

**Adolph Coors Co.**, Golden, Colo., has a program, Lifestyle/Health Insurance Link, that emphasizes an employee's personal responsibility for health by linking the level of health insurance benefits to the employee's lifestyle. Each employee is asked to fill out a health hazard questionnaire with information on diet, exercise, and other health habits. If certain habits are threatening an employee's health, the employee is asked to visit the company's wellness center for counseling on topics such as alcohol and drug abuse, prenatal care, and cardiac rehabilitation.

Questionnaire evaluations assign a point value to each response. If an employee scores within a range that reflects a healthy lifestyle, he or she receives a health plan that covers 90 percent of medical expenses. If the employee is a smoker, does not exercise, or has some other health-threatening lifestyle, coverage is reduced to 85 percent. But if the employee agrees to counseling, coverage is restored to 90 percent.

## SMOKING CESSATION

Estimates of the annual cost per smoker to industry range from a low of $624 to as much as $4,500. Smokers have an estimated 50 percent higher job absence rate than nonsmokers. Workers who smoke more than two packs of cigarettes per day have twice the job absences of nonsmokers. The on-the-job time lost simply due to the ritual of smoking may average 30 minutes per day. Smokers also run much higher risks of serious illness, accidents, and premature death than nonsmokers. They have twice as many job-related accidents and 50-percent more likelihood of being hospitalized.

Although 75 percent of smokers say they want to quit, they find it difficult to do on their own and often are helped by a supportive environment. According to a study conducted in 1985 by the U.S. Surgeon General,[2] workplace smoking cessation programs have more long-term success than broader community-based clinics, partly because of the continued support and reinforcement workers receive from each other during the crucial weeks after quitting. In the report's words:

Because of the magnitude of the health effects of smoking and the benefits of cessation, smoking cessation programs are likely to yield a higher return on investment than worksite health promotion programs targeting other risk factors such as obesity and lack of exercise.[3]

About 15 percent of American businesses provide smoking cessation programs, the Surgeon General study reported, and as many as one-half of the larger organizations have established no-smoking areas. Some employers also have begun policies of not hiring smokers.

For employees, the main advantages of a workplace program are convenience, reduced expense if the company pays all or part of the cost, and the opportunity to participate with co-workers rather than strangers. Some employees, however, may sense a lack of support from their immediate supervisors or, on the other hand, may feel coerced into participating.

For employers, the advantages are reduced job absences and medical costs, as well as increased productivity and employee morale. Disadvantages include underwriting the cost of the program and possible employee relations problems. "Nonsmoking employees may resent the time off work available to smokers and may demand that their own participation in health promotion programs be subsidized," the report warned.[4]

Long-term success rates from worksite programs are relatively high. According to the report, nearly two-thirds of those who had stopped smoking through a worksite program still were "clean" six to 24 months later, compared with the 20- to 30-percent success rate usually cited for community-based programs.

Worksite smoking modification programs range from a brief message from a doctor to long-term programs with multiple components that last up to five years. Many employers offer cash incentives to encourage workers to quit smoking either at work or entirely. Other approaches include worksite contests, distribution of self-help materials, dissemination of antismoking messages, and on-site clinics led by co-workers, health organization volunteers, or commercial stop-smoking consultants.

Workplace programs consisting mainly of self-help materials and one or two sessions produce relatively low quit rates—from 4- to 14-percent long-term abstinence. The best success rates, the study found, were achieved by "multicomponent" programs, involving group meetings over several months. Programs in workplaces with fewer than 100 employees generally were more successful than those in larger worksites, as were programs limited to smoking, and not including other health risks.

Incentive programs that award cash to employees for not smoking at work or for quitting entirely "deserve further investigation, because they appear to be effective, relatively inexpensive, and easy to implement in a variety of different settings."[5] For example, an incentive program sponsored by a small ambulance firm, which offered employees a $5 monthly bonus for not smoking at work, produced a quit rate of nearly 60 percent of the 75 participants.[6] Similarly, another program that lasted seven months and combined "sizable financial incentives" with group meetings, social support, and health information resulted in up to 91 percent of the participants abstaining from smoking six months after the program ended.[7]

No-smoking competitions among different worksites or among teams within a worksite also can produce high participation rates and "impressive" results. One worksite competition among four banks attracted 88 percent of the firms' smokers and achieved a long-term cessation rate of 15 percent.[8]

One of the major advantages of incentive and competition programs is that "they do not require large amounts of therapist or participant time." The report pointed out, however, that since some participants may "require additional guidance and support," such programs may want to consider providing participants with "self-help stop-smoking materials."[9]

Stop-smoking programs are particularly cost effective, the report observed, if aimed at workers who run the highest risk of developing cancer and chronic lung disease, such as smokers whose work exposes them to hazardous chemicals or substances.

The cost of smoke-cessation programs varies greatly. Local chapters of the American Lung Association and the American Cancer Society offer classes at no charge or for a nominal fee. SmokEnders and other for-profit enterprises charge a fee to run worksite programs.

## STOP-SMOKING GUIDELINES

Employers should incorporate these features when setting up a worksite stop-smoking program:

- Make the program convenient. Employees are more apt

    to participate in programs that offer at least some time off from work.

- Publicize the program in a variety of ways. Posters, memos, brochures, paycheck stuffers, and newsletters can be used to inform workers about the program's cost (if any) and to emphasize that the program is voluntary.

- Be sure that participants receive feedback on their progress through such methods as carbon monoxide tests and charts displaying weekly group results.

## SMOKING RESTRICTIONS

With evidence mounting that environmental tobacco smoke presents a health hazard, many employers are adopting restrictions and complete bans on smoking in the workplace. These policies aim not only at promoting a healthier work environment but also at forestalling costly litigation over nonsmokers' right to work in a safe, clean environment.

In a much-cited decision, the New Jersey Superior Court held that an employee with allergies had the right to be protected from other employees' smoke.[10] In another case, a U.S. district court held that an employee who was allergic to smoke was a handicapped person as defined under the Rehabilitation Act of 1973, and that the employer consequently was required to make reasonable accommodation to the handicap.[11] Perhaps the next question to come before the courts is whether an employee who is addicted to cigarettes also is a handicapped person entitled to reasonable accommodation.

In a number of worker compensation cases, employees have been granted disability—in a few cases permanent disability—due to asthma, bronchitis, or emphysema contracted or aggravated as a result of second-hand smoke. A number of states—among them California, Wisconsin, and New Jersey—have found that workers who quit their job because of smoke irritation are eligible for unemployment compensation.[12]

Several states and cities have adopted or are considering legislation restricting workplace smoking and requiring employers to guarantee nonsmokers smoke-free work environments. For example, effective March 1986, a New Jersey law requires employers with more than 50 workers to design a written policy that guarantees clean-air work areas for nonsmokers.[13]

A 1985 Gallup poll[14] for the American Lung Association found that 75 percent of all adults—62 percent of current smokers, 85 percent of nonsmokers, and 78 percent of former smokers—agree that smokers should refrain from smoking in the presence of nonsmokers. And 79 percent of adults, including 76 percent of current smokers, said employers should limit smoking to certain assigned areas.

Workplace smoking restrictions initially affected mainly work areas in which smoke posed a hazard to sensitive equipment, such as computer rooms, or a potential for product contamination, such as in food processing facilities. But, beginning about 1980, restrictions have been adopted in the interest of employee health, morale, or productivity. By 1985, an estimated one-third of U.S. firms had imposed some smoking restrictions. Predictions are that an increasingly large proportion of employers will adopt no-smoking policies in the future.

Once a worksite restriction on smoking takes effect, smokers tend either to quit or to cut down. At Pacific Northwest Bell, which instituted a complete ban on smoking in 1985, unofficial data indicate that about half the smokers quit within the next six months.

Employers often debate whether to restrict smoking to certain areas or to impose an outright and complete ban. Partial bans have the attraction of seeming to accommodate both smokers and nonsmokers. Such limited restrictions may take the form of policies banning smoking in all common areas and permitting smoking only in segregated, separately ventilated smoking lounges. The drawbacks of such policies are the expense of maintaining the separate lounges and the potential of lost productivity from smokers using the lounges at times other than their regular breaks.

Another form of limited restriction is to segregate common areas, such as lunch rooms and lounges, into smoking and nonsmoking sections. The disadvantage here is that smoke really cannot be segregated in most modern workplaces. Moreover, smokers and nonsmokers alike are rarely satisfied with such arrangements.

## SMOKING-RESTRICTION GUIDELINES

When employers consider placing restrictions on workplace smoking they usually fear negative repercussions from smokers.

Such reactions can be greatly alleviated by careful advance planning, particularly in regard to the following points:

- The restrictions should be realistic and clear and allow a reasonable time for smokers to adjust.

- Employees should be informed in advance of the dangers of smoking and breathing second-hand smoke. Acceptance of smoking restrictions or outright bans will be enhanced if management makes it clear there is no intent to penalize or discriminate against smokers.

- Smoking restrictions should be imposed uniformly throughout the work force. Allowing managers to smoke in their own offices, while forbidding workers to smoke in their areas, is a prescription for trouble.

- In unionized workplaces, smoking restrictions should be discussed with the union, even though it is unclear whether such policies are mandatory subjects for bargaining under the Taft-Hartley Act.

## HYPERTENSION PROGRAMS

High blood pressure affects from 15 to 25 percent of the population, yet often goes undetected or untreated. An estimated 30 million employees are at risk for heart disease, strokes, and kidney disease due to high blood pressure. Hypertensive employees are absent more often, are out longer when ill, and have significantly more premature deaths than other employees.

Hypertension also can be a predictor of alcohol abuse. Estimates are that 25 to 30 percent of all cases of primary hypertension stem from alcohol abuse. Companies with wellness blood pressure programs, combined with an employee assistance program for alcoholism, can better detect both alcoholism and hypertension in the early stages.

Worksite screening programs for hypertension have become increasingly common in recent years, and they reportedly are more cost effective than community care.[15] But most programs merely report the results to the employees and leave it up to them to seek treatment. Many employers have been reluctant to go beyond detection and become involved in treatment.

Yet a study of different forms of worksite hypertension programs found that the most significant results came from programs that went beyond mere screening and referral. A three-year study at four Ford Motor Company plants tested and compared the results of four types of intervention:[16]

1. Screening and referral only.
2. Screening, referral, and semiannual follow-up visits with hypertensive employees.
3. Screening, referral, follow-up visits with hypertensive employees as needed, and follow-up contacts with attending physicians.
4. Screening and provision for on-site treatment of hypertension.

At the end of the project, 86 to 90 percent of the hypertensive employees in the three programs offering follow-up or treatment had reduced blood pressure readings below 160/95 and of that amount, 56 to 62 percent had readings below 140/90. In contrast, only 21 percent of the employees who had only screening and referral had readings below 140/90, and only 47 percent had readings below 160/95.

Data on the cost effectiveness of these programs is difficult to assess, particularly given the uncertainties in detecting the impact on job attendance. While the long-range impact presumably is fewer absences and disabilities due to cardiovascular illness, one study found that job absences increased after a diagnosis of hypertension, perhaps because employees who heard they were sick acted accordingly.[17]

## HIGH BLOOD PRESSURE GUIDELINES

The American Heart Association (AHA) has suggested the use of these increasingly intensive levels for developing a corporate high blood pressure program:

- Health awareness or health promotion on high blood pressure, its detection, and treatment, using posters, literature, possibly films and/or a speaker, and articles in company newsletters or bulletins.

- Screening to detect high blood pressure.
- Referral of employees with an elevated blood pressure to a medical source for diagnosis of the cause and treatment.
- Follow-up to determine if referred employees visited a doctor and received a diagnosis.
- Obtaining employee's medical status regarding high blood pressure and treatment.
- Educating the individual hypertensive employee about high blood pressure, its treatment, and general heart health, and continuing blood pressure monitoring.

See Resource Center listings at the end of this chapter for information on AHA's "Heart at Work" program, which includes a high blood pressure component.

## CHOLESTEROL REDUCTION/NUTRITION

A 1-percent reduction in blood cholesterol brings about an estimated 2-percent drop in heart attack risks, which in turn lowers job absences and health care costs. Diabetic workers average twice as many lost workdays per year and have 2.3 times as many hospitalizations as nondiabetics of the same age.[18]

Blood tests performed at the worksite or during company physicals can identify individuals having high cholesterol readings or actual or incipient diabetes. A minimal-cost program might involve reporting the results to the at-risk employee with accompanying literature on specific behaviors, such as diet, weight reduction, and exercise, that improve cholesterol or blood sugar readings. More elaborate programs would involve group or individual meetings with nutrition counselors who provide diet recommendations, monitor diet plans, and give encouragement and reinforcement.

Eating habits are deeply entrenched and efforts to change them are not likely to have short-term or even intermediate paybacks for business. Lasting dietary change involves intensive, long-term maintenance procedures.

## NUTRITION GUIDELINES

The American Heart Association (AHA) suggests this checklist for conducting an employee nutrition program:

- Survey personnel to assess needs and interests.
- Pretest employees' nutritional knowledge and attitudes.
- Decide on scope of program.
- Publicize program.
- Make logistical arrangements.
- Distribute nutritional awareness brochures and publish nutrition articles in employee publications.
- Arrange for guest lectures before or after work and other special activities, such as food demonstrations at break or noontime.
- Furnish tips on using vending machines and eating out.
- Complete the nutritional screening.
- Distribute results to employees.
- Implement the program, which could include distributing pamphlets and posters, showing slide/tape presentations, arranging group sessions or cooking classes (if there is enough interest).
- Provide follow-up activities.
- Evaluate and report to management.

For materials to use with this checklist as part of AHA's "Heart at Work" program, see the Resource Center listings at the end of this chapter.

## WEIGHT CONTROL PROGRAMS

Individuals defined as obese weigh more than 30 percent above the suggested maximum weight for their height and body frame. An estimated 16 million workers—from 20 to 30 percent of the work force—meet this definition. Obese employees have higher levels of job absences, cardiovascular disease, and poor performance than other employees.

Effective diet programs now aim at permanent changes in eating behaviors, rather than rapid weight loss. The most effective programs, such as Weight Watchers and Overeaters Anonymous, combine lectures with group support, accountability, and confrontation.

Significant long-term weight reductions are difficult to achieve, but the worksite offers one of the best environments for weight-reduction programs. The availability of convenient treatment before or after work and at lunch breaks can encourage participation, and the support of co-worker participants can enhance effective maintenance.

The worksite can facilitate weight reduction management by offering better food choices in the company cafeteria and reducing calorie-dense snacks in vending machines. The company cafeteria often provides an employee's most complete meal of the day.

The costs of organized weight control programs vary widely. Many involve only providing space for meetings and publicizing their availability. Others, run under a physician's supervision, involve initial evaluation, weekly follow-up meetings, and sometimes, medication. Most organized weight-reduction programs run for at least 8 to 12 weeks. Many have follow-up reinforcement sessions with long-term involvement.

## FITNESS/EXERCISE PROGRAMS

Companies increasingly are introducing fitness and exercise programs with expectations of reducing health risks, illness, job absences, and health insurance claims. Without question, program participants have lower risk characteristics, better general health, and fewer illnesses. But those who enter and remain in these programs tend to have lower risk factors to begin with and to have previously established exercise habits. They also tend to have white-collar jobs, while nonparticipants and dropouts tend to be blue-collar workers. Employees who need exercise and fitness programs the most tend not to use them.

Moreover, these programs usually reach a relatively small proportion of the work force. If 25 percent of all employees participate initially, and if 50 percent of these remain in the program after a year (both above-average rates), the program benefits only 12.5 percent of the work force. But this rate compares well with a traditional employee assistance program, which typically involves only 1 to 5 percent of the work force.

Types of corporate physical fitness programs vary widely. At one extreme are programs that merely educate employees about the benefits of regular physical activity and possibly recommend appropriate exercises for employees to do on their own time. At the other extreme are programs that offer elaborate facilities, such as a gym, Nautilus and other equipment, aerobic exercise classes, and full-time staff.

## FITNESS GUIDELINES

The American Heart Association suggests the following increasingly intensive levels for an exercise program:

- Awareness. Use posters and company newsletters to increase employee awareness of the benefits of exercise.
- Self-help. Motivate employees to exercise on their own; encourage them to begin a walking program. Distribute maps for local running, walking, and cycling routes.
- Outside community resources. Organize and plan for the use of outside programs and facilities. Use exercise path maps, parks and recreation facilities, and/or YMCA's exercise instructors.
- Inside program. Develop on-site facilities and programs.

## STRESS MANAGEMENT

Chronic stress is a significant risk factor associated with many chronic diseases. It can lead to elevated blood pressure and then to arteriosclerosis. Recent studies suggest that stress, depression, and other emotional illnesses can impact adversely on the immune system. Stress has been linked to ulcers, mood fluctuations, increased smoking, alcoholic drinking, and use of medications, like aspirin and barbiturates.

Absenteeism clearly is one result of stress on the job. Employees sometimes stay home from work because they are unable to take another day of stress on the job. But the employer cannot eliminate stress in the workplace; a certain amount is part of the work world. Still, employers can try to keep stress at a tolerable level or help employees to cope with it.

Jobs that require high productivity but do not allow employee input on work decisions, and those that demand either more or less skill than the worker has, appear to create the most stress. Stressful jobs typically exhibit higher incidence of accidents, injuries, negligence, and such counterproductive traits as theft, vandalism, and drug abuse.[19]

Unlike physical fitness programs, workplace stress-management programs appear popular with both blue- and white-collar workers and with all levels of management. Typical efforts by firms attempting to lessen stress in the workplace center on helping employees develop better relaxation, coping, and perception skills. Time management, planning, conflict resolution, and achieving teamwork also are featured in many programs.

Formats for worksite programs to reduce stress include (1) workbooks, tapes, or other self-learning tools that employees can use privately; (2) workshops conducted by a trainer; and (3) personal coaching in such areas as dealing with a life crisis.

Stress control/reduction programs are becoming popular and are relatively inexpensive. But most studies have failed to show a direct link between these programs and reductions in serious physical illness. One of the best ways to reduce stress is to talk about it. An employee assistance program is an effective tool since it provides a counselor with whom employees can talk about stress.

## NECK/BACK INJURIES

Reducing neck and back injuries is another often ignored area in corporate wellness programs. These injuries are an expensive and prevalent problem in many work settings. Some estimates are that these maladies account for 45 million lost workdays a year in the United States. Much of this disability—estimates range from over one-half to four-fifths of the cases—could be prevented through relaxation and exercise techniques. Relatively low-cost corporate education programs can have an impressive impact.

Most of the programs currently available include relaxation, flexibility, and strengthening exercises; education about the back's anatomy and function; and advice about proper techniques for sitting, lifting, and standing. Over 100 local YMCAs offer a course for local businesses known as the Y's Way to a Healthy Back. Companies can contract with the Y to conduct the course in-house, or they can subsidize employees' fees to take the program at a Y near their homes.

## GENERAL GUIDELINES FOR WELLNESS PROGRAMS

An effective health promotion program requires careful planning and commitment of resources. Merely distributing a few pamphlets to employees will not produce desired results. These are some of the approaches to consider:

- Determine needs. The organization must decide whether its objective is to contain costs, achieve immediate results or long-term improvements, or appeal to the entire work force or to a select group of employees.

- Collect employee data. In order to tailor wellness programs to the needs of the organization and its workers, information should be gathered on the age, sex, and major health problems of employees; productivity and pay rates; absenteeism rates and disability claims; and type and frequency of accidents on and off the job. Employees should be involved either through survey participation or program planning.

- Identify resources. Staff, equipment, and operating funds are needed to launch the program, and procedures for monitoring expenditures and results can help keep it running smoothly. Tapping community resources, such as local hospitals and chapters of the Red Cross, American

Heart Association, American Lung Association, or YMCA, is a good way to reduce costs and supplement in-house capabilities.

- Consider a trial run. A trial run involving a select group of interested or motivated employees can help assess a program's potential for success. Once this group has completed the initial phase and the test results are in, the program can be revised to broaden its appeal to employees or to make it more cost effective.

- Ensure confidentiality. Central to the success of a health promotion effort is keeping data on individual employees in strict confidence.

- Consider using incentives. Incentives such as more vacation days, additional pay or special bonuses, and recognition for performance may prove effective in motivating employees to lose weight, stop smoking, use seat belts, exercise regularly, and practice other good health routines. A caveat, however, is that these incentives could end up as extra benefits for the already converted—those who would have undertaken the better health practices in any event.

- Combat denial and relapse. The most serious roadblocks to wellness programs are denial and relapse. A well-tailored worksite program can prove effective in overcoming both obstacles. Screening and testing at the workplace and aggressive outreach can help employees recognize the existence of health risk factors, while ongoing programs that emphasize group support and systematic long-term follow-up can combat relapse into old lifestyles.

## RESOURCE CENTER

American Heart Association (AHA)
7320 Greenville Ave.
Dallas, Tex. 75231
214-750-5300

The AHA offers a "Heart at Work" program to show companies how to start an in-house heart-disease prevention program. Components include (1) a high blood pressure program, (2) a smoking cessation program, (3) a nutrition and weight control program, (4) an exercise program, and (5) a program to help employees spot symptoms of a heart attack and where and how to call for help. Each component is divided into three levels of involvement depending on whether the company wants to distribute booklets and pamphlets, hold company-sponsored lectures and classes conducted by AHA volunteers or others, or hire a staff to develop and manage on-site activities. Contact your local AHA chapter.

American Lung Association (ALA)
1740 Broadway
New York, N.Y. 10019
212-315-8700

The ALA provides a variety of "Freedom from Smoking" programs. A starter option consists of self-help kits of two comprehensive workbooks to provide day-by-day guidance for the individual who wants to stop smoking. Local ALA chapters also sponsor group clinics consisting of seven 90-minute meetings over a seven-week period led by trained staffers; worksite clinics usually can be arranged. Contact your local ALA chapter.

### Community agencies

Many communities provide fitness programs through Departments of Parks and Recreation or equivalent agencies. Community programs may include maps of walking, cycling, and jogging paths, many of which may have "par course" features with calisthenic stations along the trail. Some schools open their outdoor tracks and gyms to the public, and some school gyms lease space to aerobic exercise groups.

High Blood Pressure Information Center
Kappa Systems, Inc.
2121 Wisconsin Ave., N.W.
Washington, D.C. 20007
202-944-3155

The center provides free publications with information and guidelines on hypertension treatment.

Metropolitan Life Insurance Company
Health and Safety Education Division
One Madison Ave.
New York, N.Y. 10010
212-578-2211

Based on its own experience in running health promotion programs, Metropolitan Life's Center for Health Help provides a consulting service offering needs assessment, health awareness education,
and individualized programs. A flyer describing the program is
available.

National Health Information Clearinghouse (NHIC)
P.O. Box 1133
Washington, D.C. 20013
1-800-336-4797

NHIC provides a publication listing the health risk appraisals available, with a full description, evaluation, and cost information on
each. Request "Health Risk Appraisal: An Inventory," June 1981
Publications #81–50163.

YMCA

Your local YMCA may deliver exercise services by (1) providing
programs at the company's site, or (2) offering memberships for
employees to exercise at the YMCA's facility.

---

### ENDNOTES

1. Wisconsin Association of Manufacturers and Commerce, *Primer on Managing Health Care Costs* (Milwaukee, Wis.: Wisconsin Association of Manufacturers and Commerce, 1984): 3.
2. U.S. Surgeon General, "The Health Consequences of Smoking: Cancer and Chronic Lung Disease in the Workplace," *1985 Daily Labor Report* (Washington, D.C.: BNA, 1985): 245:E-1, 248:D-1.
3. Ibid., D-1.
4. Ibid.
5. Ibid., D-7.
6. Ibid.
7. Ibid.
8. Ibid.
9. Ibid.
10. Shrimp v. New Jersey Bell, 45 U.S.L.W. 2354, 368 A.2nd 408(1976).

11. Vickers v. Veterans Admin., 29 FEP Cases 1197 (W.D. Wash. 1982).
12. The Bureau of National Affairs, Inc., *BNA's Employee Relations Weekly* (Feb. 24, 1986): 4:237.
13. Ibid., 4:238.
14. Ibid., 4:237.
15. J.E. Fielding, "Effectiveness of Employee Health Improvement Programs," *Journal of Occupational Medicine* (November 1982): 908.
16. A. Foote and J.C. Erfurt, "Hypertension Control at the Work Site," *New England Journal of Medicine* (April 7, 1983): 308:809.
17. J.E. Fielding, note 15 above.
18. Washington Business Group on Health, *Nutrition Programs in the Worksite*, (Washington, D.C.: Washington Business Group on Health, 1985).
19. Washington Business Group on Health, *Stress Management in the Workplace* (Washington, D.C.: Washington Business Group on Health, 1985).

# 7

# Enhancing Job Safety

On-the-job accidents are a major cause of job absences. Taking steps to identify and eliminate workplace hazards and to train and educate workers in job safety and health will pay off in improved attendance, lower worker compensation and medical benefit costs, improved morale, and lessened risks of citations for violating the Occupational Safety and Health Act.

## ESTABLISHING RULES AND PROCEDURES

An essential element of a successful safety program is management commitment. Management must show its continuing support for a hazard-prevention program's goals and procedures. The following list gives some ways to do this:

*Conduct both worksite and job audits.* Worksite safety and health audits should focus on such factors as the facility's layout and housekeeping needs, operation and maintenance requirements, fire protection requirements, and hazardous material distribution. Job audits call for a step-by-step study of each job to determine the safest methods of performance, applicable OSHA standards, personal protective equipment requirements, and training needs.

*Put together a safety manual.* The audit information can be used to form the basis for a manual that will serve as a guide for future periodic in-house audits, as well as employee training program purposes.

*Listen to employees' safety concerns.* Big benefits can be produced by paying close attention to employees' suggestions and complaints, investigating problems, and correcting unsafe conditions.

*Monitor safety program continually.* Supervisors usually can handle safety and health compliance in their sections. In some cases, management might rotate the duties of a "safety officer" among supervisors to reinforce their knowledge of safety and health problems and issues and their support for efforts.

*Establish emergency procedures.* These should be set up and publicized before they are needed. Relevant factors include: personal protective and first-aid equipment needs, the location of the nearest medical and emergency help, postings of emergency telephone numbers, and the location of emergency exits. Plans for mass evacuations, with special procedures for evacuation of disabled or handicapped employees, should be made. Drills should take place frequently, with and without warning to employees. Employers should draw on the expertise of local emergency service agencies, such as the fire department, in preparing emergency plans. Organizations that have hazardous materials on the premises should inform the fire department of their existence and location. Employers also should alert the fire department to the locations of computers and other sensitive equipment.

The following company example illustrates how these principles can be put into practice.

### Safety Management Program

**E.I. du Pont de Nemours & Co.**, Wilmington, Del., has a safety management program which includes these guidelines:

Organize for safety. A central safety committee, chaired by a senior management member, should be set up at each plant site.

Establish a companywide reporting system. All injuries, illnesses, and accidents should be reviewed by a small departmental committee to ensure consistent classification and tabulation of all data.

Maintain and publish corporate and departmental safety statistics. This promotes accountability and peer pressure.

Conduct companywide audits for safety, fire protection, hazardous materials distribution, and occupational health. Rate each site and report each plant's performance to top management. These audits will be useful in achieving the safety objectives that top management expects of site supervisors.

Establish short-term companywide and departmental safety goals. In addition, publish realistic but challenging annual goals. The ultimate objective should be zero accidents and injuries.

Adopt companywide off-the-job efforts. Make safety training a continuous activity.

Use annual coordinated safety themes.

Publish and use a self-instruction program to train workers and observe unsafe work practices. Training programs that teach, motivate, and retrain workers are an effective tool for eliminating injuries.

## SAFETY TRAINING

In many organizations, safety training begins as part of the orientation on a new employee's first day on the job. Each new employee receives a copy of the organization's hazard-prevention rules or other safety-oriented materials (see Exhibit 7.1 for a sample safety policy). Generally, it is easier to impress the importance of safety on newly hired employees. Safety and health training should not end, however, with completion of the orientation or probation period. All employees should be provided with ongoing training on safe working methods and procedures.

Employees in hazardous jobs should receive special training in emergency procedures. When equipment, procedures, or processes are introduced or revised, new training sessions should take place. All employees who work with new equipment, as well as any substitutes for regular workers, should receive training, including safety and emergency-procedure instruction.

Supervisors should be given special training to help them carry out their safety and health responsibilities. A number of organizations, including the National Safety Council, offer training courses targeted especially for supervisors.

Employers can draw on an abundance of outside safety and health resources, such as films, slide shows, video tapes, and programmed safety courses. For in-house training courses, supervisors and managers often make effective instructors. One-hour sessions usually are considered most effective. If safety lectures and meetings become too long, they lose their impact. It is also important to meet in a quiet place with a minimum of distractions; avoid statistical recitals; personalize the message by discussing actual accidents, or near misses, or by showing battered protective equipment; avoid holding meetings just before lunch or quitting time; and encourage employee participation.

## SAFETY COMMITTEES

Getting employees involved in job safety is regarded as a particularly effective technique. Many organizations set up safety committees composed of both rank-and-file and management members. A rotating membership with overlapping terms will involve the greatest number of employees.

A safety committee might perform the following functions:

- Establish procedures for encouraging and reviewing safety and health suggestions and recommendations.

- Make systematic inspection tours at regular times to discover and correct unsafe conditions and practices.

- Review the circumstances and causes of accidents and recommend corrective measures.

- Conduct regularly scheduled meetings to discuss accident- and illness-prevention methods, safety and health-promotion efforts, ways to eliminate recently detected hazards, the organization's injury and illness records, and other pertinent subjects.

- Provide safety and health tips and information to first-line supervisors.

- Recommend changes or additions to improve protective clothing and equipment.

- Develop or revise rules to comply with current safety and health standards.

- Arrange safety and first-aid training for employees.

- Establish good communication procedures.

- Make sure that safety materials are distributed to all employees.

# RECORDS AND REPORTS

Employers are required to record and report serious on-the-job injuries on OSHA's injury and illness log (Form 200). But injuries that need not be reported to OSHA should not be ignored. Keeping track of and analyzing the causes of injuries or accidents can help pinpoint trouble spots or weaknesses in the organization's hazard prevention program (see Exhibit 7.2 for a sample in-house accident reporting policy). The following types of information are sought in a typical accident report:

*The injured worker.* Name, address, age, sex, marital status, employee identification number, pay rate, job, length of employment, number of consecutive hours worked at the time of the accident, time of last rest break, language (if other than English), previous accident record.

*Type of accident.* Fall, slipping or tripping, electric shock, burn, machine entanglement, and so on.

*The circumstances.* Date, time, shift, place, site conditions (weather, lighting, ventilation, etc.), description of what the employee was doing (or trying to do) at the time of the accident.

*Witnesses.* Names, addresses, jobs, position of witness in relation to accident, summaries of statements.

*Injuries sustained and doctors' reports.* Description of injury and its immediate and long-term effects, estimated recovery time, names and addresses of physicians, medical costs (including doctors' fees), copy of medical report.

*Equipment involved.* Machine or mechanical device, electrical apparatus, tool, vehicle, material, obstruction, and so forth.

*Causes of the accident.* Problems with machine or equipment, job performance techniques, hazardous materials, working conditions (light, ventilation, housekeeping, etc.), availability or functioning of safety equipment, employee's physical inability to perform safely, lack of training, poor attitude toward safety, failure to use safety equipment or follow procedures, unauthorized work, or carelessness, negligence, or horseplay.

*Corrective action needed.* Safety guards or switches on machines; changes in job procedures, materials, or methods; lighting, ventilation, housekeeping, or maintenance alterations; new safety clothing or equipment; selection procedure changes, especially for jobs requiring certain physical characteristics (be careful of equal-employment-opportunity requirements here); training program

## EXHIBIT 7.1

─────────────────────── **SAMPLE POLICY** ───────────────────────

**Subject:** Safety and Health Procedures and Rules

**Purpose:** To identify the organization's safety and health rules and procedures.

**Guidelines:**

1) The employer's safety and health rules and procedures are designed to ensure that each job and area of the workplace will be be as free as possible from hazards. The employer will establish procedures to identify existing and potential hazards and to remove or guard against these dangers.

2) Employees who are aware of an unrecognized or poorly identified hazard or potential hazard in their jobs or the workplace are encouraged to report such hazards to their supervisors or a member of the organization's safety committee. Any ideas for removing or guarding against the hazard are welcome.

3) Each new employee, at the time of hiring, will receive safety and health instructional materials, which will be reviewed by the new-hire's supervisor during the job-training and orientation process. Employees are responsible for following established safety procedures. If an employee moves to another job within the company, training for that job will be given, and applicable safety procedures reviewed.

4) Supervisors will have the primary responsibility for ensuring compliance with the organization's safety and health rules in their departments. To help them carry out these responsibilities, supervisors will receive special safety and health training.

5) Penalties for employees who violate established safety and health rules or procedures will range from written warnings to dismissal, depending on the severity and frequency of the violation.

6) A safety committee composed of three rank-and-file workers and three supervisors will be responsible for steering and monitoring the organization's safety and health initiatives. All employees are eligible to serve as committee members. Memberships will rotate among employees, with each employee-member serving staggered three-year terms (i.e., one new worker-member is appointed each year). Safety committee meetings will be held as needed (but at least monthly).

7) The safety committee's responsibilities will include: investigating accidents and proposing needed corrective measures; reviewing employee safety and health suggestions and recommendations; recommending changes or additions to improve safety; conducting periodic job and workplace audits and emergency drills and making recommendations; following up on audit results; reviewing employees' safety suggestions and complaints; and planning and initiating activities to stimulate and maintain employee interest in efforts to improve safety and health in the workplace.

───────────

*Source:* Employment Guide, p. 50:65, copyright © 1986, The Bureau of National Affairs, Inc.

changes; stepped-up enforcement of safety rules; more publicity of accidents and near misses to increase worker awareness of safety problems.

Employers should periodically review all accident reports both to check that corrective steps have been taken and to spot any pattern of circumstances, conditions, or causes. All accidents, even minor ones, should be investigated and report forms should be filled out. If possible, "near misses" should be investigated and reported in the same way as actual accidents.

## ENCOURAGING EMPLOYEE ALERTNESS

To many job-safety researchers, a company's accident rate reflects the job climate, and particularly the extent of an employee's freedom to set reasonably attainable goals. A climate that encourages setting goals and facilitates their attainment gives the employee a significant sense of participation and, in turn, this promotes habits of alertness, problem raising, and problem solving.

The rewards system, including both economic and noneconomic rewards, must recognize the worker for being alert, for passing a tip to a co-worker on how best to do something or to avoid getting hurt, and for achievement out of the ordinary. Unfortunately, such orientation training interferes by overemphasizing the do's and don't's instead of encouraging new employees to do their own thinking and evaluation.

Rather than promote alertness, this type of indoctrination encourages a relatively unmotivated, resigned, and passive conformity to an apparently static situation. In such situations, an accident may take place before the worker learns to assert his or her own ideas.

Accident statistics generally support this theory. Organizations with more personnel movement among departments generally have fewer accidents. The same usually is true of departments with greater promotion opportunities. Fewer accidents occur in individual-type jobs than in crew-type jobs. And accidents take place more frequently in jobs of lower prestige.

This suggests the need for more rewards for alertness, partic-

## EXHIBIT 7.2

———————————————— **SAMPLE POLICY** ————————————————

**Subject:**  Injuries, Accidents, and Emergencies

**Purpose:**  To establish procedures for reporting and reviewing on-the-job injuries and accidents and for responding to emergency situations.

**Guidelines:**

1) Employees must inform their supervisor of any on-the-job injury or accident requiring first aid or medical attention, whether or not worktime is lost. Supervisors will be responsible for reporting all such incidents to the safety committee.

2) The safety committee will conduct an investigation of any job-related injury or illness requiring a doctor's care. Recommendations for avoiding a recurrence of the accident shall be included in the committee's report. Injuries that require only first aid and result in no loss of production or worktime will be investigated by the supervisor of the injured worker. Supervisors must submit an official accident report form on the incident to the safety committee.

3) Both employees and supervisors should inform the safety committee of "near misses" — i.e., problems or mishaps that came close to or had the potential for causing an accident, injury, or lost production.

4) During the new-hire orientation period, supervisors should inform new workers of the organization's emergency-evacuation procedures designed to vacate the building in a quick, orderly, and safe fashion. In an emergency evacuation, all employees not specifically assigned to control duties must leave the building in accordance with the instructions they have received from their supervisors. Supervisors also are responsible for periodically reviewing evacuation procedures and routes with all their workers.

5) All employees must be familiar with the location of exits, fire alarm devices, and fire extinguishers. The safety committee is responsible for making sure that emergency equipment is readily accessible and in proper operating condition.

6) A minimum of two unscheduled evacuation drills will be held each year. Employees who fail to leave the building during such drills will be subject to discipline.

7) Supervisors will designate an employee to serve as a "buddy" for each handicapped employee in their department. "Buddies" will be responsible for helping handicapped workers vacate the premises during an evacuation. Supervisors also will appoint alternates to help in the event a designated "buddy" is absent.

*Source*: Employment Guide, p. 50:45, copyright © 1986, The Bureau of National Affairs, Inc.

ularly in relatively "dead-end" jobs. Possible rewards include special economic incentives, prestige honors, extra privileges, machine and work-area "beautification" contests, and representation on special committees and councils.

## REDUCING EMPLOYEE STRESS

Another theory holds that unusual, negative, and distracting stress upon the employee increases the probability of accidents or other job performance problems. One example of this is seen in the curve of accident rates for successive age groups of industrial workers. This shows a high rate in the first 10 years of worklife, then a decline until a second peak occurs between the ages of 40 and 55. These ages are usually the greatest stress periods in the typical worker's life, which is confirmed by identical peaks in the turnover-rate curve.

According to this theory, the accident propensity of younger workers stems from stresses associated with beginning a career, adjusting to work discipline, breaking parental ties, courtship, marriage, and assumption of family responsibilities. Similarly, the middle-aged boom in accidents may be attributed to the particular stresses of that time of life.

## JOB SAFETY GUIDELINES

Job safety programs can benefit companies through reducing absenteeism, improving employee morale, and lowering workers' compensation costs. In setting up such programs, employers should implement these steps:

- Conduct worksite and job safety audits, listen to employees' concerns, and incorporate information from these sources into a safety manual.

- List preventive measures and emergency procedures in the safety manual and provide training and practice sessions to familiarize employees with these points.

- Coordinate emergency procedures with local emergency service agencies and consider using these agencies' input when developing safety policy.

- Monitor safety compliance through safety committees and accident reports/records.

- Consider using rewards to encourage employee alertness and establishing measures to help alleviate stress, a frequent cause of accidents.

## RESOURCE CENTER

E.I. du Pont de Nemours & Co.
Industrial Training Service
7450 Nemours Building
Wilmington, Del. 19898
302-774-1000

DuPont makes its "Safety Training Observation Program" (STOP) available to other companies. Write for further information.

National Institute for Occupational Safety and Health (NIOSH)
4676 Columbia Parkway
Cincinnati, Ohio 45226
513-684-8235

NIOSH publishes each year a list of all known toxic substances by generic family and the concentration at which toxicity occurs. It also will provide a set of worksheets for a do-it-yourself health hazard survey, plus an explanatory manual and a completed sample worksheet. Write for the Cooperative Exposure Survey, Hazard Section, Division of Surveillance, Hazard Evaluation and Field Studies.

National Safety Council
425 N. Michigan Ave.
Chicago, Ill. 60611
312-527-4800

A safety guide for supervisors and managers in small organizations is available from the National Safety Council. Titled "Handbook of

Occupational Safety & Health," the book offers guidance on safety problems likely to confront supervisors, as well as help in filling out required government forms. Order the guide from the membership department.

Occupational Safety and Health Administration (OSHA)
Department of Labor
3rd Street and Constitution Avenue, N.W.
Washington, D.C. 20210
202-523-8063

OSHA provides free on-site consultation services to employers upon request. The service is completely separate from OSHA's enforcement efforts. The employer's only obligation in availing itself of the professional advice is to correct any serious hazards that the consultant might find. "On-Site Consultation for the Employer," a booklet that describes the program, is available from OSHA area and regional offices, and from the OSHA Publications Office. Training programs for employer and union representatives are provided by OSHA's training branch. OSHA also issues a state-by-state directory of approved sources for OSHA-funded on-site consultation. For more information, contact the OSHA Office of Training and Education.

# 8
# Managing Disabilities

Disabled and injured workers cost employers billions of dollars annually in lost productivity, job absences and turnover, and medical and disability benefits. Short-term disability costs alone account for 2 to 5 percent of payroll, according to a 1986 survey of major U.S. employers.[1]

Psychiatric conditions, heart disease, and cancer account for the highest health-care costs, while musculoskeletal problems, pregnancy disabilities, and follow-ups to surgical procedures are the most frequent causes of short-term disabilities.[2] Catastrophic injuries account for only 1 percent of all insurance claims, but they can add up to as much as 10 percent of all dollars paid out in claims and up to half of an employer's annual health care costs. Increasingly, employers are recognizing that fragmented, uncoordinated health care in cases of catastrophic illness leads to high costs and are attempting to contain these costs by monitoring high-cost claims, encouraging cost-effective treatment, and reducing the time lost from the job.

This has led to the creation of the relatively new field of case management, which is designed to coordinate the efforts of insurers and medical providers to see that the victim of a catastrophic injury or illness is carried as far as possible toward a normal life.

## CATASTROPHIC DISABILITY CASE MANAGEMENT

The case management officer, who usually is a health-care professional with extensive clinical background, serves as the central point for communication and contact among all parties. Such a facilitator may be employed by the insurance company or by the employer. Case managers combine knowledge of both short- and long-term needs of the catastrophically disabled, with extensive knowledge of the health-care delivery system, insurance concepts, and reimbursement practices.

Early intervention is considered the key to success. The course a case manager might suggest generally follows one of three paths:

*Accelerated care* is designed to facilitate improvements in care quality to speed recovery time and allow for early hospital discharge. Such care might involve transfer to a specialized facility, additional or more intensive therapy, patient or family training, or possible recovery at home.

*Alternate care* aims at providing appropriate care in an environment less costly than that of a hospital.

*Palliative care* tries to prevent predictable medical complications that commonly occur with catastrophic injuries.

The case manager can aid in moving a patient from expensive acute-care hospitals to less costly and more appropriate settings as recovery proceeds. Indeed, such a specialist may be the only one involved in a major disability case who keeps a finger on all aspects of a patient's progress—diagnosis and prognosis; current condition; appropriate treatment and placement alternatives; rehabilitation, including vocational testing and training; technical details of insurance coverage; and family and financial considerations.

Close, continuing contact with a patient and the patient's family can make or break a recovery. A patient's progress is directly tied to the degree of acceptance of medical treatment and therapy, behavioral and attitude problems, and coming to grips with the long-term impact of a serious injury. In addition, when lawyers become involved in worker compensation or other claims relating to the disability, the case management and recovery process can be slowed or stopped altogether. An adversarial situation may develop that results in the patient regarding the disability as a permanent condition and a way to gain a reward and win a confrontation. The focus shifts from compensation as a recovery tool to compensation as the spoils of war.

Working with the patient and the family also lays the foundation for return to work following treatment. Interviews should be arranged to deal with vocational issues, such as a detailed work history and information on personal interests and hobbies, education, temperament, learning ability, adaptability to new environments, and dexterity. A rehabilitation specialist can assess the recovering worker's skills and determine what kind of work he or she can do.

The task of getting a disabled person back on the job is difficult but important, particularly if a workplace accident may have been the cause of the disability. An employee permanently disabled as the result of a job accident at age 40 can cost the employer more than $1 million over the rest of his or her lifetime.

The preferred course is to return the worker to the same job he or she had before. This often can be achieved with special workplace equipment, mobility arrangements, and similar concessions. When this is not possible, the disabled worker has to be retrained to fill a new job and then matched with job openings. Tools that may help the rehabilitated worker in a return to work include workshops aimed at helping the worker set and achieve realistic career goals, training in job application and interview techniques, and other efforts to replace the "out-of-work" routine with structured activity designed to sharpen job-hunting skills.

## RETURN-TO-WORK PROGRAMS

Many employers that have no specific case-management programs have adopted more general programs to help recovering employees return to work from any disability, not just catastrophic illness or injury. Such programs usually require that planning begin while the employee is still convalescing, in order to prevent problems from becoming complicated later on.

Return-to-work efforts may include any of the following steps:

- Reimbursement for medical rehabilitation services in rehabilitation units of community hospitals, rehabilitation speciality hospitals, or outpatient rehabilitation services.

- Reimbursement for vocational rehabilitation services, and physical therapy and occupational therapy services.

- Programs to help employees cope with or manage chronic illness.

- Return-to-work incentives, such as paid disability benefits while working.

- Job modifications to keep disabled employees in the workplace.

- Transitional employment programs.

- Coordination with state vocational rehabilitation agencies. Some states have laws requiring vocational rehabilitation programs; these laws generally apply to employees returning to work from disabling on-the-job injuries.

- Training programs for supervisors of employees with handicapping conditions.


## Setting Up a Return-to-Work Program

Gene Dent, the return-to-work coordinator of a successful program at the Lawrence Livermore National Laboratory, University of California, recommends a program including these specific components:[3]

*Counseling.* Prior to the return to work, the employer should try to determine the ill employee's motivation. The primary focus should be on whether any disabilities might impede the employee's performance of the old job. However, the counseling should explore as well any problems that the employee may have had with his old job or supervisor prior to the disability.

The employee also should be encouraged to consider the disability or sick-leave pay as salary for the important job of convalescence and re-entry preparation. Continued contact with the employee's immediate supervisor during the convalescence helps to shorten the period of disability and to prepare the employee for the return to work.

When former substance abusers or other troubled workers return to work, special considerations come into play. Suggestions for counseling these workers are reviewed in Chapter 11.

*Job Analysis.* Temporary or permanent changes in the worksite may be necessary to accommodate the disability. The physical and psychological requirements of the job should be identified, put into writing, and checked with the employee's doctor.

*Job Modification.* Some disabilities may require job modification, such as new or reduced work hours, temporary reassignment of heavier work, a modified worksite, or breaks for rest or exercise. Although the best reassignment for the employee is to the old job with its familiar skill requirements and relationships, a different job assignment may be necessary, and that job also may require analysis and modification.

*Adaptive Devices.* Simple grasping aids, orthopedic supports, or special tools can speed disabled workers' return to the job. Cleverness, rather than cost, often is the key to adapting a job to the disability. But even an expensive device may prove cost-effective from savings in continued disability payments. The employee should be involved in developing adaptive devices. Community resources—state vocational rehabilitation departments, private rehabilitation centers, hospitals—frequently can provide assistance.

*Retraining.* Retraining ideally should build upon the employee's existing skills and relationships, so that he or she does not feel lost during the return to work. Retraining should emphasize on-the-job training and continual performance monitoring.

## Examples of Rehabilitation Programs

The following programs demonstrate a variety of efforts by employers to facilitate workers' rehabilitation and return to work following an injury or illness.

### Back Injury Rehabilitation

Back strains and sprains are the most common serious workplace injury, according to the Labor Department.

**Federal Express**, the national package and messenger service, has a majority of its employees involved in work that requires bending and lifting under the high pressure demands of overnight delivery. Because of this, the company had 8,500 worker compensation claims in fiscal 1985 for back injuries.

The company has a policy that calls for return to modified duty as soon as possible after injury or illness. Federal Express believes in doing a lot of hand-holding with the injured employee. It also works closely with his or her physician and immediate supervisor. Working with the physician, who otherwise would not have a clear idea of the physical demands of the patient's job, often speeds up the date when the employee can get back on the job, the company finds.

Supervisors are told that the company considers it a routine part of their responsibilities to develop modified duty plans to expedite the return of injured workers.

## Projects With Industry Program

The **International Association of Machinists'** return-to-work effort is part of the nationwide Projects With Industry program, which links employers, government agencies, and rehabilitation agencies. The primary objective of the rehabilitation effort is to return injured employees to their previous jobs. If that is impossible, an attempt is made to place the employee in a different position with the same employer or in the same job with a different employer. The least desirable alternative is to find the worker a different job with a different employer.

Rehabilitation often does not mean that the injured workers regain their pre-injury fitness levels, but instead results in their functioning as well on the job as nondisabled employees. An example cited is a United Airlines engine maintenance worker who had been blinded in a motorcycle accident. With the help of the union-sponsored rehabilitation program, the employee was able to return to his old job at full pay. The worker's duties were modified and some duties were exchanged with those of another worker so that the disabled worker was responsible only for engine disassembly, which he was able to do as skillfully as before his injury and as accurately as a sighted machinist.

The **Perkins School for the Blind** conducts another PWI program for such clients as New England Telephone and American Telephone & Telegraph. The Watertown, Mass. school helps blind workers with job retention and worksite modification.

In one case, a customer service representative for New England Telephone suffered a vision loss that prevented her from performing her job. After conducting an analysis of jobs for which the worker was qualified and looking at adaptive technology to make up for her poor eyesight, the school suggested the company modify the position of accounts collection agent, which requires workers to use a database of account information and to make outgoing calls. The visually impaired employee now relays information normally read from the screen through a device that converts displayed data into computerized speech.

## Homework for the Disabled

**Control Data Corporation (CDC)** uses a "Homework" project to help employees return to work after experiencing such ailments as advanced heart disease, multiple sclerosis, emphysema, and quadriplegia. Homework has enabled seriously disabled employees to hold down jobs that do not require them to leave their homes. Some of these employees have been able to advance in their careers despite their disabilities.

CDC tries to get disabled employees into the program as soon as possible after the injury so as to keep interruptions to career momentum as brief as possible. Homework employees who put in a full week are treated just like any other employee, while those who work only part-time are paid for the time worked and receive insurance benefits on a sliding scale.

## Case Management & Rehabilitation

**Burlington Northern Railroad**, Chicago, Ill., has developed a rehabilitation program that combines clinical treatment and job modification to expedite return to work. A Medical Management Team, consisting of a physician, a rehabilitation counselor, an insurance claims representative, and the employee's immediate supervisor, evaluates each case and recommends different aspects of medical treatment, pain management, psychological evaluation and/or treatment, vocational evaluation, formal training, and placement in temporary modified or alternative work.

Rehabilitation professionals are involved in all aspects of the rehabilitation, including job modification, disability prevention, and individualized follow-up.

## GUIDELINES

Effective steps to follow in setting up a return-to-work program include:

- Train supervisors and managers to understand the factors that prolong disabilities and ways to encourage re-entry.
- Communicate regularly with the employee during the absence so the supervisor can monitor progress toward returning to work and maintain the employee's office linkages.
- Review all cases on an individual basis and tailor modified, light-duty job assignments for each case.
- Counsel the employee before re-entry to determine capabilities and job needs and to update the employee on changes involving the company or particular employees during the absence.
- Consider improving or adding rehabilitation benefits to long-term disability policies.
- Give a specified individual responsibility for coordinating disability programs and return-to-work policies.
- Consider creating an internal review board to monitor and evaluate disability cases.
- Consider implementing the program as part of an overall employee assistance program or offering the services of outside vocational rehabilitation experts.

## ENDNOTES

1. Institute for Rehabilitation and Disability Management, "Corporate Behavior in Disability Management" (Washington, D.C.: Institute for Rehabilitation and Disability Management, 1986).
2. Ibid.
3. The Bureau of National Affairs, Inc., April 1985 address by Gene Dent to the American Occupational Health Conference, *Benefits Today* (May 24, 1985): 2:178.

# Part 3

# Corrective Measures

# 9

# Utilizing First-Line Supervisors

First-line supervisors are the key to any attendance improvement program because of their obvious influence on the way an employee is likely to answer the question: Should I go to work today? The answer to that question often hinges on the responses to secondary questions, such as: Does management care whether or not I show up? What will be the consequences if I don't? Do I really care about my job or my boss? The answers to these questions depend a great deal on the employees' relationships with their supervisors and on the attitudes their supervisors have communicated regarding job attendance.

This sounds self-evident, yet it often is overlooked in developing attendance improvement policies. Many companies install elaborate procedures for monitoring attendance, disciplining chronic absentees, and rewarding good attendance but neglect any training or guidance to help the first-line supervisor influence the attendance of subordinates.

A 1986 study by the Department of Health and Human Services,[1] which involved 2,700 employees in 374 work groups, found that employee use of sick leave was directly related to how the work groups were managed. Of the measures found to be significant in predicting the use of sick leave, the most important were morale, fairness of management, communication, climate for innovation, and strength of authority. Work groups with high morale and strong leadership used less sick leave.

The study also found that the potential for management action to influence sick leave use is greatest in work groups with younger employees. When co-worker cooperation and the climate for innovation are high, these groups were found to use less sick leave. Groups with younger, less experienced, less educated employees were found to use more sick leave, and by implication were most susceptible to improvement through management action.

As the study shows, supervisors can have a clear impact in improving employee attendance, and accordingly companies should provide managers with training and guidelines on how to implement effective programs to promote good attendance. (See Exhibits 9.1 and 9.2 for managerial guidelines used in two companies' attendance programs.)

## THE HIRING DECISION

The first-line supervisor usually has the decisive say in selecting new employees and should therefore be trained and encouraged to assess the "work ethic" of job applicants in making these decisions. Examination of virtually any work group will show that some employees report to work no matter how ill they feel while others call in sick at the slightest ache. Probably the most decisive factor influencing the job attendance record of a work unit is this work ethic of the individual members of the unit.

The hiring manager can try to gauge this by asking applicants about their past attendance patterns and by conducting thorough reference checks. Previous employers who may be reluctant to relay subjective judgments concerning the applicant usually are willing to report objective attendance records.

## THE NEW-HIRE ORIENTATION

Attitudes formed in the first 90 days of employment usually determine future attendance patterns. While newly hired employees may carefully avoid unnecessary absences during their probationary period, their impression as to the importance of good attendance is formed from what they observe during the first few months.

At a new employee's orientation, supervisors should emphasize the necessity of good attendance and explain the company's

## *EXHIBIT 9.1*

### Management Guidelines on Attendance

#### 1 Expectation

- Employees are expected to be at work everyday and to arrive on time
- Any deviation requires careful individual consideration and attention

#### 2 Orientation

- All employees must understand IBM's expectation:

  Orientation for new employees
  Periodic reviews for all employees

- The manager sets the example

#### 3 Track/Understand

- Accurate/timely records must be kept
- Reason(s) for absence must be understood

  Sickness/accident?
  Personal/family problems?
  Motivational/job dissatisfaction?
  Past lenient management?
  Other?

#### 4 Immediate follow-up

- Express concern to employee immediately after every absence/ tardiness

Concern for employee
Concern for absence/tardiness

- Determine if action is required
- Take appropriate action

#### 5 Periodic reviews/ reinforcement

- Review data
- Review actions
- Consult with Personnel and Medical as appropriate
- Reiterate expectations to all employees
- Review employees' attendance records with them
- Document as appropriate

#### 6 Closure

- Don't allow problems to continue indefinitely
- Set reasonable resolution date—the sooner the better
- Keep upper management informed
- Resolve each situation by careful consideration of individual circumstances and the needs of the business

---

*Source*: This policy statement, reprinted with permission, is taken from the in-house guide for supervisors used by International Business Machines Corp., "Managing Attendance: An On-Going Process."

## EXHIBIT 9.2

### SUPERVISOR CONTROL OF ABSENTEEISM

Excessive and avoidable absenteeism is a serious and growing problem in our company. To reduce and control it, the policies and procedures outlined below are to be aggressively followed by all concerned.

1) *Pre-Employment Interview—Applicant Screening.* During the pre-employment interview, in-depth inquiry into the job applicant's prior attendance and work habits will be made. Stress the importance our company places on good attendance and overall dependability. When checking the applicant's school records and his work history with former employers, always ask for specific information concerning his/her attendance record.

2) *Orientation of New Employees.* When the new employee is introduced to his job and is undergoing general orientation, be sure to emphasize that avoidable absenteeism and tardiness will not be tolerated. Any tendency toward absenteeism must be watched carefully during the probationary period.

3) *Stress the High Cost of Absenteeism.* Don't let your people take absenteeism for granted. Point out the high cost of non-attendance in terms of disrupting work schedules, inefficiency and waste, production delays, costly overtime, job pressures, and customer complaints.

4) *Maintenance of Records.* Keep a good running record for each employee in your unit, department or terminal and let the people know you are doing it. Don't let healthy stay-aways get away with absences. Make them report to you when they get back; require full explanation. Let your weekend- and holiday-stretchers know that you are wise to their pattern.

5) *Publicize Our Attendance Control Program.* Post a list of individuals' standings on bulletin boards at least every six months. Submit stories of outstanding records to the [company newsletter]. Tie attendance performance to promotions. Convince your people that good attendance is a key factor in helping them get ahead on the job.

6) *Supervision and Counseling.* A tough attitude toward unexcused absenteeism and a tighter control must be exercised by all members of management. Quick and decisive disciplinary action should be taken with continuous offenders when counseling fails to correct the problem.

Each supervisor will be expected to examine his/her philosophy and leadership style and to learn much more about why an employee avoids his work. (It is the consensus that most employees will come to work when able if someone cares if they come.) Establishing the proper climate and working environment is essential.

---

*Source:* This policy statement was developed by a large southern transportation firm to detail the supervisor's role in controlling absenteeism and was published in BNA Policy and Practice Series, Personnel Management, p. 241:801, copyright© 1981, The Bureau of National Affairs, Inc.

policy on monitoring attendance and disciplining offenders. Supervisors should make it clear they are not merely parroting the "company line" and will view attendance as an important part in their future evaluation of the employee.

## JOB SATISFACTION

All other things being equal, an employee's job attendance is likely to rise or fall in direct proportion to his or her job satisfaction. This of course is highly subjective; the same job may be boring to one person, challenging to another, and too stressful for a third. But management in general and the first-line supervisor in particular can do much to enhance job satisfaction through employee involvement, job enrichment, career development, quality of work-life, and similar programs. Books have been written on these subjects, and it is beyond the scope of this book to address this issue in detail.

## DOCUMENTING AND MONITORING

Although each immediate supervisor should collect the initial data on attendance, all records should be accumulated, analyzed, and maintained in one central location. Periodic analytical reports from this central location should be fed back to supervisors. Requiring supervisors to keep records on each employee's absences serves two purposes. It helps managers to spot trends and potential problems, and it lets the employees know their attendance is being recorded and consequently is viewed as important. Accurate records should detail all lost time, including lateness.

Supervisors should keep in mind that virtually all absences are for "personal reasons." Therefore, just recording "personal business" to explain the absence is not particularly helpful. The record should show the specific reason for an absence, such as "had to go to the bank." But the employee should not be asked why he or she had to go to the bank; this is private.

Supervisors should avoid using the word "excused," either orally or on the absence record. One supervisor may accept a particular reason as an excuse, another may not. Further, employees may feel that an "excused" absence should not be counted against them when their overall attendance record is appraised.

An employee's attendance record should be reviewed each time an absence occurs. These routine reviews will alert supervisors as to the frequency of absences and any pattern in the reasons given. To make this timely review, supervisors should keep attendance records near at hand.

## RETURN-TO-WORK INTERVIEW

When an absent employee returns to work, the supervisor should welcome the employee back and make it clear that he or she was missed. This is the best time to find out what the trouble was and how to prevent its recurrence.

In this interview, the focus should be on the attendance record, not the person. The supervisor should determine the reasons for the absence, show the employee the past attendance record, and communicate awareness of any pattern of absences. The supervisor should express sympathy about the difficulty that caused the absence as well as concern about the impact of the absence on operations. It is important to specify the dates of past absences to make sure the employee is fully aware of the number of days missed and also to show personal concern for improvement.

Before the interview, the supervisor should plan specific questions. After reviewing the record, the supervisor should see if a pattern exists and compare the employee's attendance record with others. During the interview, the supervisor should use open-ended questions to pin down the reasons for the absence. If the employee responds, "I was sick," the supervisor should seek a more definite explanation. But the supervisor should only record the reason for the absence, not challenge it.

The employee also should be asked for specific ideas on ways to improve attendance. If the employee says, "I guess I will just try harder to get a ride to work," the supervisor might ask, "How do you plan to do that?"

If illness has caused the absence, the supervisor should express concern about the state of the employee's health. The supervisor might ask, "Have you fully recovered?" or "Do you foresee any future complications or problems?" The tone should be solicitous, not adversarial.

To make sure the employee knows that management views every absence seriously, a written summary should be made of the interview, including both the employee's explanation of the absence and any agreement on specific employee action for the future. At the end of the interview, the supervisor should summarize the discussion.

## EVALUATING ATTENDANCE RECORDS

While an interview should accompany each employee's return to work, the supervisor should concentrate on the worst offenders in subsequent evaluations of attendance records. Typically 10 percent of employees account for more than half of the job absences. Supervisors also should give the greatest weight to absences over which employees have a great deal of control. (See Exhibit 9.3 for a company checklist used to determine whether an employee's absences merit disciplinary action.)

Relevant factors in evaluating an attendance record include frequency, causes, and patterns of absence; tardiness record; total time absent over a representative period; and compliance with call-in policies. Attendance records should undergo review at least monthly to identify employees who have unsatisfactory records or who seem to be heading in that direction. The focus should be on employees with one- or two-day absences that occur around scheduled days off; these employees may require additional attention.

Probably no specific absence percentage should automatically trigger a counseling session. For example, a senior worker who loses a month due to major surgery but who otherwise has had acceptable attendance does not need counseling. But a relatively new employee who misses a Monday or Friday once a month might be a candidate. Employees with serious medical problems should be encouraged to request a leave of absence. Similarly, employees

*EXHIBIT 9.3*

## Pre-Discipline Checklist

Before making a disciplinary decision, supervisors should review the following list of questions. Too many "no" answers may indicate that the supervisor is on shaky ground and should consult with higher management before proceeding with discipline.

▶ Is the rule at issue a clearly applicable, published standard that is expressed in easy-to-understand wording?

▶ Was the violated rule, standard, or order reasonably related to the efficient or safe operation of the organization?

▶ Is the discipline contemplated for the employee consistent with penalties meted out to other employees who committed similar infractions in the past?

▶ Do you have records documenting all violations of this rule or order?

▶ Has this employee received a previous oral or written warning within the past 12 months for a violation of the same or another rule? Has the employee ever received a final warning for the violation of any published rule or order?

▶ Has the incident that triggered the final warning or discharge been carefully investigated? Has all available evidence been gathered, including the names of witnesses, dates, times, places, and other pertinent facts?

▶ Is there a written record of any previous steps taken to correct this employee's unsatisfactory performance or behavior?

▶ Does the degree of discipline contemplated for this employee reflect the seriousness of the offense and the worker's past record and length of service?

*Source:* Employment Guide, p. 40:3, copyright© 1986, The Bureau of National Affairs, Inc.

suspected of having special problems like alcoholism, mental illness, or drug addiction should be given the opportunity to rehabilitate themselves by taking a leave of absence. When an employee requests a leave of absence, the first issue concerns whether a leave of absence probably will correct the problem, or if the problem is likely to continue following the leave and to interfere with the employee's future attendance.

## COUNSELING AND CONFRONTING

When an evaluation of attendance records turns up someone who is showing signs of chronic absenteeism, the supervisor should confront the employee. Here are some generally accepted guidelines for supervisors to use in conducting such an interview:

- Consult with your immediate supervisor, the personnel department, and/or the employee assistance program counselor before undertaking a confrontation. It always helps to get the perspective of someone who is not as closely involved in the situation. Advise the other person of your recorded observations, your evaluation of the problem, and your plans for action. If there is a potential job discrimination complaint, you also should consult with the EEO/Affirmative Action staffer.

- Select a private and comfortable setting for the interview where you will not be interrupted or overheard.

- Begin by being supportive. Tell the employee you want to help. Don't lecture or become angry.

- Use the documentation you have maintained to show evidence of declining attendance. Don't rely on memory—have the documentation in front of you. Keep your description of the problem brief, and give the employee a chance to respond. When the employee gives excuses, keep going back to the record. Make it clear that there are no excuses for prolonged job absenteeism. If the employee is sick, he or she should get treatment.

- Encourage the employee to talk about the problem without appearing to make any judgments about the excuses given.

The goal is to get beyond the excuses and gain an insight into the underlying problem.

- Don't try to act as a therapist. Leave diagnosis to the professionals. But if you suspect a substance abuse or emotional illness problem, don't give the impression that by speaking to you, the employee is getting all the necessary help.

- Describe, don't evaluate. Say, "You have missed work on Monday five times in the past two months." Don't say, "You must be drinking a lot on weekends to miss work so often on Monday."

- Don't refer to off-the-job behavior. This will alienate the employee and most likely will be viewed as an infringement of the employee's privacy.

- Be clear that you expect improvement. Stress that it is the employee's responsibility to maintain an acceptable attendance record. Obtain the employee's commitment to correct the problem, with specifics on how this is to be done and the appropriate time period. Put this commitment in writing. Have the employee sign it and give him or her a copy. Whatever the plan, the employee should play a part in developing it. A proposed solution that does not reflect the employee's ideas is not likely to elicit commitment.

- Remember that attendance problems may stem from personal problems on or off the job. Be sure to inform the employee of help that may be available either through the company's employee assistance program or other resources. You should have information on appropriate sources of help and stress the confidential nature of such help. Remember, however, that the employee's personal problems are not your responsibility. You are responsible only for the employee's job performance.

- Make it clear that additional action will be taken unless attendance improves. Specify both the further action and the time interval.

- Summarize at the session's end the extent of the problem, the employee's explanation, and plans for improvement. The summary then can be incorporated into a brief memo for the employee and the files.

# FOLLOW-UP

Once a plan for improvement is drawn up and the employee's commitment is elicited, the supervisor should reinforce good behavior. If the employee is not immediately successful, the supervisor should avoid being critical and instead try to provide support. The supervisor should carefully examine the employee's reasons for failing and try to adjust for them in a positive way. Similarly, when the employee succeeds, the supervisor should recognize this and encourage the new behavior.

If the supervisor finds that the first session has not produced a significant change within a reasonable period of time, a second counseling session should be scheduled. Participants in this session should include the supervisor, the employee, a union representative (if applicable), and a higher management official.

The presence of the higher management representative is designed to underscore the seriousness of the situation and to ensure the employee an opportunity to present his or her case to another echelon of management. Results of this second session also should be documented.

If the employee shows no improvement after the second session, another session can take place, which also should include a higher-level manager. At this stage, the employee should be directly confronted with the decision either to meet the attendance standards or to terminate.

To dramatize the seriousness of the situation, the employee might be given a day off with pay in which to decide whether to undertake a long-term improvement in attendance. See the discussion on "Positive Discipline" in Chapter 19.

If no improvement occurs after this step, discharge may be necessary.

# GUIDELINES

These objectives should guide the first-line supervisor when dealing with chronic offenders:

- Either correct or separate the chronically absent employee.

- Spend a minimum of time administering the program.
- Avoid antagonizing the 90 to 95 percent of the employees who do not have an attendance problem.
- Establish solid proof of nondiscriminatory treatment in the event of grievances or lawsuits filed by employees.

## ENDNOTES

1. National Technical Information Service, "Implications for Reducing Sick Leave Through Improved Managerial Practices," (Springfield, Va.: National Technical Information Service, 1986).

# 10

# Using Rewards and Penalties

One option for improving attendance is the use of incentives and rewards. Another option is to penalize poor attendance by deterrents other than traditional discipline.

## PROS AND CONS OF REWARDS

Some managers object to rewarding employees merely for showing up at work because, presumably, this is what employees already are being paid to do.

Proponents of a reward system point out, however, that incentives often are used effectively to motivate employees to improve the quality or quantity of their output, even though they are being paid to do these things. From their standpoint a reward for perfect attendance is not unlike a production bonus.

The bottom line is whether attendance reward programs produce a net saving. Here the opponents argue that such programs merely reward the employees who would have good attendance in any event and have little if any effect on chronic offenders. Proponents, on the other hand, cite statistics showing improvements in attendance rates after a rewards system is installed.

Other studies, however, have found that absenteeism reverts back to previous levels when the novelty wears off or the reward for good attendance is withdrawn. Motivational programs that are more effective in the long run may involve making more fundamental changes in the organization, such as through job enrichment or worker participation programs.

Programs that reward attendance generally have been highly

praised in studies reported in management literature, and many of these positive reinforcement techniques are rated by personnel managers as fairly effective in reducing absenteeism. Yet such programs are used relatively infrequently.[1]

# REWARD PROGRAMS

Rewards and incentives focused on job attendance can be in either a tangible or an intangible form. The system's success depends on the type and frequency of the reward and the way it is communicated and granted. It is essential that employees know what is expected of them and what the rewards will be for meeting those expectations.

## Tangible Rewards

Good attendance can be rewarded in any of the following tangible forms:

- *Cash bonus.* Employees with perfect attendance can earn cash bonuses on a weekly, monthly, or bimonthly basis. Under one organization's plan, employees could receive the greater of $100 or 40 hours' pay for six months of perfect scheduled attendance, or $50 or 20 hours' pay for having only two incidences of absence or tardiness. During the life of the program, unscheduled absence rates dropped from 2.47 percent to 1.53 percent for production workers and from 2.53 to 2.13 percent for office workers.[2]

- *Sick leave bonus.* Employees can be paid a cash bonus for each unused sick leave day per month or quarter. For example, at one company an employee who has accumulated 20 sick leave days in his or her sick leave bank has the option of receiving cash for all days in excess of 20 that are in the bank at the end of the year or of continuing to carry the days in the bank. At another company, employees have the choice of cashing unused sick days annually at half value or banking for future illnesses at double value.[3]

- *Profit sharing.* The extent of each employee's participation in a profit-sharing plan can be tied to his or her attendance record. Or the profit-sharing pool for the entire work force can be based in part on the overall attendance record.

- *Retirement benefits.* Accumulated unused sick leave can go toward extra credits in computing retirement benefits, or unused sick leave can be paid in a lump sum at retirement. Thus a small southern college gives half pay to retirees for unused sick leave up to 120 days (maximum of 60 days' pay).[4]

- *Time off.* Employees can earn extra hours or days of paid leave for perfect attendance. The Atlanta Envelope Company, for example, developed a program under which an employee who is present every workday of the month gets approximately two hours' pay as a bonus. Perfect attendance for six consecutive months is rewarded with eight hours' extra pay in addition to the monthly bonuses. And for missing no working time for a full year, a worker receives a full week's pay. In the first year after the plan was adopted, man-days lost per month dropped 50 percent and production increased 15 percent with no added hires.[5]

- *Lotteries.* These can take a variety of forms: (1) employees with perfect attendance records can qualify for a monthly cash award; (2) several lottery prizes can be awarded each month, with the number varying according to the group's overall attendance record; or (3) each employee who arrives on time can draw from a deck of playing cards, and the employee with the best five-card hand at the end of the week wins a cash bonus.

   At one company, a monthly lottery for $10 was held for all employees with perfect attendance during the month. Compared to the year preceding the lottery, absenteeism decreased by more than 30 percent and sick pay costs were cut by more than $3,000.[6]

The following programs demonstrate how two employers have used rewards as incentives to improve attendance.

**Strux Corp.**, Lindenhurst, N.Y., adopted a comprehensive program of rewards for days spent on the job to combat absenteeism rates that had been averaging 25 percent a year.

Under the program, which was based on suggestions from

employees, any employee with three consecutive months of perfect attendance gets one extra leave day. Employees with perfect attendance for a year are awarded a $200 savings bond and another bonus leave day. Thus, a year's perfect attendance can result in five leave days plus the savings bond.

Employees who have perfect attendance for the month also are recognized by the company in its newsletter.

The prior absenteeism rate of 25 percent has been reduced to between 3 and 4 percent. Turnover also is down.

The cost of the program is $15,000 to $20,000 a year for the 60 hourly paid employees (an average of about $300 per covered employee). Management feels it has saved many times that amount.

**New United Motor Manufacturing, Inc. (NUMMI)** adopted an innovative effort to tie vacation eligibility to attendance in its 1985 agreement with the United Auto Workers. (NUMMI is the experimental venture between General Motors and Toyota at the Fremont, Calif. plant.) This agreement links vacation eligibility to both seniority and attendance.

Three categories of attendance are listed: below standard, standard, and perfect. To meet the standard requirement, an employee may not miss more than 10 days' work in the previous eligibility year, or more than six days in the previous six months' eligibility period. Perfect attendance is defined as missing no days, except for excused absences.

Employees with standard attendance earn 28 hours of vacation in the first six months, 80 hours for one to three years, and so on up to 140 hours for 10-12 years. In all but the first six months, employees with perfect attendance earn eight hours more than those with standard attendance. Employees with below-standard attendance earn up to 28 hours less than those with standard attendance.

Company contributions to a savings plan are tied to attendance as well. For example, for each five-year employee who contributes $1 to the plan, NUMMI contributes 50 cents for those with standard or better attendance, compared with 20 cents for those with below-standard attendance.

## Intangible Incentives

Recognition for good attendance can be based on intangible rewards. These can include an honor roll of employees with perfect attendance on the bulletin board or in the company newsletter, a year-end recognition ceremony, or an employee-of-the-month or employee-of-the-year citation.

---

## EFFECTIVENESS OF INCENTIVES

In a study that won the 1985 research award of the American Society for Personnel Administration, four different attendance incentive programs were tested in a one-year experiment at six similar contract sewing plants of the Maid Bess Corp.[7] Two additional plants were used as controls.

The four rewards programs were:

(1) a financial incentive program that provided an annual $50 cash bonus for employees who had no absences and $25 for those with one or two absences;

(2) a recognition program under which quarterly citations were issued to employees with no more than one absence and an engraved piece of jewelry was awarded to employees who had no more than one or two absences during the year;

(3) a quarterly lottery that awarded a prize worth about $200 from a drawing in which employees with perfect attendance each had two entries while those with one absence had one entry; and

(4) an information feedback program under which each employee received his or her year-to-date absence record once a month with the paycheck.

Job absences decreased significantly at the plant using the recognition program. At the plants using cash bonuses and information feedback, no statistically significant reduction occurred. At the plant using the quarterly lottery, absences actually showed a statistically significant increase.

The researchers noted some features of the recognition program that might have contributed to its success. Employees with perfect or good attendance records were recognized both at work (names posted on the bulletin board) and at home (congratulatory cards signed by the plant manager and sent to the home). The employees also seemed enthusiastic about the personalization of the jewelry award.

One control plant had an unanticipated statistically significant decrease in job absences. This may have been partly due to a reduction in work orders and the employees' recognition that poor performers would be laid off first.

## NONDISCIPLINARY PENALTIES

Discipline is the traditional way of using the stick, rather than the carrot, to improve attendance. But some companies have experimented with using financial penalties for chronic absenteeism. The following program is one leading example of such discipline policies.

**General Motors (GM),** beginning with its 1982 agreement with the United Auto Workers, tied employee benefits to hours worked. Benefits are reduced, however, only for employees whose "controllable" absences amount to 20 percent or more of the available hours during a base period.

For these chronically absent employees, individual attendance rates during the base period are calculated and, for the next six months, this rate determines their benefit entitlements. For example, an employee absent for 20 percent of the base period would receive only 80 percent of benefits in the next six months.

The affected benefits include holiday and vacation pay, paid absence allowance, bereavement pay, and jury duty pay. The rate also is used to calculate sickness and accident benefits and supplemental unemployment benefits. Thus, an employee with an absence rate of 30 percent would receive only 70 percent of holiday pay for any holiday falling in the six-month period.

In 1981, GM had an 11-percent rate of "controllable" absences, which includes sickness, casual absence without leave, and excused absences. In 1984, the rate had dropped to under 9 percent. Counting just sick leave and casual absences, the rate dropped to under 5 percent.

Despite the size of its work force, GM looks at each case before imposing penalties. The computer kicks out those whose job absences exceed 20 percent, but each situation then is reviewed to determine reasons for the absences. If the absences are largely accounted for by something like open heart surgery or participation in a drug/alcohol treatment program, the employee is not penalized.

If the absences are not clearly accounted for by such factors, the employee is called in for counseling. Teams of peer counselors, consisting of a salaried employee and a bargaining unit employee, are trained and set up to work with each employee. The team has full control over how often it meets with the employee, and all information is kept confidential. If a problem relating to drugs or alcohol is suspected, the employee is turned over to the employee assistance program. But the attendance-control penalties are imposed nevertheless.

In June 1985, 1.1 percent of the work force was affected by the reduction in benefits.

In 1984, GM and the UAW modified the program so that employees absent due to a workplace accident would not be penalized. The parties also added an attendance recognition award that gives a quarterly $50 bonus for perfect attendance and an extra $300 bonus (for a total of $500) for perfect attendance in all four quarters. This reward program was designed in part to meet employee complaints that the penalty program gave all of the attention to problem employees.

An employee can have approved absences and still be eligible for perfect attendance. Approved absences include vacations, jury duty, education, military and union leave, and snow days. A year of perfect attendance can earn an employee $500—the equivalent of a 25-cent-per-hour raise.

For the first quarter of 1985, 66 percent of the work force qualified for the perfect attendance bonus of $50.[8] During the first year of the program, approximately $125 million was paid out.

---

## ENDNOTES

1. K.D. Scott and S.E. Markham, "Absenteeism Control Methods: A Survey of Practices and Results," *Personnel Administrator* (June 1982):73.
2. The Bureau of National Affairs, Inc., *BNA Policies & Practices Series, Personnel Management* (BNA: Washington, D.C., 1987): 241:134.
3. The Bureau of National Affairs, Inc., "Job Absence and Turnover Control," *Personnel Policies Forum*, Survey No. 132, October 1981 (Washington, D.C.: BNA, 1981): 9.
4. Ibid.

5. The Bureau of National Affairs, Inc., note 2 above, at 135.
6. L.M. Schmitz and H.G. Heneman, "Do Positive Reinforcement Programs Reduce Employee Absenteeism?" *Personnel Administrator* (September 1980): 87.
7. K.D. Scott, S.E. Markham, and R.W. Robers, "Rewarding Good Attendance: A Comparative Study of Positive Ways to Reduce Absenteeism," *Personnel Administrator* (August 1985): 72
8. Letter to author from K.J. McCormick, UAW-GM Human Resource Center, June 3, 1985.

# 11

# Dealing With Alcohol/
# Drug Abuse

Substance abuse in the workplace costs an estimated $80 billion a year and is responsible for a job absence rate five to 15 times greater than normal. Alcoholics face a three to four times greater risk than other workers of being involved in on-the-job accidents, use three times the amount of sick benefits, and file three to five times the number of worker compensation claims.

Substance abuse often is described as "a family illness." The implications of this for employers is pointed up by a study that found that nonalcoholic members of alcoholics' families use 10 times more sick leave than other employees.[1]

Employers generally view alcoholism and drug addiction as illnesses and deal with them accordingly. For example, sickness and/or disability leaves and other benefits frequently are made available to alcoholics. However, an employer that suspects absenteeism is due to addiction may treat it somewhat differently from absences caused by other illnesses. In part this may be because of the perception that addiction, though considered a chronic illness under today's medical definition, is treatable, and that the addict who abstains from alcohol or drugs can return to work as a healthy employee. Another reason for different treatment is the protection that may be accorded substance abusers under the federal and state laws barring discrimination against the handicapped. These legal constraints are discussed in Chapter 4.

Identifying alcoholics and drug abusers is difficult because they typically deny their problems up to—and often even beyond—the point of jeopardizing their jobs. In addition, supervisors and coworkers sometimes protect such employees—particularly in cases of alcohol abuse—because of their personal popularity, long service, talent for generating sympathy for their other problems, or valuable skills and knowledge. Yet most professionals who treat substance abusers agree that job threats often are the most effective means of breaking down denial and getting the substance abuser to accept help. Issues involved in the discipline of alcoholics or drug abusers are discussed in Chapter 16. This chapter will focus on overall policy considerations in dealing with attendance problems that may result from alcoholism and drug abuse.

## DEVELOPING A POLICY

The first step for the employer is to develop a policy on substance abuse. The policy can treat the problem as a medical one, a disciplinary one, or a combination of the two. Most organizations adopt a policy that recognizes substance abuse as an illness but also provides discipline for those who fail to seek treatment and continue to exhibit deficient job performance.

Substance abuse policies will differ from company to company and industry to industry. Some, like the airline and railroad industries, require strict procedures to avoid disaster and to instill public confidence. But the important element is a top-level corporate commitment to recognize and deal with the problem in a firm but fair manner. The policy should not only let employees know that substance abuse will not be tolerated but also provide managers with guidelines for handling workers who need help.

Topics that might be addressed by a substance abuse policy include:

1. the use or possession of alcohol or drugs on company premises;

2. selling or providing drugs to co-workers on company premises;

3. reporting to work, or working, while impaired by alcohol or drugs;

4. the use of sobriety or drug tests, or searches of employees' lockers, desks, lunchboxes, handbags, and so on.

For a sample policy statement on drug/alcohol abuse, see Exhibit 11.1, which was developed by a group of Minnesota companies, including public utilities, transportation companies, and manufacturing and high technology firms.

To avoid wrongful discharge suits, employers should clearly state their substance abuse policy, carefully investigate any violations, consistently enforce the policy, and apply progressive discipline when appropriate.

To avoid charges of discrimination, management should check applicable federal, state, or local laws and regulations regarding handicapped individuals and the duty to make reasonable accommodation for chemically dependent people. (See Chapter 4.) Similarly, management should check statutes or court decisions dealing with employee privacy rights that may restrict investigations and testing to detect substance abuse.[2]

If employees are represented by a union, the policy should be incorporated into the collective bargaining agreement through the negotiation process.

For the supervisor, three basic issues are involved: (1) identifying the substance abuser; (2) confronting him or her with the need to seek treatment; and (3) providing referral to effective treatment. These are discussed below.

## IDENTIFYING THE PROBLEM

Employees who have drinking or drug problems often begin using excessive amounts of sick leave. These absences typically occur in patterns, such as missing Mondays or Fridays or days after a holiday or three-day weekend. Substance abusers also are likely to become candidates for "on-the-job absenteeism," which occurs when the employee comes to work only marginally able to function. Similarly, the substance abuser frequently may be inefficient or inattentive due to hangovers, lack of sleep, the "jitters," or other drinking- or drug-related physical or emotional ailments. Frequent restroom breaks, constant borrowing of money, frequent accidents, and confusion in carrying out instructions also may be indicators.

A critical aspect of any corporate substance-abuse program is training supervisors to recognize and document job performance problems. Information on the behavioral effects of substance abuse in the workplace is readily available, and supervisors should fa-

## EXHIBIT 11.1

### Statement on Alcohol/Drug Abuse

Company X recognizes alcohol and other drug dependency as an illness and a major health/behavior problem. The company also recognizes alcohol and drug misuse/abuse as a potential health, safety, and security problem. Employees needing help in dealing with such a problem may use an employee assistance program, disability plans, and health coverage plans as appropriate. Conscientious efforts to seek and use such help will not jeopardize an employee's job.

At the same time, the company is also concerned about the potential for adverse effects of alcohol or other drug use on employee health and safety and corporate security. Employees are expected and required to report to work on time and in the appropriate mental and physical condition for work. It is the intent of this policy to provide a drug-free, healthy, safe, and secure work environment.

It is prohibited to use or have consumed any amount of mood-altering substances on company premises and/or while conducting company business and during working hours, including breaks. Further, any possession, transfer, or sale of such legal or illegal substances while working on or off company premises is also prohibited. This includes all forms of alcohol, narcotics, depressants, stimulants, hallucinogens, and marijuana. (See procedure in regard to the use of legitimate medical prescriptions.) Violation of this policy will result in disciplinary consequences, including possible termination and possible criminal prosecution.

### PROCEDURE

When there is possible and/or reasonable cause, people suspected of violating this policy shall be required to report to corporate medical services or a designated physician or clinic on company time and at company expense for a fitness for duty examination which will include appropriate testing. People determined to be in violation of this policy or who refuse to submit to an examination will be removed from the work site and subjected to disciplinary action.

Since physician-directed use of drugs can affect behavior and performance, employees are encouraged to advise their supervisor whenever they are taking drugs for medical reasons. When such use of drugs adversely affects job performance, it is in the best general interest of the employee, co-workers, and the company that sick leave or personal leave be used.

The company's authorized representative shall have the right to search an employee suspected of use, sale, or possession of alcohol, narcotics, depressants, stimulants, hallucinogens, and marijuana while on the job or on company premises. Substances confiscated will be turned over to the local law enforcement agency and may result in criminal prosecution.

The company recognizes the confidentiality and data privacy due applicants, current employees, and former employees. The disclosure of information will be restricted through the procedures that enforce compliance with data privacy regulations.

Employees who are convicted for drug-related charges may be subject to company disciplinary action. This action will be dictated by the nature of the charges, the employee's present job assignment, the employee's company record, and other factors relative to the impact upon the company of the employee's arrest.

---

*Source:* Reprinted with permission from "Drugs in the Workplace: Everyone's Business—Everyone's Problem," by R.P. Neuner, copyright © 1985, Hazelden Educational Materials, Center City, Minn.

miliarize themselves with the symptoms of substance abuse and document how it affects job performance.

Unfortunately, there is no simple way to identify users and no single profile of who has a problem. One National Institute on Drug Abuse study found higher rates of drug use among employees with above-average responsibilities and job pressures. Another study found drug problems among workers whose jobs were repetitious, tedious, and unsupervised. Both are probably true.[3]

Moreover, different drugs produce different behavioral effects. For example, frequent users of cocaine and amphetamines may appear high-strung and irritable and exhibit erratic mood swings. Users of barbiturates and tranquilizers, on the other hand, may appear listless, slower in their reaction time, and less motivated.

Employees with drug or alcohol problems try to hide their problem in different ways. Lower-status workers who are more closely supervised resort to staying away from work to avoid detection. Conversely, white-collar and managerial workers force themselves to attend work, but find ways to be absent on the job.[4]

Supervisors usually are the first to observe falling job performance due to substance abuse, and their early intervention is important both for the employee and the employer. Supervisors should be instructed to make a written record of their observations, citing specific incidents or behaviors exhibited by the employee. But they should be cautioned against attempting to diagnose the underlying problem. Diagnosis and treatment are best left in the hands of medical and counseling professionals. The supervisor's focus should be on job performance.

Rather than hastily deciding to fire a worker based on incomplete information, it generally is better to suspend the employee pending further investigation. Also, employees should never be told that they are being disciplined or terminated because of alcoholism or drug abuse. Discipline should be based on poor job performance or violation of company rules.

## USING TESTING PROGRAMS

One strategy for detecting substance abuse in the workplace is to administer blood or urine tests for evidence of chemicals. These tests can be used for the following purposes:

- To screen out job applicants who abuse drugs.

- To confirm an employee's successful participation in a substance-abuse recovery program.

- To protect employees in safety-sensitive positions.

- To determine fitness for duty following an accident or behavior problem on the job.

- To make a random check for drug use among all employees.

According to a 1985 survey, one-fourth of all Fortune 500 companies screen for drugs in pre-employment physicals, up from one-tenth in 1981.[5] Since then many more companies have begun drug-screening programs for job applicants. Estimates are that half of the larger companies will be testing applicants for drugs by 1988.[6] More complex issues of employee relations and legality come into play when employers extend testing to employees already on the job, which explains why companies screen job applicants instead.

In early 1986, the President's Commission on Organized Crime submitted a report to President Reagan recommending that all U.S. companies "consider the appropriateness" of using drug tests. The Commission urged the government not only to test its own workers but also to withhold federal contracts from private firms that decline to test their workers.

Opponents of drug testing contend that the tests delve into the personal lives of employees, who should be measured only by their on-the-job performance. They point out that late-night television viewing or extramarital affairs can also affect absenteeism and productivity, and yet such off-the-job behavior generally is considered none of the employer's business. Furthermore, if alcohol or drugs are impairing job performance, it is up to managers and supervisors to detect the problem employees and work out a way of dealing with their performance deficiencies. Indiscriminate reliance on drug testing in effect is a cop-out from managerial responsibility.

The critics also cite the unreliability of the tests. Although test manufacturers recommend confirming test results through a second test that uses a different method, not all labs do this. In addition, a positive reading does not mean that the employee was under the influence while on the job. Other than a "walk-a-straight-line" test, researchers have yet to devise an accepted method to show actual impairment by drugs.[7]

Moreover, drug testing programs tend to focus on illicit drugs, while most studies suggest that abuse of legal drugs causes more problems in the workplace than illicit drugs. Alcohol, caffeine, and cold medicines are examples of legal drugs that can be abused and impair job performance.

Some drug testing programs look for prescription medications, as well as illegal drugs, on the theory that these are commonly abused. But a positive urine test cannot distinguish between someone who is abusing a prescription drug and one who is taking a therapeutic dose. For a variety of reasons—fear of discrimination, fear of social stigmatization, or a simple desire for privacy—many individuals are reluctant to disclose their medical conditions that call for the use of prescription drugs. An employee or job applicant, for example, may want to keep a history of epilepsy or psychiatric treatment private.

Drug testing of employees is more generally accepted if safety is an issue, particularly among employers with a responsibility to protect the general public, such as railroads, airlines, and protective service agencies. Employers also have a recognized obligation to safeguard factory or construction workers from the hazards of co-workers who are on drugs. But if safety is not an issue, compulsory testing may be deeply resented by employees who give no signs of addiction.

Proponents of drug testing argue that unannounced, intermittent, and random testing of employees is the best way to reduce drug use in the workplace and that employee awareness of such a policy can be an effective deterrent. Many employers who use tests to spot drug use among current employees explain that their intent is to refer detected employees to treatment, not to immediately fire them.

Any testing program should be carefully thought out and explained to affected employees. The policy should be applied consistently and with regard for employee privacy. A policy that is applied to blue-collar workers but not to managers is sure to cause resentment. Management must choose appropriate tests, ensure reliable analysis, provide for retesting when necessary, and avoid potential disparate impact on groups of employees protected under equal employment opportunity laws. If a drug/alcohol-testing program will apply to employees after hire, employees should be told in advance the circumstances under which testing may be required and the consequences of refusing to submit to testing.

Instituting a drug-testing program for employees may well be viewed as a change in a "term of condition of employment" that requires negotiation with an incumbent union and that would leave an employer open to unfair labor practice charges if imposed unilaterally.

---

## CONFRONTING THE EMPLOYEE

One of the most effective—and widely used—methods of motivating employees suspected of substance abuse to seek help and improve their job performance is the "constructive confrontation" technique.

Recommendations and pointers on using this technique have been suggested by researchers Harrison Trice and William Sonnenstuhl of the Program on Alcoholism and Occupational Health, sponsored by Cornell University's School of Industrial and Labor Relations. Their research involved a two-year study of supervisory approaches toward problem employees in a major U.S. corporation employing 120,000 workers in more than 50 facilities nationwide.[8]

The constructive confrontation process calls for a supervisor to hold a number of private discussions with an employee whose job performance is deteriorating or unacceptable. In unionized workplaces, a union representative usually is present.

During these discussions, Trice and Sonnenstuhl suggest, the supervisor should confront the employee with specific examples of the worker's unacceptable behavior and warn that continuation of the problem could lead to formal discipline. The supervisor then should offer constructive assistance—without specifically diagnosing the cause of the performance problems—through reminders of the availability of counseling, rehabilitation, and other employee assistance programs.

If performance does not improve after several discussions, a supplementary tactic—"crisis precipitation"—is added to the constructive confrontation process. This consists of progressive formal discipline, such as a written warning, followed by suspensions, and, finally, discharge. At each step of crisis precipitation, the supervisor urges the employee to seek help.

Major findings from the two-year study of supervisors' actual use of this technique include the following:

- Constructive confrontation is a viable and effective strategy. Particularly for alcoholic employees, the technique can motivate workers to seek treatment, attain sobriety, and improve job performance.

- Employees are most likely to show marked improvement when confrontation occurs before job performance seriously deteriorates. Performance appraisals should be an ongoing process, not a static event that occurs at prescribed intervals. Supervisors should be prepared to confront employees at the earliest signs of performance problems.

- Formal discipline may negatively affect an employee's willingness to accept assistance and improve performance. While discipline cannot be delayed indefinitely and should be part of the constructive confrontation strategy, positive outcomes are more likely when supervisors constructively confront employees early.

- Troubled employees are most likely to accept assistance when a supervisor balances constructive and confrontational topics in the performance discussion. While supervisors should sympathize with employees' problems, they also must be firm about the inevitable consequences of unacceptable job performance.

- The supervisor's use of confrontational topics is needed to break down an alcoholic's denial system. The supervisor should realize that most substance abusers or otherwise troubled employees will attempt to shift the focus away from their job performance and on to their personal problems. The supervisor's job is to keep the discussion centered on the deficient job performance.

## MAKING HELP AVAILABLE

Since the standard recommendation for dealing with suspected substance abusers is to give them a firm choice between rehabilitation or discipline, it is important that the employer be prepared to suggest rehabilitation resources.

More than three-fifths of the Fortune 500 companies now have employee assistance programs (EAPs) to provide counseling and referral services to troubled employees, particularly those with alcohol- and drug-abuse problems. Larger companies may provide a fairly sophisticated in-house EAP with a full-time staff. Other organizations contract with outside independent EAPs or consultants to provide similar services as needed. For a full discussion of EAPs, see Chapter 12.

A variety of outside resources are available to companies that do not have a formal EAP. (See Resource Center at the end of this chapter.) Most group health plans cover both inpatient and outpatient alcohol and drug rehabilitation.

## Cost Savings of Company Plans

Several studies suggest that offering EAP services and health insurance coverage for counseling, treating, and rehabilitating chemically dependent employees saves employers health care costs. Most estimates are that savings of $2 should result for every $1 spent. The savings are even more dramatic if the benefits of reduced absenteeism, increased productivity, and fewer accidents and injuries are taken into account.[9]

Some have questioned, however, whether providing unlimited coverage for alcohol- and drug-abuse treatment is cost effective and whether this merely enables the afflicted individuals to avoid responsibility for their own recovery. Hughes Aircraft Co., for example, decided that its former liberal coverage led some people covered by the plan—especially retirees, dependents, and spouses, whom Hughes could not discipline for poor job performance—into a "revolving door" of treatment.[10]

Hughes came to the conclusion that its costly unlimited coverage often enabled addicts to continue their habits indefinitely, rather than get them off chemicals once and for all. So in 1985, it imposed a once-in-a-lifetime cap on treatment coverage. The cap allows exceptions for extenuating circumstances and does not reduce access to the company's EAP or stop substance abusers from re-entering treatment. It just makes them pay for it after the first time.

## Effectiveness of Inpatient Programs

An ongoing and largely unresolved debate concerns the effectiveness of inpatient versus outpatient rehabilitation programs for alcohol/drug recovery. A typical 28-day inpatient substance-abuse treatment program might cost $10,000 or more. Consequently, employers and EAP professionals increasingly are looking at innovative and cost-effective day and evening outpatient treatment programs.

Many substance abuse counselors report seeing a younger, healthier clientele that do not need a 28-day inpatient program. Outpatient counseling and referral to support groups such as Alcoholics Anonymous and Narcotics Anonymous may prove just as effective for this population and at a greatly reduced cost. Employees also may be more willing to accept treatment that does not require a month's absence from the job and the associated fears of being stigmatized as an alcoholic or drug abuser.

One example of a company-sponsored outpatient program is the counseling center opened by United Technology Corp. (UTC) in a refurbished old mansion in New Britain, Conn.[11] At this site, the company offers counseling and a day-treatment program for substance abusers among UTC employees who live in the area.

UTC initially tried to encourage the traditional inpatient treatment centers to develop an outpatient program, but they were dubious about the profitability of such a program. The UTC center offers a two-week program from 8:30 a.m. to 4:00 p.m. Monday through Friday and a half-day on Saturday. More than 2,000 employees used the program in its first five years.

Most evidence points to continuing aftercare as the key to effective recovery, regardless of whether the initial treatment is inpatient or outpatient. Yet this is the aspect that providers of treatment most often neglect. Job-centered rehabilitation efforts should emphasize the importance of aftercare and should be prepared to reactivate a constructive confrontation at the first sign of relapse.

## GUIDELINES

In developing a policy for assisting chemically dependent employees, an employer can take these steps:

- Review current medical plans to determine the extent to which substance-abuse treatment is covered.
- Decide whether to adopt an in-house EAP or contract outside EAP services.
- Decide whether to make leaves of absence available to employees who seek treatment.
- Determine which local organizations provide effective in-patient and outpatient alcohol and drug rehabilitation programs. (This usually is done by an EAP if available.)
- Devise a constructive confrontation strategy and train supervisors to use the strategy.
- Take special care to protect employees' rights of privacy and confidentiality in all substance-abuse matters. Information on discipline, rehabilitation, or test results for alcohol or drug use should not be divulged to prospective employers, co-workers, or anyone without a clear need to know.

---

## RESOURCE CENTER

*Note*: Since programs on occupational alcoholism and drug abuse have evolved in recent years into broader employee assistance programs, the resources for dealing with both substance abuse and other employee problems are listed in Chapter 12.

Much has been written about substance-abuse problems and how to deal with them in the workplace, and it would require a separate book to provide a comprehensive listing of the literature available. Two of the most authoritative sources of books, booklets, and pamphlets on the subject are provided below. Publication catalogs are available from both of these sources.

A.A. Publications
Box 459
Grand Central Station
New York, N.Y. 10017

Hazelden Educational Materials
Pleasant Valley Road
Box 176
Center City, Minn. 55012-0176

## ENDNOTES

1. The Bureau of National Affairs, Inc., 1985 *Daily Labor Report* 211:C-1, October 31, 1985 (Washington, D.C.: BNA, 1985).
2. T.E. Geidt, "Drug and Alcohol Abuse in the Work Place: Balancing Employer and Employee Rights," *Employee Relations Law Journal*, vol. 11, no. 2 (1985):181, 199.
3. R.P. Neuner, *Drugs in the Workplace: Everyone's Business—Everyone's Problem* (Center City, Minn.: Hazelden, 1985): 9.
4. H. Trice and P. Roman, *Spirit and Demons at Work: Alcohol and Drugs on the Job* (Ithaca, N.Y.: Cornell ILR Press, 1972).
5. R. Marcus and M. Engel, "Many Workers Fighting Use of Drug Tests," *The Washington Post* (February 2, 1986):A-14.
6. Ibid.
7. The Bureau of National Affairs, Inc., *Alcohol & Drugs in the Workplace* (BNA: Washington, D.C., 1986): 32.
8. H. Trice and W. Sonnenstuhl, "Constructive Confrontation and Counseling," *EAP Digest* (March/April 1985): 31.
9. The Bureau of National Affairs, Inc., 1985 *Daily Labor Report* 211:C-2, October 31, 1985 (Washington, D.C.: BNA, 1985).
10. Ibid., 211:C-5.
11. The Bureau of National Affairs, Inc., *Employee Assistance Programs: Benefits, Problems & Prospects*, BNA Special Report (Washington, D.C.: BNA, 1987): 123.

# 12

# Assisting Employees With Problems

Personal problems clearly can—and often do—have a direct impact on an employee's job attendance. Yet only recently have employers recognized the need to help employees deal with these personal problems. Today three-fifths of the Fortune 500 corporations and many smaller organizations have established employee assistance programs (EAPs) to provide employees with counseling to help them through personal difficulties, such as alcoholism, drug abuse, marital discord, other relationship troubles, financial difficulties, legal problems, and emotional or mental illness.

## EMPLOYEE ASSISTANCE PROGRAMS (EAPs)

EAPs grew out of occupational alcoholism treatment programs that evolved in the 1960s and early 1970s, and many EAPs still remain focused largely on alcohol- and drug-abuse problems in the workplace. (See Chapter 11.) But EAPs increasingly are broadening their reach to encompass problems other than alcohol and drug abuse and to provide help to family members as well as to employees. An EAP can be simply a referral service that will direct employees to agencies that can provide required care or it can be a full-service program staffed by professional counselors and medical and paramedical personnel. It can be designed to assist employees and their families with a limited number of problems or with a wide array of needs. EAPs can be available to employees who recognize the need for help or they can be suggested by supervisors as resources for subordinates whose personal problems appear to be affecting job performance.

In short, an EAP can be as little or as much as the sponsoring organization wants it to be. Some firms provide these services through an in-house EAP with a full-time staff such as the following.

### Comprehensive EAP

**United Technologies Corp. (UTC)**, Hartford, Conn., uses four separate EAP models to provide appropriate treatment for its 118,000 domestic employees located at 207 plants. An umbrella EAP coordinator at corporate headquarters helps local plant managers set up workable programs suited for the plant size and location. Regardless of the model, the policy is the same—all employees have a chance at working out their personal problems confidentially and without fear of retribution.

At the largest locations, United Technologies provides in-house counselors who maintain a caseload and provide counseling as well as assessment and referral. These EAPs also do patient follow-up. At mid-size plants, one person may manage the program and handle initial assessment and referral, while contracting out the clinical services. At smaller plants, management may contract out the entire program, with the consultant doing the assessment and referral.

At very small locations with 350 or fewer employees, the corporation has experimented with regional EAP models under which several UTC operations in a similar region band together in seeking outside counseling services. This consortium approach allows the units to receive more exclusive attention from the contractor who can assign one person to the group.

UTC trains managers on how to refer employees to the EAP, and it tries to get every employee "into a conference room or cafeteria to explain what an EAP does" and how to use it. Over 50 percent of the employees are covered by either the in-house or the in-house plus consultant models. In recent years, high-level executives have also taken advantage of the EAP services now that credibility and confidentiality have been established.

Overall costs in 1986 were estimated at $12 to $18 per

capita. The EAP coordinator estimates that management gets at least a five-to-one return on its investment through increased productivity, reduced absenteeism, and lower insurance costs.

Other organizations contract with outside EAP specialists or consultants to provide services as needed; similar arrangements may be made with one or more community agencies.

## Outside Consulting Firm

**NI Industries**, Los Angeles, Calif., offers all full-time employees and members of their immediate families free, professional counseling and referrals to deal with "people problems" as well as drug and alcohol abuse. The service, which is provided by an independent consulting firm, is available to employees 24 hours a day by dialing a hotline number. Formal "book-in" appointments also can be arranged.

Strict confidentiality is maintained, and no information on the counseling or subsequent treatment is entered into personnel records. Employees seeking help can become involved in the EAP through self-referral or formal supervisory referral.

Managers are encouraged to suggest that an employee seek counseling if there appears to be a personal problem affecting attendance or job performance. The usual disciplinary procedures for handling performance problems are otherwise followed.

If the employee accepts the referral, the supervisor receives periodic reports on the employee's progress but is not given the specifics of the problem or the counseling. Employees also can be referred to the EAP by a union representative. In all cases, employee participation is voluntary. Sick, personal, or vacation time may be used to meet with a counselor during working hours.

**The Counseling and Referral Elective**, Charleston, S.C., is run by the Charleston County Substance Abuse Commission. Headed by two occupational program consultants, the program contracts with any business, industry, or government agency that wants its services.

A participating company's supervisors are trained by program officials to detect any drop in an employee's attendance or productivity. Once the decline has been confirmed, the employee is referred to one of the two consultants who interviews the worker to try to determine the cause of the problem. The consultant then refers the employee to an appropriate counselor, usually a commission staff expert, to work on a solution. Employees also may refer themselves to the program.

The emphasis of the program is on providing help to the employee while he or she continues to put in a full day's work for the employer.

Smaller companies may provide more informal assistance by training the personnel department staff or supervisors on how to counsel troubled employees and on referral resources in the community.

According to a 1986 Hewitt Associates survey of 293 companies, almost half (47 percent) sponsored an EAP, with an additional 10 percent considering establishing one. Substance abuse was the problem most often covered (99 percent), followed by nervous disorders (92 percent), marital or family discord (91 percent), stress (83 percent), and financial problems (81 percent). Less than half of the EAPs extended coverage to more specialized services such as termination (33 percent) or retirement counseling (28 percent).[1]

One study of the effects of an EAP in reducing absenteeism was conducted by the Imperial Oil Corp. of Canada. The study showed that 295 employees were absent a total of 3,033 days for one year before their involvement with the EAP; a year after the EAP began, the same individuals were absent only 873 days—a reduction of 74 percent. Imperial placed a value on the non-lost days of $311,318. It also estimated that it had saved $44,744 in recaptured supervisory time that would have been spent on counseling "troubled" employees if the EAP had not been available. When the total cost benefit was computed, the company figured it had saved $2.74 for every $1 spent on the EAP.

## ENCOURAGING EMPLOYEE PARTICIPATION

Whatever their form, EAPs use two primary means to encourage employees to get help for personal problems that affect job attendance and performance:

1. Employees are alerted through communication and education programs to the availability of confidential counseling and referrals for assistance and are encouraged to use these services. (See Exhibit 12.1.)

2. Supervisors and managers are encouraged to identify employees whose deteriorating job attendance or performance may indicate personal problems and to refer such employees for counseling and referral. (See Exhibits 12.2 and 12.3.)

Most EAPs provide several hours of counseling at company expense to help the employee identify the exact nature of the problem. Once the problem is identified, the employee is referred to a resource for assistance, and the company's direct financial subsidy usually ends. According to a 1986 survey by Hewitt Associates, the cost of the EAP counseling service is fully company paid by four out of five companies, although the number of times an employee may use it sometimes is limited. Annual employer costs average $18 per employee, with a range of $1 to $135 per year.[2]

If employees have chemical dependency, psychiatric, or other medical problems, they are referred to professional treatment resources that often are covered by the company medical insurance. Other possible referrals include family social service agencies, legal clinics or law firms, financial counselors, or other known resources. The EAP counselor helps the employee work out the most suitable financial arrangements.

Many organizations make use of hotlines or other well-publicized telephone numbers for employees to use confidentially in seeking help. Some large organizations provide a 24-hour hotline staffed by telephone counselors trained to make referrals to local services and to handle emergency situations.

Maintaining employee privacy is the key to any EAP's success. Employees need assurances that all information disclosed to an EAP counselor is strictly confidential. Many organizations have found that, particularly at the outset, employees' confidentiality concerns are somewhat allayed if an outside contractor rather than the personnel department provides the counseling.

EAP counselors usually are available to help supervisors cope with problem employees. The counselor can suggest ways to identify and document job performance deficiencies and to confront the employee in a constructive manner. (See the discussion on constructive confrontation in Chapter 11.) In helping managers deal with troubled employees, a good EAP will emphasize that the job

# EXHIBIT 12.1

## COMPANY LETTER TO EMPLOYEE AND FAMILY

Dear (Company) Employee and Family:

The purpose of this letter is to acquaint you with a new program (Your company) is installing for its employees. Referred to as the Employee Guidance Service Program, the program deals with a wide range of human problems which, if unattended, often result in poor work performance and attendance.

(Your company) is aware that human problems not only create difficulties on the job but hardships at home as well. In some cases neither the efforts of the employee nor the supervisor are successful in resolving the employee's problem and unsatisfactory job performance persists.

It is a fact that most human problems can be successfully treated if identified early and a referral is made to appropriate care. This applies whether the problem is one of physical illness, mental or emotional illness, finances, drinking, drugs, marital or family stress, legal problems or other difficulties. Unfortunately, most people are unaware of the helping resources available in the community and often too ashamed or too afraid to admit a problem exists. While (company) is primarily concerned about job performance and attendance, experience shows that the cause of problems must be dealt with first. We also realize that diagnosis is best done by someone who is professionally trained and competent.

The Employee Guidance Service Program is designed to help employees get assistance on a confidential, professional and humane basis without jeopardizing one's job, future, or reputation. You need only call (Your company contact or outside counselor).

The purpose of this program is to help people get assistance with problems at the earliest possible time so human and financial loss can be kept at a minimum. The alternative is that such problems usually get worse and employees can end up jeopardizing their jobs.

Remember, waiting to do something about a problem usually makes the problem worse.

Sincerely,
(Signed by Chief Executive)

---

*Source:* BNA Policy and Practice Series, *Personnel Management*, pp. 245:803–245:804, The Bureau of National Affairs, Inc., 1979.

## EXHIBIT 12.2

Subject:　ER 1—Employee Relations
　　　　　　7—Employee Benefits & Services
　　　　　　J—*Employee Assistance Program*

### POLICY

### 1.　GENERAL

It is the policy of Security Pacific National Bank to offer confidential
professional assistance to the staff member whose job performance has
deteriorated as a result of a severe personal problem. The Bank is only
concerned when a staff member's personal problem affects performance or
attendance and has no interest in intruding upon an individual's private life.

The Bank recognizes that alcoholism is a progressive disease which can be
successfully treated, usually without interruption of employment. Other major
problems may also be successfully treated while the staff member continues
employment. Staff members with major personal problems who seek assistance
will be referred to competent professional treatment resources in the
community.

The Bank also recognizes that a staff member's job performance may also be
affected when a member of the family has severe personal problems. For this
reason, assistance is also available to any member of the immediate family.

### 3.　OBJECTIVE

The objective of the Employee Assistance Program is to retain valued staff
members whose job performance is affected by personal problems through
motivating the staff member to seek help. However, the decision to accept
assistance is the responsibility of the staff member.

### 5.　PERFORMANCE

The implementation of this policy provides no privileges or exceptions to the
Bank's standard policy governing job performance.

### 7.　EVALUATING PERFORMANCE

It is the responsibility of the supervisor to evaluate a staff member's
performance.

　　a.　When a staff member's performance slips to an unsatisfactory level and
　　normal supervisory action does not improve performance, it is the

*EXHIBIT 12.2—Continued*

responsibility of the supervisor to determine if the staff member should be referred to the Assistance Program. In such cases, the supervisor is to discuss the matter with the Employee Assistance Coordinator. The supervisor *does not diagnose* the problem, rather the supervisor is concerned with job performance and attendance.

Prior to referring a staff member, the following steps must be taken.

(1)   Document examples of deteriorating job performance, (i.e., excessive absences, decreased productivity, poor judgment).

(2)   Inform the staff member of the inadequate work record. Give the staff member an adequate period of time to improve.

(3)   If job performance does not improve, refer the staff member who desires help to the Assistance Program for evaluation and assistance. Advise the staff member that the decision to seek assistance is confidential and is *not* included in the personnel file.

Staff members who do not desire assistance will be expected to improve performance. If performance is not improved, the supervisor must take the appropriate disciplinary action in accordance with guidelines in ER 1–5F.

b.   Once the staff member is referred to the program, the supervisor is to follow through with the required job performance evaluations.

9.   ASSISTANCE COORDINATOR

a.   An Assistance Coordinator is available to review cases requiring evaluation and referral. Supervisors should refer such cases to their Personnel Relations Officer or the Assistance Coordinator. All cases must be treated in a confidential manner and must not be discussed with anyone except the Personnel Officer or Coordinator.

b.   A confidential interview by the Assistance Coordinator with the staff member provides an opportunity to discuss the nature of the problem and to outline an approach to the solution.

If it is determined in the interview that:

(1)   Alcoholism is the major source of difficulty, the nature of the disease, its progressive stages of deterioration, and the sources of treatment available will be reviewed. Community resources directed toward the treatment of alcohol problems will be outlined with the staff member. The staff member may be referred to Alcoholics Anonymous or to other resources appropriate to the specific needs.

*EXHIBIT 12.2—Continued*

(2)　If some other severe personal problem is affecting the staff member's job performance, an open discussion of the situation confronting the staff member will result in a suitable referral. The staff member will be referred to competent professional treatment resources in the community.

The Coordinator will arrange a follow-up schedule with the supervisor, staff member, and treatment resource. The information, gathered through follow-up, will support the use of treatment resources and the staff member's efforts to improve job performance.

If the staff member's response is favorable and job performance is restored, after a periodic follow-up schedule, no further contact will be made unless further assistance is requested by the staff member.

When the staff member does not respond to the assistance offered and job performance does not improve, the supervisor must take the appropriate disciplinary action in accordance with the guidelines in ER 1–5F.

## 11.   SELF REFERRAL

Self referral to the Program is also available on a confidential basis to any staff member who wishes to request assistance with a personal problem affecting job performance and no contact will be made with the staff member's supervisor.

## 13.   MEDICAL BENEFITS

Staff members and their dependents who are covered by the Bank's Medical Plan will receive benefits allowable under the Plan. However, alcoholism is excluded from Long Term Disability.

---

*Source:* Reprinted with permission from the Security Pacific National Bank Employee Relations Manual.

*EXHIBIT 12.3*

## CORPORATE POLICY DIRECTIVE

### EMPLOYEE ASSISTANCE PROGRAM

I.   POLICY

Northrop Corporation recognizes that behavioral-medical problems such as alcoholism, drug dependency, and psychological disorders, can be treated successfully. While the company has no intention of interfering in an employee's private life, it is the policy of Northrop to become involved and endeavor to help when an employee's job performance is affected on a continuing basis or when an employee requests help. The Employee Assistance Program has been established to provide help for the troubled employee. Employee referral to and participation in this program shall be treated in a confidential manner, and associated information shall neither appear in the employee's personnel records nor be released to anyone without the written approval of the employee.

II.   RESPONSIBILITIES

A.  The Corporate Medical Director shall assist each element of the company in establishing procedures to provide for management orientation and for appropriate diagnosis and referral of employees to outside agencies for treatment.

B.  Supervisors and managers shall be responsible for recognizing that an employee may have a problem. Although it is often very difficult to judge whether or not an employee's unusual behavior or poor performance is due to a behavioral-medical problem, early identification is the key to successful treatment. Therefore, when there are indications that such a problem exists, the Administrator of the Employee Assistance Program or the company element medical department should be contacted immediately.

C.  The Administrator of the Employee Assistance Program shall conduct management briefings, counsel employees (when appropriate), refer employees to treatment programs in the local areas, and generally administer the program.

D.  Employees who refer themselves or are referred by their superiors to the Employee Assistance Program shall cooperate fully in their recovery program and shall receive the same consideration as employees having any other illness. However, continued unacceptable job performance by employees who fail to cooperate fully may result in disciplinary action which could include termination of employment. While it is understood that relapses may occur, they will be evaluated on an individual basis depending upon the employee's progress and attitude towards the recovery program.

Thomas V. Jones
Chairman and
Chief Executive Officer

*Source:* Reprinted with permission from Northrop Corp., Corporate Policy Directive, 1978.

of the manager is to monitor and motivate, not to become inappropriately involved in personal, nonwork-related issues.

The participation rate in EAPs varies dramatically depending on the work force, the corporate climate, the program, the publicity it receives, and its reputation for confidentiality. Conservative estimates are that at least 10 percent of the work force have problems serious enough to impair job attendance or performance and that 10 percent of this group can be encouraged to seek help—in other words, a minimum of 1 percent of the work force will avail themselves of an EAP.

But organizations with comprehensive programs that are trusted and accepted have found that 10 percent of the employees may use the EAP. The most effective and well-utilized programs are tied closely to an overall corporate medical and employee wellness program.

Accessibility is a key to utilization of an EAP. The time when an employee or family member is willing to reach out for help is typically short. A 24-hour hotline usually may be provided. Ideally the initial contact should be handled by a professional equipped to respond to the problem immediately. In any event, the waiting time for professional assistance should be kept to a minimum.

## EAP PROVIDERS & CONSULTANTS

With the rapid growth in corporate interest in broad-brush EAPs, many mental health agencies, treatment facilities, and consultants have seen this as a new source of added revenues. Too often, those advertising themselves as EAP resources have limited ability to deliver an effective comprehensive program. Moreover, some agencies and treatment centers offer low-cost EAP services in the expectation of feeding business to the provider. Management should be careful to check the credentials and independence of prospective EAP contractors.

The EAP field at present is in a period of turmoil and transition. In the past, most EAP directors and consultants were drawn from the ranks of recovered alcoholics, but today many EAP practitioners have advanced degrees in such fields as psychiatric social work or psychological counseling. Whether a recovered alcoholic or a social worker with a master's degree, the EAP practitioner needs to understand employee relations and know how to tailor a program to a particular company's culture and needs. This is the talent most often lacking among the otherwise qualified health-care counselors who print up business cards and claim to provide EAP services.

The Association of Labor-Management Administrators and Consultants on Alcoholism (ALMACA) has adopted a credentialing program to certify employee assistance professionals. ALMACA is the leading professional organization in the EAP field and has about 4,500 members, up from 1,500 ten years ago. As its name suggests, it started out as an organization of alcoholism consultants, but it has paralleled the growth in EAPs and now represents professionals involved in comprehensive programs. Its first credentialing exam was given in spring 1987.

A similar credentialing program is being instituted by the Employee Assistance Society of North America, which was started in 1983 and now has about 1,500 members.

## EAP COST-EFFECTIVENESS

How do EAPs fit in with the current concern for containing escalating health care costs? Initially it might appear that EAPs are part of the problem rather than the solution, since they result in increased referrals of employees and family members for treatment. EAP proponents argue, however, that studies show EAPs encourage successful early treatment that ends up saving money in the long run. The case for the cost-effectiveness of EAPs is stronger when total costs and benefits, including job attendance, are tallied.

A 1985 study by the International Foundation of Employee Benefit Plans found that EAPs can lower the rates of increase in employer health insurance costs, even though employees at firms with EAPs file more claims for treatment.[3] Other studies have confirmed that EAPs can have a "gatekeeper" effect by early referral to non-intensive therapy, thereby forestalling later use of more extensive inpatient care or long-term psychiatric therapy. Moreover, early mental health care has been shown to reduce the cost of physical health care. Some companies have tailored their health insurance plans to provide incentives for treatment that is referred and monitored by the EAP on the assumption that the EAP would provide the most cost-effective treatment.[4]

## REHABILITATING TROUBLED EMPLOYEES

Special job-readjustment needs arise when former substance abusers or other troubled employees return to work after medical leaves to participate in treatment programs. A return-to-work conference, if properly programmed, can help the employee and supervisor.[5]

Such a conference typically involves the rehabilitated employee, the employee's supervisor, a counselor involved with the employee's treatment, and, if there is an employee assistance program, the EAP coordinator. Each participant should be asked to state what he or she wants from the meeting. The employee should be encouraged to participate in this process rather than assume the more passive role of just listening to what those in authority have to say.

The conference might cover these topics:

*The employee's performance problems.* The participants should review the employee's prior job performance problems. The supervisor and the employee can then develop a corrective plan.

*Job-related treatment issues.* The employee should be given a chance to describe what was learned in treatment that will affect job performance and attitude. Typical issues include the employee's relationship with co-workers, attitude toward authority, and career goals.

*Workplace events during the employee's absence.* The employee should be updated on job-related developments, including specific information about the job and the organization in general and personal news about co-workers.

*The employee's concerns.* The conference should focus on the employee's anticipations, questions, and anxieties about returning to work. Common concerns include what co-workers are thinking, how much will have to be explained about the treatment, and whether the company wants the employee back.

Benefits of a return-to-work conference include easing the

employee's transition back to the job, re-establishing and strengthening the supervisor-employee relationship, and giving the supervisor and the organization insights about workplace conditions that may hinder performance.

## GUIDELINES

Employee assistance programs can go a long way to improve job attendance and performance. An employee with a problem—whether related to the job or strictly personal—is likely to let the job suffer. Just knowing there is someone who can provide help and guidance on further assistance may be enough to alleviate major job problems.

In setting up an employee assistance program, management should take these actions:

- Determine employees' needs. A work force with a large component of young, relatively unsophisticated employees may have more need for counseling than a work force largely made up of employees who know where to get help on their own.

- Determine the availability of outside resources. In some locations, community agencies may be so lacking that the employer may have to rely more on its own staff or on specialized EAP contractors.

- Based on these determinations, decide whether to set up an in-house program or contract services from an outside agency.

- Address issues such as on-site or off-site location, hours of operation, cost-sharing with employees, method of reimbursement, and confidentiality.

- Provide autonomy for the EAP, even if an in-house program, so that the integrity of the program and client confidentiality is preserved.

- Give supervisors special guidance and training that covers how to detect problems, counsel or refer employees to counseling, and confront the employee firmly but sympathetically. The supervisor has the delicate task of balancing a sympathetic concern for the employee with a firm insistence on remedying job performance deficiencies.

- Review the malpractice/general liability coverage of the EAP provider, whether an in-house or an outside contractor.

- Communicate the availability of the program at all levels of the company and emphasize protections of confidentiality.

- Emphasize to employees that the program is voluntary. Even if the EAP is suggested by the supervisor, the employee should realize that he or she has a free choice to make a personal commitment to work on the problem through the EAP or to decline to make that commitment and suffer the consequences.

- Review utilization reports as barometers of areas of stress or other problems within the organization (provided the numbers are large enough to protect the confidentiality of the individual).

## RESOURCE CENTER

For information on how to start an employee assistance program, contact these groups:

Association of Labor-Management Administrators
  and Consultants on Alcoholism, Inc. (ALMACA)
1800 North Kent St., #907
Arlington, Va. 22209
703-522-6272

The name of this association is a bit misleading, since it is a nonprofit organization of professionals dealing with employee assistance programs, not just alcoholism programs. It has more than 50 local chapters and some 4,500 members.

Employee Assistance Society of North America (EASNA)
P.O. Box 3909
Oak Park, Ill. 60303
312-383-6668

This relatively new group was started in 1983 and has about 1,500 members.

National Institute on Alcohol Abuse and Alcoholism (NIAAA)
Occupational Program Branch
5600 Fishers Lane
Rockville, Md. 20850
301-443-1273

This federal agency provides information on occupational alcoholism, EAPs, and local resources.

National Institute on Drug Abuse Clearinghouse (NIDAC)
P.O. Box 416
Kensington, Md. 20795
202-443-6500

This federal agency provides information on guidelines for identifying substance abusers and for establishing a company program.

National Clearinghouse for Alcohol Information (NCIA)
P.O. Box 2345
Rockville, Md. 20852
301-468-2600

This group maintains a regularly updated list of state and territorial occupational program consultants. These agencies, particularly in larger states or communities, may employ trained program consultants.

## Private Consulting Organizations

Hazelden Consultation Services
1350 Nicollet Mall, Suite 103
Minneapolis, Minn. 55403
612-338-2960

Personal Peformance Consultants, Inc.
211 N. Lindbergh Blvd.
St. Louis, Mo. 63141
314-981-4422

## Emergency Help

If an employee faces a crisis requiring immediate attention and no employee assistance program exists, possible contacts may include those listed below.

*Alcoholics Anonymous/Al-Anon.* In most communities, the local phone book has a listing for the AA "desk" that often is staffed round-the-clock to provide help to individuals and families.

*Local hospital emergency rooms, mental health clinics and institutions.* Many employers maintain a list of licensed mental health resources that provide emergency help and referrals.

*Veterans Administration hospitals.* If the employee or family member is a veteran with an honorable discharge, the nearest VA hospital will offer treatment for medical, psychiatric, and substance abuse problems.

---

**ENDNOTES**

1. Hewitt Associates, *On Employee Benefits*, November/December 1986 (Atlanta, Ga.: Hewitt Associates, 1986): 3.
2. Ibid.
3. The Bureau of National Affairs, Inc., "Employee Assistance Programs: Benefits, Problems and Prospects," BNA Special Report (Washington, D.C.: BNA, 1987): 33.
4. Ibid., 34.
5. G. Singer, "Return-to-Work Conference for Rehabilitated Workers," *EAP Digest*, vol. 6, no. 3 (February 1986): 51.

# Part 4

# Disciplinary Measures

# 13

# Traditional Discipline

Discipline traditionally has been used to handle problems of employee performance in the workplace. However, in dealing with job absences, the most common performance problem in the United States, the disciplinary approach encounters particular problems. This is because our system of workplace discipline assumes that the employee has engaged in misconduct and that the employee has it within his or her control to correct the misconduct. Disciplining the employee is intended to correct, not punish such behavior.

## JOB ABSENCES AND MISCONDUCT

Applying this concept to causes of job absence creates confusion, however, because an absent employee may or may not be guilty of misconduct. For example, an employee who is working on a second job while on sick leave is clearly guilty of misconduct, and traditional disciplinary concepts are appropriate. But more often than not, the issue is not misconduct but excessive job absences that have become intolerable to management regardless of the reason.

As noted in Chapter 1, most company policies make a distinction between excused and unexcused absences. Generally it is the supervisor who determines whether or not an excuse given by the employee is valid, after asking the employee to explain the absence and, in doubtful cases, to offer proof, such as a doctor's note.

If management decides certain absences are not justified, it

167

must also decide at what point to apply corrective discipline. Since different supervisors assess the validity of the reasons for absences and determine the appropriate penalty, management runs the risk of seemingly disparate treatment. But even if management accepts the reasons given for an absence or a string of absences, it may decide at some point that the absences have become so disruptive to efficiency as to warrant taking corrective action.

With chronically absent employees, however, there often is no clear-cut distinction between valid and invalid or excused and unexcused absences. For example, the employee who is "sick" on a Monday or Friday once or twice a month may come under some suspicion.

Employees, as well as management, can be frustrated by the confusing application of normal discipline-for-misconduct concepts to job absences. They may argue that they need clear and consistent attendance rules, but when management attempts to provide such rules, the affected employees may complain about the lack of flexibility. Nevertheless, the generally accepted principle is that management can expect attendance with some degree of regularity and can impose discipline for failure to adhere to this standard.

## GENERAL PRINCIPLES

In adopting and implementing traditional disciplinary rules, these principles should be followed:

- The rules should be clearly stated, reasonable, and communicated to those affected.

- The rules should be applied consistently. The same penalty should be applied to all violators unless mitigating circumstances clearly warrant special treatment. The progressive disciplinary steps should be consistently and patiently observed.

- Employees should not be entrapped. Tempting suspected employees to violate the rules breeds hostility.

- Management should get all the facts before acting. The employee's view of the incident should be obtained.

- During a reprimand, care should be taken to maintain the dignity of both the supervisor and the employee. Verbal abuse and physical contact should be avoided.

- After a reprimand or disciplinary layoff, the employee should be given a fresh start and treated the same way as any other employee.

## ATTENDANCE RULES

Two main issues are involved in attendance discipline cases: (1) the reasonableness of the company's attendance policies in general; and (2) the appropriate application of these policies in particular cases.

The following discussion stems largely from awards by labor arbitrators dealing with these issues under union contracts. But the principles discussed usually arise from standards of basic fairness, or the "common law of the shop," and consequently apply to both union and nonunion situations.

## COMPANY POLICY

Management's best defense against complaints of arbitrariness is adherence to an established policy clearly defining permissible leave situations. For example, one arbitrator upheld an employer's attendance control program as reasonable and fair after concluding that the program was "definitely calculated to stimulate the interests of the employees in being regular in their attendance."[1]

Any attendance control policy must pass this test of reasonableness and will be found flawed if it has discriminatory, arbitrary, or capricious features. Thus, an employer was ordered to change its new attendance control program that excused most absences for which a doctor's certificate was produced but contained a 5-percent absenteeism calculation that triggered an attendance counseling requirement regardless of excuse. "An absence excused for medical reasons is a legitimate reason to excuse an employee from counseling," the arbitrator held.[2]

Before imposing discipline for unexcused absences, a company should make clear what constitutes an excused absence.[3] Similarly, management also should spell out how many absences or late arrivals will trigger disciplinary action.[4]

Employees also should receive notice of any changes in attendance policies. Arbitrators will not enforce a rule or practice of which employees are not informed or are informed of only as a consequence of their behavior.[5]

In one such case where three employees were disciplined for taking off from work to go deer hunting, Arbitrator Harry Platt reinstated one employee with full back pay. This man, unlike the other two, had not been informed that the company was rescinding a past practice of permitting employees to be absent at the start of hunting season.[6]

## CONSISTENT ENFORCEMENT

Even if management establishes reasonable rules and clearly notifies the employees of them, it still can be faulted for inconsistent application of the rules. Employees guilty of the same offense should get the same disciplinary treatment, although allowance may be made for mitigating circumstances such as long service with a good work record.

Consistent enforcement of attendance rules is not easy, given the seemingly endless variety of excuses for absences, the inevitable difficulties in comparing different absence records, and the idiosyncrasies of individual supervisors. What counts is uniform purposes rather than rigid application.[7] The humane exercise of discretion in individual cases may justify different responses in situations with surface similarities.[8]

## PROGRESSIVE DISCIPLINE

Once a problem is determined to warrant correction, the next step is to effect a course of progressive discipline. With certain exceptions, a discharge for absenteeism generally is not justified unless the individual first has been warned about unsatisfactory attendance and of the possible consequences of failing to correct the situation.

The last element is particularly important. The employer should make good-faith efforts, over a reasonable period of time, to eliminate the cause of absenteeism before resorting to the "capital punishment" of discharge. This particularly applies in the case of an employee with long and satisfactory service.[9]

A progressive discipline system is intended to give the employee a chance to correct the attendance problem. The penalties become increasingly severe under such a system. The common steps in such a program are listed below.

## Oral Warning

Here the supervisor clearly explains the company's attendance policies and how the employee's record fails to meet this standard. The supervisor should attempt to determine if any special circumstances contribute to the problem and should counsel the employee on the consequences if the problem persists. Although the warning is oral, the supervisor should make a written record of it.

## Written Warning

If the employee continues unsatisfactory attendance, a written warning is usually the next step. An official notice is given to the employee and placed in his or her personnel file. The supervisor again should attempt to counsel the employee, find out the underlying cause for the poor attendance, and offer to work with the employee in overcoming the problem. Frequently the seriousness of the situation is stressed by asking the employee to read and sign the written statement that is going into the files.

The supervisor can add to the impact of the written warning by not apologizing for it and by emphasizing that more serious consequences will follow if the behavior is not changed.

## Suspension

The next step if attendance does not improve is a disciplinary layoff without pay. Since the idea is to get the employee's attention, a short-term suspension generally is effective.

## Discharge

The final step is termination. At the exit interview, the supervisor should stress the reasons for the discharge, review the employee's attendance problems, and remind the employee of previous efforts to encourage correction of the behavior. Since a small number of employees usually account for most of the company's absenteeism, termination of the major offenders frequently can have a ripple effect on attendance.

Most employers agree that this system of progressively harsher actions is the most effective disciplinary approach toward the employee who is chronically and sporadically absent. There is less agreement, however, on the merits of using progressive discipline when the employee's absence clearly is due to illness or injury.

When a company has an established system of progressive discipline, arbitrators generally uphold its enforcement absent unusual circumstances.[10] Implicit in this doctrine of progressive discipline is a "correlative duty on the part of the employee to progressively improve." Repetition of misconduct after warnings and/or suspension will constitute evidence that the worker has failed this obligation.[11]

Since progressive discipline is designed to correct employee misconduct, it may seem inappropriate when applied to absences due to illness or injury where misconduct is not an issue.[12] An alternative approach in such cases is to notify the employee that the health problem, if not corrected, may cause termination.

## MITIGATING CIRCUMSTANCES

Although attendance is ranked by management as the most serious disciplinary problem, it also produces the greatest number of exceptions from standard disciplinary procedures. Since employee culpability is not necessarily a part of an attendance problem, employers and arbitrators are more prone to find mitigating circumstances that justify waiving or ameliorating normal disciplinary rules.

Long seniority is probably the most frequently cited circumstance warranting retaining an employee whose attendance record otherwise would justify discharge.[13] This is particularly true when it is reasonable to expect the employee will be able to resume work and maintain an acceptable record.[14]

For example, Arbitrator George Roumell set aside a discharge and held that a company owed an employee with an admittedly poor attendance record more than just a mechanical application of the company's disciplinary policies, given that the employee had 27 years of service and was 58 years old. Moreover, the arbitrator noted, the employee's most recent spells of absenteeism had occurred during a period when he was suspected of having cancer. Since that fear subsequently was proved false, there was reasonable hope that the employee could return to work with an acceptable attendance record.[15]

On the other hand, a company does not have to prove that the future holds no hope for improvement in order to sustain a discharge for poor attendance. The only requirement is that the employer make a reasonable judgment, based on the employee's past performance and attitude, that the employee's attendance is not likely to improve.[16]

Among the mitigating circumstances that might justify overlooking an absence or imposing a less severe penalty is evidence that the employer somehow was responsible for the absence. In a case where an employee's absence pushed her over the sick leave allowance, an arbitrator found that the absence was caused by illness from toxic fumes in the workplace.[17]

## OTHER DISCIPLINARY PENALTIES

Warning, suspension, and discharge are the traditional penalties for absenteeism. But employers sometimes try other techniques to encourage better attendance.

Withholding privileges such as vacation pay or bonuses has been used by employers as a penalty for excessive absenteeism. Arbitrators, however, do not look favorably upon such attempts to restrict employee benefits unless specifically sanctioned by the collective bargaining contracts.[18]

## Denial of Promotion

Denying a promotion to an employee with a poor attendance record generally is upheld. The theory here is that denial of a promotion does not punish the employee but rather reflects management's evaluation of the employee's ability to handle the new job.

Thus, an arbitrator held that an employer did not act in an "arbitrary or capricious" manner by deciding that an employee "did not meet minimum qualifications for the job" because she had "a significantly higher absence rate than other employees considered to be high-absence people." Even though the employee had not been warned or disciplined for absenteeism, this did not preclude the employer from denying her the promotion, the arbitrator ruled. Management can take attendance records into account in promotion decisions without regard to the separate issue of discipline for absenteeism.[19]

## Demotion

Demotion for poor attendance is a different matter. While good attendance may be required for advancement, this requirement may not be imposed retroactively to demote an employee. Instead, standard disciplinary procedures should be used in an effort to correct deficiencies in the employee's performance of his current job.[20]

## GUIDELINES

Here are some of the general principles applied by arbitrators in determining whether discipline for absenteeism is justified:

- The attendance rule on which discipline is based must be reasonable and based on economic or safety concerns.

- The rule and disciplinary policies and procedures should be clearly communicated to employees.

- The disciplined employee should have known and understood the rule or policy and been forewarned that discharge might result from a continued failure to observe the policy.

- The employee should be accorded "due process." The employer's investigation should be conducted fairly and objectively, and the employee should be given a chance to explain his or her side of the story.

- Discipline should be applied consistently, equitably, and without discrimination.

- The degree of discipline should be reasonably related to the seriousness of the offense and the employee's record.

- Discharge usually should occur only when the probability of a future change in the behavior pattern is remote.

- Recognition should be given to any mitigating circumstances that might call for modification of standard disciplinary policies.

## ENDNOTES

1. Celanese Piping Sys., Inc., 66 LA 674 (McIntosh, 1976).
2. Amax, Inc., 76 LA 607 (Moats, 1981).
3. John A. Volpe Constr. Co., Inc., 45 LA 535 (Dunlop, 1965); American Standard Co., 30 LA 231 (Thompson, 1958).
4. W.R. Grace & Co., 62 LA 779 (Boals, 1974); Shepard Niles Crane & Hoist Corp., 71 LA 828 (Alutto, 1978).
5. General Elec. Co., 72 LA 809 (MacDonald, 1978); Wilson Paper Co., 73 LA 1167 (Rose, 1978); J.R. Redeker, *Discipline: Policies and Procedures* (Washington, D.C.: BNA Books, 1985): 57.
6. Shakespeare & Shakespeare Prods. Co., 9 LA 813 (Platt, 1950).
7. B.A. Aaron, "The Uses of the Past in Arbitration," in *Proceedings of the Eighth Annual Meeting, National Academy of Arbitrators* (Washington, D.C.: BNA Books, 1955): 11.
8. H. Block and R. Mittenthal, "Arbitration and the Absent Employee," in *Arbitration 1984*, Proceedings of the Thirty-Seventh Annual Meeting, National Academy of Arbitrators, ed. W. Gershenfeld (Washington, D.C.: BNA Books, 1985): 88.
9. Peerless Laundry Co., 51 LA 331, 335 (Eaton, 1968).

10. General Mills Fun Group, 72 LA 1285 (Martin, 1979) and cases cited therein.
11. Amax, Inc., note 2 above.
12. Atlantic Richfield Co., 69 LA 484 (Sisk, 1977) and cases cited therein.
13. Peerless Laundry Co., 51 LA 331 (Eaton, 1968); Menasha Corp., 71 LA 653 (Roumell, 1978); Drexel Univ., 85 LA 579 (Kramer, 1985).
14. Pullman-Standard Co., 36 LA 1042 (McCoy, 1961); Union Carbide Chems., 35 LA 469 (Hale, 1960); Menasha Corp., note 13 above, at 657 and cases cited therein.
15. Menasha Corp., note 13 above.
16. Shell Oil Co., 85 LA 767 (LeBaron, 1985).
17. ITT Power Sys. Corp., 84 LA 288 (Elkin, 1985); *see also* Kansas City Power & Light Co., 84 LA 393 (Kubie, 1985).
18. Liberty Plating Co., 9 LA 508 (Fearing, 1951); Terre Haute Malleable & Mfg. Co., 9 LA 526 (Greene, 1951).
19. Pierce Governor Co., Inc., 75 LA 1282 (Petersen, 1980).
20. Owens-Corning Fiberglas Corp., 78 LA 21 (Clarke, 1982).

# 14

# Discipline for Abuse
of Sick Leave

Sick-leave policies are exceedingly difficult to police. Most employers decide it is impractical to check on each and every claim, because constant surveillance would be cumbersome, expensive, and irritating to both the company and the employee. Nevertheless, the substantial benefits of paid sick leave place an equally substantial obligation on employees to use leave only when justified. Only the dishonest employee—until detected—comes out ahead in abusing sick leave; in the long run, the rest of the work force has to foot the bill.[1]

## STANDARDS OF PROOF

An employer's sick-leave policy should provide standards on what is abuse and what is not. Most questions of abuse arise when employees on sick leave are found to have engaged in activities other than lying at home on a sick bed. Although such activities are difficult to detail, employees should have some guidelines as to what they can or cannot do while on sick leave.

Clearly an employee need not be completely immobilized in order to claim sick leave. When one employer argued that its policy prohibited employees from performing any physical acts while on sick leave, an arbitrator noted that a strict interpretation of that policy "might prohibit a newly wed employee with a broken arm from consummating a marriage, an act most will agree is taxing physically."[2]

177

When an employer attempts to restrict the activities of workers on sick leave, this arbitrator said, three areas are involved:

- a "pure white one," consisting of activities in which the employee clearly has the right to engage in while on sick leave;

- a "pure black one," consisting of activities that clearly would be inconsistent with a claim for sick leave; and

- a "gray one," in which an employee's activities may or may not be justified depending on the circumstances.

Activities engaged in "for recreational purposes which are inconsistent with prescribed treatment," he remarked, are a "typical gray area." Engaging in other paid employment with physical demands similar to those of the regular job normally is in the "black" area.

In this particular case, the arbitrator upheld the discharge of a worker who was seen plowing his corn field for spring planting while he was on sick leave for an alleged eye problem. This was in the "black" area, the arbitrator said.

But in a "gray" area case, another arbitrator set aside the suspension of an employee for playing golf while under doctor's orders to perform no manual labor.[3]

The standards for testing the fairness of management's policing of sick-leave abuse differ depending on whether the situation involves discharge and other discipline or merely denial of sick leave.

If an employee is discharged or suspended for undertaking other work during sick leave, the alleged misconduct involves asserted moral turpitude on the employee's part and the employer must prove the misconduct "beyond reasonable doubt," arbitrators hold.[4]

Even if the case involves recreational activities, arbitrators may hold the employer to a stringent standard of proof before upholding a discharge. Thus, an arbitrator reinstated two workers who were fired for playing ball the nights before and after their days of sick leave. In this case, the arbitrator said, the quantum of proof lay somewhere between "clear and convincing evidence" and "proof beyond a reasonable doubt," particularly since the discharge could affect the employees' chances of obtaining other jobs.[5]

## OUTSIDE EMPLOYMENT

Probably the strongest case for disciplining sick-leave misrepresentation concerns the employee who is found to have worked outside jobs while claiming sick leave. Thus, an arbitrator upheld the discharge of an employee with a good work record and 20 years' employment who feigned disability to continue receiving disability compensation while doing equally strenuous work at his own business.[6]

But proof that an employee on leave performs some work for himself or another company would not necessarily justify discharge. Absent a rule specifically prohibiting such conduct, one arbitrator held, a company had no business firing an employee who operated an undertaking business while on sick leave. This other employment was not sufficient ground, the arbitrator said, for the company to disregard the doctor's certification that the employee suffered from a mental and nervous condition that made him unable to perform his regular job.[7]

Similarly, an arbitrator reinstated, but without back pay, an employee who, while on sick leave, promoted his fishing equipment business, set up and manned a booth at a sports show, and went on a fishing trip in another state. The employee had an ulcer and had been extremely upset over his brother's suicide. His doctor had suggested that he do "whatever he would best relax at," and fishing seemed to fit the bill.[8]

The decisive point in these discharge cases is whether the demands of the outside employment differed sufficiently from those of the regular job so that the employee's asserted medical problems could permit performing the outside job but not the regular job.

## SPORTS ACTIVITY

A similar standard determines the appropriateness of discipline when an employee on sick leave is found to have participated in bowling, baseball, or similar sports. These two cases demonstrate application of the test:

Discharge was upheld when an employee claiming workers' compensation had indicated that he needed help getting out of bed, dressing, and eating because of lower back pain when, in fact, he had been playing basketball.[9]

But discharges were set aside for employees who had played basketball either the night before or the night after the days on which they claimed sick leave. "Mere participation in a sport is not proof that the participant is healthy," the arbitrator said. "The employee may have played the game while he was sick; or, his physical condition may have deteriorated during the period for which he took leave."[10]

## OTHER ACTIVITIES

The same issues and tests affect cases in which employees engaged in other activities while on sick leave. Thus, an arbitrator upheld the discharge of an employee who was seen at an amusement park with his family on the day his wife reported that he could not come to work because of illness.[11]

## FRAUD VS. ABUSE

Some of these cases distinguish outright fraud from mere abuse of sick leave, with more severe discipline reserved for the fraud cases.

In one case, an employee was told by his doctor to remain at home and rest for three days. During those three days, however, he went bowling one night to prevent his team from forfeiting a game, and he took his girlfriend to a party the next night. On the bowling night, he scored considerably lower than usual, and on the night of his date, he became so ill that he had to be taken to a hospital. The arbitrator set aside the discharge because he concluded that the employee had not falsified his sick-leave claim. But the employee was denied back pay since he nevertheless had abused his sick leave.[12]

## GUIDELINES

Management will not want to police every sick-leave claim for possible misrepresentation. The company policy should provide standards as to what is abuse. In disciplining employees for abuse or misrepresentation of sick-leave claims, management should consider these factors:

- The nature of the employee's illness and any medical opinions regarding permitted activities.
- The nature of the employee's activities while on sick leave.
- The degree of similarities or differences between the demands of the employee's regular job and the questionable activities performed while on sick leave.

## ENDNOTES

1. Alaska Airlines, 53 LA 860 (Gilden, 1969).
2. Farmland Foods, Inc., 67 LA 607, 608 (Hutcheson, 1976).
3. Lilly Indus. Coatings, Inc., 68 LA 1061 (Leahy, 1977).
4. Western Rubber Co., 83 LA 170 (Cohen, 1984) and cases cited therein.
5. Northrop World Aircraft Servs., 75 LA 1059 (Mewhinney, 1980).
6. Emery Indus., Inc., 72 LA 956 (Ipavec, 1979).
7. United States Steel Corp., 26 LA 712 (Garrett, 1956).
8. National Cash Register Co., 51 LA 1165 (Teple, 1968); *see also* Standard Brands, Inc., 52 LA 918 (Trotta, 1969).
9. Bethlehem Steel Corp., 75 LA 1201 (Sharnoff, 1980).
10. Northrop Worldwide Aircraft Servs., note 5 above.
11. General Tel. Co., 74 LA 1052 (Laybourne, 1980).
12. Safeway Stores, Inc., FMCS Case No. 84K/26868 (Richman, 1985) (unreported).

# 15
# Discipline for Chronic Illness

Dealing with employees who are absent due to chronic illness or injury probably is the most difficult attendance issue for management. On the one hand, it seems inappropriate to discharge employees for absences beyond their control. Yet, on the other hand, it seems unfair to require an employer and other employees to shoulder the burdens created by an employee who is unable to fulfill the responsibilities of full-time, regular employment. In addition, the nebulous area between genuine chronic illness and malingering continues to be a thorny problem for both management and arbitrators.

An important distinction should be made at the outset between two types of chronic illness cases involving excessive job absences and their differing justifications for discharge.

In the first situation, the absence is recognized as resulting from chronic illness or injury, and the question is whether discharge is justified under the particular circumstances. The basic issue here, as in discharge-for-misconduct cases, is whether there is "just cause" for discharge given the facts of the case, including the underlying reasons for the absences, mitigating circumstances, prospects for improvement, and so on.

In the other situation, the absences are viewed as excessive regardless of the underlying reason, and the issue is whether management may impose discharge under a no-fault absenteeism program without regard to the reasons for the absences or extenuating circumstances. As we shall see in Chapter 19, the focus here is on overall policy and not on the facts of a particular case.

This chapter will deal only with the first situation, "just cause" for discharge, and will discuss only those cases in which absences are recognized as resulting from illness or injury. In cases where the employee fails to give valid reasons for the absences or engages in malingering or abuse of sick leave, the issue is wrongdoing and the usual discipline-for-misconduct rules discussed in Chapters 13 and 14 apply.

## "JUST CAUSE" FOR DISCIPLINE: THRESHOLD QUESTIONS

The first question to consider is whether management should even have the right to discharge an employee who is absent because of illness or, stated another way, whether a bona fide illness is always a legitimate excuse for absence. A related question is whether management may act against an employee for using sick leave authorized under the union contract or company policy.

### Minority View

Discharge is not warranted for excessive absenteeism due to illness, according to a minority view. While recognizing that an employee cannot expect to be carried along indefinitely for extended absences that are within the employee's control, the minority view argues that when the employee is incapacitated by injury or illness, a leave of absence rather than discharge serves the interests of both the employer and the employee.

As Arbitrators Howard Block and Richard Mittenthal noted in a paper presented at the 1984 National Academy of Arbitrators meeting,[1] arbitrators who take this position usually rely on contract provisions or company policies that grant sick leave or protect employees' seniority rights during disability. They also noted that a forceful argument supports the proposition that these clauses represent the agreed-upon method of handling disabled employees. Consequently, the parties could hardly have contemplated discharge for the very same disabilities. "Behind all this," Block and Mittenthal observed, "lies the equitable notion that an employee who is truly disabled and who has not through carelessness brought about his own disability is simply a victim of forces beyond his control."[2]

## Majority View

The majority view, however, is that discharge may be justified for chronic, excessive absenteeism even when due to illness. Those who adopt this position focus on the adverse impact of the absences on the employer's business.

This view holds that termination of the chronically ill and chronically absent employee is not discipline for misconduct but rather an act of self-defense by the employer that is necessary for the efficient and profitable operation of the business. No matter how good the excuse for the absence, one arbitrator observed, management is entitled to insist upon certain minimal standards of attendance. Merely because an employee's absences are due to illnesses does not mean he cannot be guilty of excessive absenteeism.[3]

While acknowledging that absences due to illness normally fall outside the scope of discharge/discipline policies, majority view proponents say that at some point discharge becomes the only appropriate recourse.

---

## NONDISCIPLINARY DISCHARGE

In some of these cases, discipline for offenses against the company is distinguished from nondisciplinary discharge. An example of a nondisciplinary discharge, one arbitrator said, would be the termination of a man who had lost both arms and no longer could work. This right of nondisciplinary discharges would permit firing an employee who is absent so often as to be of little worth to the company, the arbitrator said. Whether such absences were excused or not makes little difference, since termination is not based on misconduct, but on inability to perform the job in a satisfactory manner.[4]

An employer should not have to retain employees whose persistently poor health holds no foreseeable hope for improvement, Arbitrator James Duff observed. "The inability of employees to satisfy their end of the fundamental work-for-wages bargain in essence releases the employer from any obligation it might otherwise have to retain them," he said. "Such employees may ultimately be terminated if they amass an unreasonable number of total absences, but they may not be disciplined."[5]

## MAJOR ISSUES

The majority view does not support discipline in every case of excessive absenteeism due to illness or injury. Unlike the no-fault approach, the particular circumstances of each case are still evaluated. Three major, but often overlapping, questions occur in these cases:

- When does the absenteeism become so excessive or disruptive as to warrant discipline?

- What is the nature of the underlying illness and its prognosis?

- Is discharge or other discipline reasonable under all of the circumstances of the particular case?

## EXCESSIVE ABSENCES

Employees and their advocates usually argue that if an employee has not exceeded the sick leave available under the company policy or union contract, discipline for excessive absenteeism is not warranted. Employers, on the other hand, argue that even absences excused under a sick-leave policy may become so disruptive as to justify discipline.

One arbitrator, after an extensive review of other arbitration awards, found support for these propositions:

- Sick leave is not an earned right in the same sense as vacation benefits and therefore, by the nature of its use, sick leave may be excessive, although not used up or exceeded in any one period.

- An employer, within reasonable limits, may judge an employee's use of sick leave by its impact on business operations even though the sick leave taken has not reached the maximum available in any given period and is excused.[6]

If the amount of sick leave available under the employer's sick-leave policy is not determinative, then what considerations should be used in deciding when an employee's use of sick leave has become excessive? Two of the most commonly used yardsticks are statistical comparisons with the other employees' absenteeism and the extent of disruption to the employer's operation.

## Statistical Comparison

The most meaningful comparison of an employee's absentee rate is with that of other employees in the same department or facility. Other comparisons may not be appropriate. For example, an assembly-line worker in an inner-city plant should not be judged by the absence rate of white-collar workers in a suburban high-tech park. Thus, arbitrators have upheld these discharges for absenteeism:

- The employee's absence record for two and one-half years was from five to seven times the plant average.[7]

- The employee's absence rate for an extended period of time was 16.6 percent compared with the plant average absence rate of 2 percent.[8]

- The employee had 20 unexcused absences during a 12-month period and an absenteeism rate well above the plantwide average during the prior two years.[9]

## Disruption of Business

In upholding the discharge of an employee whose absenteeism disrupted the employer's operation, one arbitrator commented: "One may certainly argue that the Company has a duty to other employees to maintain their schedules on a regular basis and to terminate employees who interfere or prevent the Company from fulfilling its duty to those employees."[10]

Discharges based on disruption to business have been upheld

in the following situations: (1) a large number of absences over a two-year period made it difficult to operate a refinery safely and efficiently,[11] (2) the employee worked in a continuous-operations department, which required the employer to pay overtime and rearrange other employees' schedules when the employee was absent,[12] and (3) the employee held a critical and important job.[13]

## SPORADIC VS. LONG-TERM ILLNESS

Before discharging or disciplining an employee for excessive absenteeism, management should attempt to determine the underlying cause of the absences. Two employees may have identical records of lost time but, depending upon the reasons for the absences, only one may merit discharge.

A discharge for excessive absenteeism is relatively easy to justify when the employee has had frequently recurring brief illnesses over an extended period of time and showed symptoms of psychosomatic origin or chronic bad health. On the other hand, termination of an employee with several genuine illnesses, each lasting a long time, may be more difficult to justify. For example:

Employee A has missed 25 days of work during the past two years with virtually all of the absences occurring one day at a time and for varying reasons. Most of the absences fell either on a Monday or a Friday and were without prior notice.

Employee B has the same record of 25 days of absence during the past two years. But his absenteeism consisted entirely of one five-week absence due to a heart attack from which he is now fully recovered.

Clearly a much stronger case can be made for discharging Employee A than Employee B. The chronic AWOL like Employee A requires management to juggle work schedules on short notice and disrupts efficient operations. Employee A is a major headache because the absences cannot be anticipated or planned for.

In contrast, an absence caused by serious illness or injury, such as with Employee B, is far less disruptive. It does not cause unexpected intermittent vacancies and last-minute work force adjustments. This type of absence usually is exempt from discharge or discipline provided the employee is likely to recover and resume regular attendance in the near future. Such an absence makes the company no worse off than would a maternity leave or an extended leave of absence for reasons other than illness.

Arbitrators generally recognize this distinction and hold that management's right to discharge for excessive absence due to illness pertains more to frequently recurring short-term illnesses showing symptoms of psychosomatic origin or of chronic bad health, rather than to several long-term illnesses that undoubtedly are genuine.[14]

---

## OTHER JUST-CAUSE ISSUES

In deciding whether just cause exists for discharging a chronically ill employee, management should consider two issues: (1) Was the individual's absence record "excessive"? and (2) What was the nature of the illnesses or injuries that caused the absences?

But a number of other questions may be raised. Arbitrator Sylvester Garrett pointed out that the presence or absence of just cause can be determined only after all relevant factors in a case have been weighed carefully. Pertinent factors, Garrett said, include the length of the employee's service, the type of job involved, the origin and nature of the claimed illness or illnesses, the types and frequency of all of the employee's absences, the nature of the diagnosis, the medical history and prognosis, the type of medical documentation, the possible availability of other suitable jobs or a disability pension, the employee's personal characteristics and overall record, the presence or absence of supervisory bias, and the treatment of similarly situated employees.[15]

In cases of discipline for excessive illness-related absence, arbitrators tend to impose more stringent just-cause standards on management. Unlike most unacceptable behavior for which discipline is administered, these absences may have occurred through no fault of the worker.[16] Some of the major issues that are examined in deciding whether just cause existed for discharge are described below.

### Progressive Discipline

Before upholding a discharge, arbitrators usually require that the employee receive progressive discipline and a clear warning that discharge will result if attendance fails to improve.[17]

This generally accepted requirement of progressive discipline demonstrates the confusion about handling chronically ill employees. Presumably, if the employee has bona fide illnesses or injuries, warnings and suspensions will not cure the underlying physical disabilities. Yet employers, unions, and arbitrators seem to accept the applicability of the progressive discipline principle in these cases. This suggests that all the concerned parties suspect that at least some of the illness-caused absenteeism may be controllable and could be reduced by the employee's efforts.

## Need for Clear Warning

If management has winked at violations of attendance rules or has failed to carry out prior threats of discharge, arbitrators frequently hold that drastic penalties are not in order until the employee has been put on notice that the past laxness must come to an end. One arbitrator ordered the reinstatement of an employee discharged for excessive absenteeism when the employer's "lax enforcement of its policy concerning excessive absenteeism" had led the worker to conclude that the employer did not view the absences as an employment-threatening violation of rules.[18]

But past leniency toward an employee's absenteeism does not preclude a subsequent crackdown as long as the employee has adequate warning of this more stringent attitude. To rule otherwise would not be a happy state of affairs from the standpoint of other employees, one arbitrator noted.[19]

An oral warning, by itself, usually will not suffice to drive home the fact that the employee is risking discharge. A verbal warning is a rather mild penalty, usually assessed for minor rules violations, one arbitrator observed. Something of a more drastic nature, such as a written reprimand or a disciplinary layoff, should have been imposed before discharge.[20]

## Investigation and Counseling

Management will have a stronger defense for the discharge of a chronically absent employee if it first has attempted to counsel the employee, determine the underlying cause of the problem, and provide rehabilitation assistance. Such efforts will be expected particularly in cases of long-service workers.[21]

"If the Company insists on asserting its right to manage the working force, as it has the right to do," Arbitrator Harry Seligson commented, "it must also assume the responsibility—as part of this management function—to find out the causes behind employee deviations from rules before it imposes punitive discipline. This is not to suggest that the Company has an obligation to run a psychiatric clinic. Each case will suggest the nature of the investigation necessary."[22]

## Prospects for Improvement

An important just-cause consideration is whether the employee's absence record is likely to improve. A related question is whether the employee has displayed a sense of responsibility regarding this obligation to improve attendance.

In a case where an employee had been absent about one-third of the two years before his dismissal, the arbitrator noted that the worker often had not sought a physician's treatment and when he did, he frequently failed to follow the prescribed regimen. Since the employer had made reasonable efforts to encourage the employee to take care of his health and the employee had made little attempt to improve, the arbitrator concluded that the employer had not acted arbitrarily or capriciously in dismissing the worker.[23]

Another arbitrator, in a case where an employee was discharged only after he had disregarded warnings and reverted to his pattern of frequent absences, observed that "it does not seem unreasonable to expect one in Grievant's position to come forward with evidence that will show that he is taking steps to eliminate the cause or causes of his frequent absences."[24] On the other hand, when an employee with a history of chronic absenteeism alters the cause of the absences or otherwise makes a bona fide and successful effort to overcome the problem, a properly certified illness may be accepted as an excuse for sick leave.[25]

## Other Considerations

Long service with the company, particularly if it includes an unblemished record apart from the absenteeism, is a factor in the employee's favor. On the other hand, a poor work record displaying other disciplinary infractions will buttress the case for discharge.[26]

Evidence of discrimination or disparate treatment, such as

proof that employees with similar absentee records were treated less severely, may be held to preclude discharge.[27]

## MENTAL ILLNESS

One estimate is that emotional problems account for 20 to 30 percent of employee absenteeism. In recent years, discipline increasingly has been viewed as an inappropriate means of compelling the mentally ill employee to adhere to attendance and other production standards. One study of reported decisions found that arbitrators impose a stiff evidentiary burden and uphold discharge "only when a mental disability exposes the employee or others to serious risks of injury or harm, or alternatively, prevents the employee from performing his duties."[28]

If an employee's poor attendance resulted from mental illness, an arbitrator may direct reinstatement, but without back pay, if evidence shows that the employee has subsequently undergone successful treatment and has become employable. Some reinstatements may be conditioned on continued treatment or satisfactory completion of a trial period.[29]

As in cases involving alcoholism,[30] the typical approach of arbitrators to cases of mentally ill employees who have been terminated for excessive absenteeism is to give them one last chance to prove their ability to meet normal attendance standards. Most arbitrators also require, however, that the employees seek or have obtained professional help for their psychological problems and present medical certification that they are able to return to work.[31]

Application of the just-cause test in cases of absenteeism presents some special problems when mental illness is alleged to be the underlying cause. Erratic attendance often suggests the possibility of deeper problems than mere irresponsibility.

Habitual absenteeism often involves a psychosis, one arbitrator noted, and the only solution lies in the realm of psychotherapy. Nevertheless, an employer cannot be required to put up with chronic erratic attendance if no remedy is in view. The arbitrator in this case held the discharge justified, but gave the worker one final chance to keep his job if he got a clean bill of health from a licensed psychiatrist.[32]

While an employee's precarious mental health may be a "mitigating circumstance," it does not completely absolve the employee's responsibility for job-related behavior, another arbitrator noted. Simply receiving psychiatric care did not insulate the employee from discipline, the arbitrator said.[33]

If there are conflicting medical opinions about the chance of a mentally ill employee recovering sufficiently to return to gainful employment, arbitrators generally resolve the question in favor of the employee.[34]

# GUIDELINES

Before terminating a chronically ill employee, management should consider these issues:

- The impact of the employee's absences on safety, efficiency, and/or profit.

- The pattern of absences—one long illness vs. several short-term absences.

- The nature of the illness and the likelihood the employee will return to regular employment in the near future.

- The possibility of redesigning the employee's current job or transferring the employee to another job so as to accommodate handicaps.

- The efforts by management to correct the problem through progressive discipline, including a clear warning that continued excessive absenteeism could result in discharge, and through counseling.

- The attendance records of other workers in comparable posts.

- The employee's length of service, compliance with notice requirements, overall work record and attitude, and response to management's efforts to correct the attendance problem.

## ENDNOTES

1. H. Block and R. Mittenthal, "Arbitration and the Absent Employee," in *Arbitration 1984*, Proceedings of the Thirty-Seventh Annual Meeting, Na-

tional Academy of Arbitrators, ed. W. Gershenfeld (Washington, D.C.: BNA Books, 1985): 77.
2. Ibid., 91.
3. R.C. Mahon, XII Steel Arbitration Reports, Pike & Fisher, Inc., 1819 (Mittenthal) quoted in Block & Mittenthal, note 1 above, at 91.
4. Courtaulds North Am., Inc., 44 LA 733 (McCoy, 1965).
5. J.C. Duff, "The Quantitative Monitoring of Absenteeism: Do 'No-Fault' and Just Cause Standards Conflict?," 40 *Arbitration Journal* No. 1 (March 1985): 62.
6. Husky Oil Co., 65 LA 47 (Richardson, 1975).
7. Anaconda Aluminum Co., 48 LA 182 (Luckerath, 1966).
8. Phillips Petroleum Co., 48 LA 402 (Jenkins, 1967).
9. Anaconda Aluminum Co., 55 LA 1164 (Volz, 1970).
10. National-Standard Co., 79 LA 837, 839 (Ferguson, 1982).
11. Avco Corp., 64 LA 672 (Marcus, 1980).
12. Phillips Petroleum Co., note 8 above.
13. McLean Trucking Co., 36 LA 1307 (Volz, 1961).
14. Husky Oil Co., note 6 above; Courtaulds North Am., Inc., note 4 above.
15. United States Postal Serv., 73 LA 1174, 1181 (Garrett, 1979).
16. Oblebay Norton Co., 82 LA 652 (Duda, 1984).
17. Stokely Van Camp, Inc., 81 LA 677 (Schaffer, 1983); Menasha Corp., 71 LA 653 (Roumell, 1978).
18. New Castle State Hosp., 77 LA 585 (Deitsch, 1981).
19. The Bureau of National Affairs, Inc., *Bulletin to Management* (December 26, 1957): 3.
20. The Bureau of National Affairs, Inc., *Bulletin to Management* (July 18, 1957): 3.
21. *Compare* Union Camp Corp., 80 LA 156 (Coxe, 1982) *with* Butler Mfg. Co., 70 LA 426 (Welch, 1978).
22. American Smelting & Refining Co., 31 LA 351, 354 (Seligson, 1958).
23. Gehl Co., 70 LA 630 (Seidman, 1978).
24. National Standard Co., note 10 above, at 840.
25. Stokely Van Camp, Inc., note 17 above.
26. Union Oil Co. of Cal., 77 LA 428 (Winton, 1981).
27. National Standard Co., note 10 above; Gartland-Haswell Foundry Co., 45 LA 108 (Altrock, 1965); Worthington Corp., 47 LA 1170 (Livengood, 1966).
28. B. Wokinson & D. Barton, "Arbitration and the Rights of Mentally Handicapped Workers," *Monthly Labor Review* (April 1980): 41.
29. M. Greenbaum, "The 'Disciplinatrator,' the 'Arbichiatrist,' and the 'Social Psychotrator'," *The Arbitration Journal* (December 1982): 59.
30. *See* Chapter 16.
31. D. Cramer, "Arbitration and Mental Illness," *The Arbitration Journal* (September 1980): 20–21.
32. Allied Maintenance Co., 46 LA 1014 (Sembower, 1966); *see also* Babcock & Wilcox Co., 72 LA 1073 (Mullin, 1979).
33. Clevepak Corp., 73 LA 641 (Archer, 1979); *see also* Plastomer Corp., 81 LA 700 (Roumell, 1983) and cases cited therein.
34. City of Hartford, 69 LA 303 (Mallon, 1977).

# 16

# Discipline for Alcoholism and Drug Abuse

This chapter will focus on the use of traditional disciplinary procedures in dealing with attendance problems that may result from alcoholism and drug addiction. Nondisciplinary approaches to the attendance problems of substance abusers are discussed in Chapter 11; the possible legal constraints under federal and state laws protecting handicapped employees are reviewed in Chapter 4.

## DEALING WITH ALCOHOLISM

Perhaps the most succinct description of the employer's role in disciplining the alcoholic employee is found in *Alcoholics Anonymous*, the "bible" of members of Alcoholics Anonymous. In a chapter, "To Employers," this book advises:

> It boils right down to this: No man should be fired just because he is alcoholic. If he wants to stop, he should be afforded a real chance. If he cannot or does not want to stop, he should be discharged. The exceptions are few.

> We think this method of approach will accomplish several things. It will permit the rehabilitation of good men. At the same time you will feel no reluctance to rid yourself of those who cannot or will not stop. [1]

## APPROACH OF ARBITRATORS TO ALCOHOLISM

An extensive review of the approach arbitrators take to this issue is provided in a book by Tia Schneider Denenberg and R.V. Denenberg. They find an emerging consensus among arbitrators,

194

advocates, and treatment specialists that an alcoholic employee should not be exempted from the normal progression of corrective discipline. The employee should be held accountable for his or her conduct, but also should be given opportunities to recover.

Given objective grounds for imposing discipline, such as heavy absenteeism, a finding of just cause depends, the Denenbergs suggest, on such factors as how obvious the alcoholism was to the employer, how much assistance was offered to the employee, and how well the employee utilized the offers of assistance.[2]

From extensive review of arbitration awards, the Denenbergs draw these conclusions on the proper use of discharge and discipline for the alcoholic employee:

- An alcoholic employee is ultimately dischargeable for misconduct or poor performance, including excessive absenteeism.

- Reinstatement, unaccompanied by constructive measures to deal with the underlying alcoholism, is not realistic. Without a recovery plan, a second chance tends merely to delay the employee's inevitable termination, and it may cause harm by enabling self-destructive drinking to continue.

- The challenge is to devise second-chance reinstatements with conditions that facilitate corrective action without being unduly onerous.

- Ideally, discharge should occur only after an effort to deal with the underlying problem through an employee assistance program or other counseling has failed.

- If an employee's alcoholism is recognized only at the time of the discharge or later, the termination might be stayed if the employee agrees to make an intensive attempt at recovery, such as entering a residential treatment facility covered by the health benefit plan.[3]

On the basis of their review of several hundred arbitration awards involving drug and alcohol abuse by employees, the Denenbergs have identified three general schools of thought:

*The "progressive discipline" school.* In this category, arbitrators base their decisions on whether progressive discipline took place, regardless of the possible implications of the underlying cause. In some instances, the parties may even fail to mention the employee's alcoholism as a factor in a discharge. This approach leaves the arbitrator grappling with symptoms without getting to the cause of the misconduct.

*The "therapeutic" school.* Arbitrators in this group look for proof that the employee's problems are due to the "sickness" of alcoholism, and recommend treatment as a remedy. The problem with this approach, the Denenbergs caution, is that arbitrators "can't really say who will benefit from treatment or whether treatment is a success—even treatment professionals have trouble with these questions."[4] This can bring arbitrators outside the realm of their competence and have them substituting the prescription pad for the award sheet.

*The "middle ground" school.* This group seeks a compromise between the other two. The employee is held broadly accountable but is given one last chance to overcome a treatable case of substance abuse. The problem with this approach is that mixing treatment and punishment often resembles "trying to mix oil and water."[5]

## REHABILITATION EFFORTS

The importance attached to management's responsibility to make rehabilitation efforts is underscored by the following case:

An employee compiled an extremely poor absence and tardiness record. Although management issued a series of warnings and suspensions in an effort to correct her attendance problem, the employee continued to miss work for a variety of alleged reasons, including illness, auto troubles, and "personal" problems. When the absenteeism continued for several months after a "final" warning, management discharged her.

Two months after discharge, the employee informed management that she was an alcoholic and asked to be reinstated to her job and allowed to participate in an employer-sponsored alcoholism rehabilitation program. She claimed that she had recognized her drinking problem only after being fired and that management had neglected to tell her about the availability of the rehabilitation program.

The arbitrator ordered the discharge reduced to an eight-month suspension but conditioned the worker's reinstatement on successful completion of a 28-day alcohol rehabilitation program.

Perhaps because the employee did not project the typical

"profile" of an alcoholic and consistently denied any substance abuse, the arbitrator observed, management felt no further need to investigate the cause of the attendance problem. Conceding that the employer was not required to be psychic, the arbitrator concluded nevertheless that when an employee's attendance problems are linked to alcoholism or drug abuse, the employee is "entitled to a reasonable opportunity" to "deal forthrightly and constructively" with the addiction before dismissal.[6]

## EMPLOYEE RESPONSIBILITY

Although the employer has some responsibility to offer rehabilitation, the employee has an obligation to make a good-faith effort to resolve his or her problem. Take this case for example:

An employee periodically appeared at work physically unable to perform his duties because of the effects of alcohol abuse. He also was habitually absent on Fridays and abused his sick leave.

The employee received progressive discipline for his misconduct, including written reprimands and two suspensions. On several occasions, his supervisor referred him to the employee assistance program, but he refused to participate. While on probation for his poor job record, he rejected a recommendation that he enter a hospital's alcoholism treatment program. Subsequently, he was fired for continuing to arrive at work incapacitated from alcohol and for misusing sick leave.

An arbitrator upheld the discharge. Management should treat workers with substance-abuse problems as "salvageable" employees who are "suffering from a disease" and should support their efforts to overcome their problems, the arbitrator said. But, he added that the employee has an obligation to take specific action to resolve the alcohol or drug problem. This employee failed to demonstrate that commitment to his own treatment, the arbitrator concluded.[7]

Another arbitrator emphasized that while alcoholism is an illness, it is an illness that only the patient can "cure."[8] (Treatment professionals would argue that there is a continuing process of recovery, not a cure, for substance abuse.)

## DRUG ADDICTION

While alcoholism increasingly is recognized as a treatable ill-ness, employers and arbitrators still have difficulty accepting the idea of rehabilitating the drug-dependent employee. There are several reasons for this.

Drinking alcoholic beverages is both legal and an openly ac-cepted part of social life for most people. Drug use, on the other hand, is often illegal and is stigmatized, at least by the older rule-setters in the workplace.

The drug abuser today often is viewed the way alcoholics were a few decades ago—as weak-willed individuals who choose self-indulgence over their responsibilities to family, job, and society. Unlike past and present attitudes toward alcoholics, the public also tends to regard drug addicts as criminals.

But a study of drug abuse commissioned by the Ford Foun-dation concluded that the common distinction between alcoholism and drug abuse is not pharmacological but social—that alcohol is known and accepted in the culture. "It is entirely possible that alcohol is inherently more dangerous than most of the other drugs," the study noted.[9]

Employers also should keep in mind that the most abused drugs in the workplace are not the illegal ones—marijuana, heroin, cocaine—but those prescribed by physicians—tranquilizers, bar-biturates, amphetamines—or those bought over the counter, such as sleeping pills.

Concentrating on the issue of job attendance avoids the ques-tions of drug use on the premises or the possession or sale of drugs, issues that are complicated by the taint of criminality. When the focus is solely on absenteeism, it makes little difference whether the attendance problems are caused by abuse of alcohol or other drugs.

## GUIDELINES

In considering discipline of alcohol or drug abusers, these factors should be considered:

- The employee's performance and employment record. In cases where a competent long-time employee begins to miss work because of substance-abuse problems, discharge should be a last resort after progressive discipline, counseling, and the offer of treatment.

- The employee's commitment to and participation in treatment programs. When employees recognize their problems and take specific action to resolve them, such as enrolling in an appropriate treatment program, management is in a better position to condition employment on continuing self-help efforts. On the other hand, suspending normal disciplinary rules for an alcohol or drug abuser who shows no signs of recognizing or dealing with the problem usually only postpones the inevitable and may actually harm the employee by enabling the self-destructive behavior to continue.

- Distinction between pretreatment and post-treatment absences. If an employee with a past record of absenteeism attributable to substance abuse treatment undergoes successful rehabilitation, consideration should be given to forgiving part or all of the pretreatment absences. Post-treatment disciplinary action based on the employee's total absenteeism record—before and after treatment—may constitute a failure to accord "reasonable accommodation" to the needs of a "handicapped" employee.

---

## ENDNOTES

1. AA World Services, Inc., *Alcoholics Anonymous* (New York, N.Y.: AA World Services, Inc., 1976): 148.
2. T.S. Denenberg and R.V. Denenberg, *Alcohol and Drugs: Issues in the Workplace* (Washington, D.C.: BNA Books, 1983): 143.
3. Ibid., 144.
4. Ibid.
5. The Bureau of National Affairs, Inc., 1985 *Daily Labor Report* 235:A-3, December 6, 1985 (Washington, D.C.: BNA, 1985).
6. Allegheny Ludlum Steel Corp., 84 LA 476 (Alexander, 1985).
7. Michigan Dep't of Social Servs., 84 LA 1030 (Borland, 1985).
8. Caterpillar Tractor Co., 44 LA 87 (Larkin, 1964).
9. J. DeLong, "Drugs and Their Effects," *Dealing with Drug Abuse: A Report to the Ford Foundation* (New York, N.Y.: Praeger, 1972): 116.

# 17

# Discipline for Imprisonment

When management is contemplating disciplining an employee for an absence caused by confinement in jail or a mental institution, it should first clarify its reason for the discipline. It should answer the following questions:

- Is the problem due to the underlying criminal offense or mental illness?

- Or is the problem instead the mere fact of the absence or failure to report?

## NATURE OF OFFENSE

If discipline is to be based on the employee's underlying behavior, management may have a harder time justifying its action. Discipline in these cases is easiest to justify when the conduct that led to the incarceration occurred on the job or on company premises. "There is little doubt among arbitrators," one arbitrator concluded, "that criminal conduct which occurs on the Company premises itself is sufficient to merit discharge."[1]

But when off-the-premises behavior is involved, management should have evidence that the behavior had some direct and negative impact on the organization's reputation or product. Thus, public agencies were upheld for discharging corrections officers who had been arrested for barroom brawling[2] or drunk driving.[3]

But an arbitrator concluded that a conviction for grand theft in no way impaired an employee's ability to perform his job.[4] And the discharge of an off-duty pilot for arrest for assault while under the influence of alcohol and marijuana was overturned when the incident had not resulted in adverse publicity.[5]

The conduct also justifies discharge when it reasonably could cause other employees to refuse to work with the arrested employee or otherwise impair the work relationships. Thus, a discharge was upheld when the employee had been charged with a much-publicized violent crime, and the employer feared that putting the employee back to work might cause altercations with his co-workers and make his supervisors reluctant to provoke him.[6]

Some crimes, by their very nature, may render the perpetrator unfit for continued employment. Thus, one arbitrator observed that most people would agree that an employee's discharge is justified for a felony conviction such as rape, but he also noted that, conversely, most people would argue against discharging an employee for a first offense of speeding. And yet both offenses violate the law.

The difference, as the arbitrator pointed out, lies in the general public's belief that a person who commits rape has personality disorders that make it unlikely he will function properly on the job whatever the job. Consequently, it is argued, a rapist's discharge is justified, even if there is virtually no chance that he will commit rape while on the job.[7]

But another arbitrator declined to uphold the discharge of an employee jailed for nine months on a morals charge since the employee had 37 years of unblemished service with the company.[8] As in most discipline cases, mitigating circumstances, particularly length of service, may lead to differing outcomes for similar behavior.

## MIXED CONSIDERATIONS

Discipline for jail-caused absences sometimes may be based on both the nature of the crime and the fact of absence. This is particularly true if the company's rules or the union contract refers to discipline for absenteeism unless the absence is for a reason "beyond the employee's control" or a "justifiable reason."

When one contract specified that absence from work for three successive workdays "without justifiable reason" is considered a resignation, an employer's rule specifying that any confinement in jail would be viewed as such an absence was held improper. Under common usage, the arbitrator said, "justifiable" means free from blame, and viewed this way, an innocent employee who mistakenly is confined in jail may have a justifiable reason for absence.[9]

Even if not required by company policy or contract language, the nature of the offense may be considered in evaluating the reasonableness of the disciplinary action. For example, when an employee received a two-day jail sentence for the relatively minor offense of driving without a driver's license, an arbitrator ruled that those days of absence could not be held against the employee since the absences were caused by reasons "beyond his control."[10] Another arbitrator concluded that confinement in jail fell within the meaning of contract language excusing absences for a "justifiable reason."[11]

But one arbitrator concluded that a company was not obligated to view an employee's imprisonment as forced upon him for reasons beyond his control. Management, the arbitrator said, "is not required to sit idly by and, in effect, carry an employee who is serving a jail sentence for acts committed against society." Finding that the employer had no contractual obligation to place the worker on annual leave, the arbitrator concluded that the worker's confinement, in light of his prior discipline and significant absenteeism problem, warranted discharge.[12]

If management bases discipline to some extent on the jailing, rather than the mere fact of absence, an important consideration may be whether the jailing was followed by a conviction. As one arbitrator explained, "Until convicted, the presumption of innocence accorded all accused would place his absence in the category of an excused absence until conviction."[13]

When one employee was discharged four months into an eight-month incarceration, an arbitrator held that the employee should have been reinstated upon release. The absence of a conviction led the arbitrator to conclude that the employee's "absence was occasioned by circumstances beyond his control and should be treated as though he had been incapacitated due to a cause such as an extended illness."[14]

## ALCOHOLISM/MENTAL ILLNESS

Special considerations may apply if an employee's incarceration is related to alcoholism or a possible mental illness. Both would suggest that the employee had not been in control of the actions that landed him in jail and consequently, that the employee's absence was not "unjustified" or "unexcused." On the other hand, the company does not necessarily have to take the employee back without some evidence of his rehabilitation.

In one relevant case, an employee with 33 years of service was fired after his second arrest and incarceration on charges of indecent assault on a minor. Citing a hospital report finding that the employee had a personality disorder and recommending psychotherapy, an arbitrator decided that the employee deserved a chance to demonstrate, through competent medical evidence, that he had improved to the point that he was a good employment risk.[15]

But a discharge was upheld when the employer had fired a man who could not get back in time from his vacation because he was serving a sentence for drunken driving. In this case, the contract gave the company authority to discharge for "willful neglect of duty." The arbitrator interpreted this to cover "reckless indifference, as well as an intentional and deliberate purpose to injure, particularly where the public has an interest or a question of safety to persons is involved."[16]

## NOTIFICATION REQUIREMENTS

An employee who is jailed or otherwise incarcerated may fail to meet an employer's requirement that employees provide advance notice of absences. As with other issues of notification, the question may turn on whether the employee made a good-faith effort to comply with the absence notification requirement.

One arbitrator decided that jail or hospital confinement should qualify as recognized exceptions to an employer's requirement that employees call in every absence by 9 a.m.[17] Another arbitrator, on the other hand, held that discharge of employees for failing to give notice of absence was upheld when they had telephone privileges in jail but nevertheless failed to notify their employer.[18]

# MITIGATING CIRCUMSTANCES

Even when the employer has been reasonable and even-handed, discharge may be viewed as too severe if there are mitigating factors. Thus, management should consider such factors as the length of the employee's service, the dependability of the employee, the employee's period of incarceration, the employee's prior disciplinary record, and the relative ease or difficulty of replacing the employee temporarily.

Of the mitigating factors, the length of an employee's service appears to carry the most weight. For example, if an employee is incarcerated for a relatively short period and has 20 or more years of service with a good work record, most arbitrators would conclude that these factors mitigate against an immediate discharge.

# GUIDELINES

In determining whether discharge is appropriate for absence due to confinement in jail or another institution, these are among the considerations:

- The underlying nature of the employee's conviction, and its effect on other employees' attitudes toward the offender and on the company's public image.
- The duration of the absence, and the ease or difficulty of having the employee's work done in his absence.
- The employer's past practice toward absenteeism generally and toward incarceration-caused absences in particular.
- The employee's length of service, dependability, and prior disciplinary and absenteeism record.
- The employee's ability and effort to notify the employer of the absence.

- The employee's degree of responsibility for the underlying conduct that led to the incarceration.

## ENDNOTES

1. McInerney Spring & Wire Co., 72 LA 1262, 1265 (Roumell, 1979).
2. New York State Dep't of Correctional Servs., 69 LA 344 (Kornblum, 1977).
3. Polk County, Iowa, 80 LA 639 (Madden, 1983).
4. Mansfield Tire & Rubber Co., 31 LA 775 (Shaw, 1958).
5. Eastern Air Lines, Inc., 64 LA 828 (Wycoff, 1975).
6. Pearl Brewing Co., 48 LA 379 (Howard, 1967).
7. Eastern Air Lines, Inc., 45 LA 932, 933 (Ables, 1965).
8. United States Steel Corp., 41 LA 568, 571 (Garrett, 1963).
9. Capital Mfg. Co., 48 LA 243 (Klein, 1967).
10. Kansas City Structural Steel Co., 24 LA 251 (Beatty, 1955).
11. Glasgow-Adrian Co., 25 LA 614, 618 (Bowles, 1955).
12. United States Steel Corp., 69 LA 225, 227 (Garrett, 1977).
13. National Carbide Co., 26 LA 176, 179 (Warns, 1955).
14. Owens-Illinois, Inc., 71 LA 1095, 1098 (Foster, 1978).
15. Pittsburgh Steel Co., 37 LA 909 (Joseph, 1961).
16. Minneapolis Brewing Co., 23 LA 418, 422 (Piper, 1954).
17. Cowin & Co., Inc., 81 LA 706 (O'Connell, 1983).
18. Crown Cork & Seal Co., Inc., 72 LA 613 (Daly, 1979).

# 18

# Discipline for Special Types of Absences

This chapter will examine special attendance problems that arise when employees use personal or emergency leave, overstay leaves of absence or vacations, fail to report for weekend work or other special assignments, or engage in wildcat strikes or other concerted activities. The issues in these cases also may involve questions of insubordination.

## PERSONAL LEAVE

Granting short-term paid leave is a widespread personnel practice, particularly for salaried workers. Paid leave, generally from two to five days, may cover specified occurrences, such as jury duty, serious illness or death in the family, short military or National Guard duty, and the like.

In recent years, however, employers increasingly are permitting employees a designated number of days as annual personal leave without any restrictions on its use. Often such personal leave days are in addition to authorized leave for specific purposes such as funerals, jury duty, or military duty.

If personal leave is authorized, management may have difficulty requiring an acceptable reason as a condition for granting leave. For example, when employees previously had to supply reasons for taking personal leave only if two or more workers wanted time off, an arbitrator decided that this past practice barred the employer from suddenly requiring "adequate reasons" before au-

206

thorizing personal leave. The arbitrator added, however, that the employer does have the right to:

- Deny personal leave requests when it has "good and sufficient reason to believe" that an absence should be covered instead by sick leave or vacation.

- Determine whether reasons voluntarily given by workers warrant the use of personal leave.

- Base personal-leave use on departmental needs and on the time reasonably needed by employees to fulfill the purpose of the leave.[1]

In another case, an arbitrator disagreed with an employer's contention that an employee's looking for another job did not qualify as a legitimate "personal reason" for leave.[2] He noted that granting leave of absences for "personal reasons" establishes an extremely broad company policy.

Even when paid personal leave is not allowed, management may be faced with situations in which employees cite "personal business" as an excuse for an unpaid absence. Management generally has discretion to grant or deny requests for such leaves and to require explanations or documentation provided it does not act in an arbitrary or unreasonable manner. See Chapter 3 on verification of absences.

## PERSONAL-LEAVE GUIDELINES

Management needs to decide at the outset whether to grant a specified number of days for personal leave regardless of the reason, or to limit paid leave to specified events, such as family emergencies, weather conditions, transportation problems, and so on. Under the first approach, authorization of personal leave may amount to granting additional vacation leave, since most employees will make use of their personal-leave days. But under the second approach, management should be prepared to spend time and energy resolving disputes over whether the listed reasons apply to actual situations.

Once this basic decision has been made, the formal leave procedure should be spelled out in writing and applied consistently. The policy should cover the following areas:

- Spell out which types of leave require advance approval, from which management authority, and how far in advance employees must make their request.

- Specify whether leave requests and approval can be oral or must be in writing.

- Describe procedures for handling leave extensions, return from leave, and cancellation of leave grants.

- Clarify the leave pay arrangements, such as whether overtime pay or shift differentials are excluded.

- Specify whether employees are required to produce any applicable documents—training orders, jury summons, and so forth—before receiving leave.

## EMERGENCY LEAVE

When paid leave is specifically authorized for "emergency" situations, disputes inevitably will arise over the proper definition of an "emergency." "Within the context of labor arbitration terminology," one arbitrator said, an emergency would be defined as "an unexpected and unforeseen occurrence which leaves no time for deliberation or demands prompt attention."[3]

Here are some examples of attempts to apply emergency-leave policies to specific cases:

One arbitrator, while sympathetic with an employee's desire to attend a parent orientation program at her son's college, said he could not "find any rational way of equating" the trip with "what is commonly and logically considered to be 'an emergency'."[4]

In another case, the three-year-old son of a two-career couple came down with a common childhood illness, and the mother stayed home with him for the first three days of the week. The father decided to spell her for the next two days and claimed that his absence should be covered by the employer's policy of paid leave for "serious distress" family situations. The arbitrator held that the employee's decision to provide personal care for his ill son, rather than obtain the services of a babysitter or nurse, was a "personal choice." But since the illness was "of a routine nature" and created "no cause for undue alarm," management "could rationally say" that the parents had adequate time to arrange for their son's care. Consequently, the situation was not an emergency entitling the worker to serious distress pay.[5]

But another arbitrator held that an employee should have been paid sick leave for the worktime he missed helping his wife take their daughter to a hospital. In this case, however, the employer's policy allowed sick leave for serious family illness and thus was not restricted to emergencies.[6]

Another employee's request for emergency leave should have been granted, an arbitrator decided, when the employee's roommate had unexpectedly moved out and had tried to steal his stereo, and the employee was afraid the roommate might return to remove more property. But the arbitrator limited the emergency leave to four hours' pay, rather than the eight hours taken by the employee, since this should have been sufficient time to handle the crisis.[7]

How far can management go in attempting to verify the nature of the claimed emergency? One arbitrator said a supervisor seemed to go "beyond the normal call of duty" when an employee had left work because his "live-in friend" was bleeding and needed his help. The supervisor not only called the home of the worker's parents but also demanded the names of the worker's friend and her doctor. The employee's reluctance to disclose his friend's identity, the arbitrator observed, was in line with "an old-fashioned and commendable code—a gentleman does not kiss and tell."[8]

Even if a company's rules or union contract do not specifically authorize emergency leaves, arbitrators may take emergencies into account in determining whether management had just cause for disciplining the absent worker. It is "fundamentally unfair to discharge an employee" for responding to an emergency, one arbitrator commented. "A reasonable distinction can be drawn between employee absences compelled" by emergencies and those caused by circumstances that are not "urgent and overriding," he added.[9]

In this case, the arbitrator set aside the discharge of an employee, despite her record of 28 warnings for absenteeism that had placed her under threat of discharge for additional absences, since the absence that precipitated the discharge occurred when the employee was informed that her four-year-old daughter had been taken to the hospital. In leaving work to go to the hospital, the employee was not "continuing her pattern of regular absenteeism," the arbitrator said, pointing out that she could not have "prevented" or "rescheduled" the accident.

Another arbitrator decided that suspension without pay, rather than discharge, was the proper remedy for an employee with a poor attendance record who had been advised to devote full-time attention to her daughter who had been suspended from school due to threatening and potentially violent behavior. "It is important in cases such as these," an arbitrator said, "that society—and all those affected—recognize the individual problems of an employee."[10]

## EMERGENCY-LEAVE GUIDELINES

In developing a policy to handle emergency absences, employers should keep these pointers in mind:

- Decide whether to grant a specified and limited number of days of paid personal leave for use at the employee's discretion for family emergencies and other personal business. (See earlier discussion of personal leave.)
- Define key terms as clearly as possible, such as who is "family," if policy allows leave for family emergencies.
- Balance management's need to verify the reason for an absence against the employee's interest in privacy in personal matters.
- Recognize that emergencies, by their very nature, cannot be completely codified in advance.

## INCLEMENT WEATHER

Often employers use a "liberal leave" policy when bad weather creates transportation difficulties. Under such policies, employees who are unable to report to work because of inclement weather may be granted annual leave or excused absences without loss of pay, depending upon the circumstances.

These ad hoc determinations often lead to disputes between the individual worker and management. According to one arbitrator, the "basic criterion" that management should follow in deciding if a worker should be charged annual leave in such situations is "whether the employee made a reasonable effort to get to work."[11] He said the factors to be considered include the commuting distance traveled by the worker, the mode of transportation the employee normally uses, and the success of other similarly situated employees in getting to work.

Under this test, the employee has an obligation to show that he or she had made "every reasonable effort" to report to work. Leave properly was denied, the arbitrator held, when the employee simply described the "climatic and geographic conditions without showing that she made any effort to use some other form of transportation."[12]

To avoid possible complaints of discrimination by removing subjectivity from decisions regarding inclement-weather leave, some employers adopt a blanket policy of forgiving all absences on bad-weather days. Usually such policies take effect only when weather conditions cause a substantial proportion of the work force to be absent.

In one such case, an arbitrator held "not unreasonable" a policy under which a weather-related absenteeism rate of 50 percent or more would mean that the absences would not be counted against the employees under the employer's no-fault absenteeism program. But the arbitrator found the policy's application defective because it was adopted unilaterally and without advance notice to the employees.[13]

In another case, the company made an exception to its absenteeism control program for "Acts of God." It refused to apply this exception, however, on the day after a severe snowstorm when 80 percent of the employees were able to report for work. An arbitrator disagreed, holding that the company could have extended the Act-of-God allowance to the other 20 percent without retarding or impairing the overall effectiveness of the absence program.[14]

If a company previously has followed a liberal policy regarding absences during inclement weather, it may have difficulty shifting gears in favor of a more stringent policy. Some advance notice of the change in policy may be required.

Thus, an arbitrator faulted an employer for applying a new policy of requiring employees who could not get to work during a snowstorm to use paid sick leave or go AWOL. The employees could not be penalized, the arbitrator held, for relying upon the past practice of granting leaves in similar situations. Even if the employer had the right of unilaterally changing this policy, the employees could not be expected to follow the new policy unless informed of it.[15]

---

## INCLEMENT-WEATHER GUIDELINES

Many employers, particularly those in the snow belt, adopt general guidelines on operation and attendance during inclement weather. Such policy pronouncements may cover these points:

- How employees can learn if the company will be open.
- Whether and under what circumstances no-shows will be unexcused, granted annual leave, or excused without penalty.
- Whether employees who do report will receive compensatory time off or extra pay.

Note that some employers prefer not to spell out such policies in advance but prefer instead to make ad hoc determinations based on such factors as the proportion of shows to no-shows.

---

## OTHER TRANSPORTATION PROBLEMS

Since most employees commute by car or public transportation, breakdowns in transportation equipment are a frequently cited reason for absences or tardiness. Such excuses generally are accepted, at least when accompanied by objective proof that the trouble actually occurred, that it was unforseeable, and that the employee had no alternative way of getting to work.

An employee improperly was denied emergency leave, an arbitrator held, when his automobile broke down on the way to work, the employee conscientiously tried to get his car repaired as quickly as possible, and no public transportation was available.[16]

But, one arbitrator suggested that if an employee persistently and repeatedly has "car trouble," there comes a point when management justifiably can fault the employee for not doing what is necessary to keep his car properly repaired. However, the arbitrator decided that an employer acted unreasonably in adopting a policy that recognized only one "car trouble" excuse over the three-year life of the union contract.[17]

## OVERSTAYING LEAVES & VACATIONS

Vacations, layoffs, and leaves of absence often give rise to attendance problems when employees report back late. Employers should judge these situations as they would any other attendance problem, but with particular attention to the reason for the absence and the consistency of the company's discipline for leave-stretching. Here are examples of arbitrators' rulings in these cases:

- Discharge of an employee for not returning to work until one week after the end of her scheduled two-week vacation was upheld by an arbitrator. The employee claimed that she could not get transportation back from the distant vacation spot unless she waited for her husband to finish his three-week vacation. In the arbitrator's view, she probably had deliberately chosen not to return to work on time. In any event, she had demonstrated an irresponsible attitude toward her job.[18]

- But in another case where an employee overstayed her vacation by a week, an arbitrator found reason to reduce her discharge to a suspension without pay. Her excuse for the absence was an attempt to save her marriage, which the arbitrator felt outweighed the employer's need for her presence.[19]

- An employee on medical leave who failed to return on the date approved by the company doctor was reinstated by an arbitrator. The employee was able to show that her own doctor had advised further postoperative care that made return to work inadvisable.[20]

The importance of past practice was pointed up in a case where a man who was fired for returning late from leave was reinstated, but without back pay, because past experience had led the employee to believe that his offense would be overlooked.[21]

# ABSENCE WHEN SCHEDULED TO WORK ON REGULAR DAY OFF

When management schedules work on a Saturday, holiday, or other days outside the normal workweek, it usually runs into a higher than normal absenteeism. However, management's right to schedule work is generally recognized, except when this right has been specifically limited by contract. It follows that if management has the right to schedule the work, it has the right to discipline employees who fail to report.

Even when employees have the right to refuse work on a Saturday or holiday, arbitrators usually hold that an employee who has accepted an assignment to work on a normal day off has the usual duty to report.[22]

Similarly, when a company's overtime policy noted that management expected employees to perform a "reasonable" amount of overtime but would consider requests for relief, an arbitrator upheld the discharge of an employee who missed roughly two of every three Saturdays of regularly scheduled overtime. Taken together, the absences added up to just cause for discharge even though family responsibilities may have limited the employee's control over the absences.[23]

But since employees will have to give up a day off, management should look carefully at extenuating circumstances before imposing discipline on no-shows. Such considerations include whether employees had sufficient advance notice of the extra work, the importance of the employee's previous commitments for the normal time off, and the difficulty in changing those plans.

# CONCERTED ACTIVITY

Wildcat strikes are grounds for severe discipline, arbitrators overwhelmingly agree, unless the workers were prevented from reporting to the job through "duress, coercion, intimidation or the like." Declaring that "willing participation in a work stoppage is among the most henious of industrial offenses," one arbitrator stressed that dismissal in such circumstances would not be too severe a penalty.[24]

For practical purposes, however, many employers do not go to the extreme of firing all wildcat strikers. As one arbitrator explained, "A company that is the victim of an illegal strike cannot be expected to 'cut off its nose to spite its face' by firing all participants."[25]

Consequently, most arbitration cases dealing with wildcat strikes involve selective discipline, with the focus on whether management acted in an arbitrary, capricious, or discriminatory manner. Some arbitrators may require clear proof that the disciplined workers either instigated the illegal activity or at least were more active in it than other employees.[26]

Neither contract provisions nor obligation to justice compels a company to discipline every case of employee misconduct, Arbitrator Harry Platt noted. Unequal treatment in disciplinary matters does not amount to discrimination if distinction exists between those disciplined and those not. "It is only where the grounds for distinction are irrational, arbitrary, or whimsical that disciplining of some employees and not others may be looked upon as unjust and discriminatory," Platt said.[27]

Another arbitrator upheld management's application of its absenteeism program to some, but not all, wildcat strikers. He found a "fundamental prerogative of management to select the form and extent of disciplinary action as long as it is not specifically restricted from doing so by the agreement, as long as cause is demonstrated, and as long as equal treatment is accorded."[28]

When more than half of a work group called in sick on the day a black was promoted to foreman, the arbitrator agreed with the company that an unjustified sick-out had taken place and that "the group absence was a form of protest which was impermissible." The arbitrator chided the company, however, for not differentiating between the protesters and the legitimately sick. The arbitrator awarded sick pay to three workers who, he concluded from the testimony, were genuinely sick.[29]

## GUIDELINES

Before disciplining an employee for the various types of absences discussed in this chapter, management should review these factors:

- How much notice did the employee have that the absence could result in discipline, as communicated by policy or past practice?

- Did the incident reflect an irresponsible attitude on the employee's part?

- Would it have been possible for the employee to notify the company of the absence, and, if so, did the employee make a reasonable effort to do so?

- If the incident involved a conflict between the company's needs and the employee's personal needs, was a reasonable balance struck?

---

## ENDNOTES

1. Consolidated Papers, Inc., 79 LA 1209 (Yaffe, 1982).
2. Briggs & Stratton, 64 LA 1155 (Kassoff, 1975).
3. Wadsworth, Ohio, City Bd. of Educ., 68 LA 418, 420 (Siegel, 1977).
4. Ibid.
5. Indiana Bell Tel. Co., 84 LA 255 (Seidman, 1985).
6. Michigan Gas Utils. Co., 73 LA 885 (Coyle, 1979).
7. Mare Island Naval Shipyard, 78 LA 552 (Boynton, 1982).
8. Naval Air Rework Facility, 79 LA 412, 414 (Levitan, 1982).
9. Knauf Fiber Glass, 81 LA 333 (Abrams, 1983).
10. County of Monroe, 72 LA 541, 543 (Markowitz, 1979).
11. United States Army Training Center, 73 LA 1003, 1007 (Flannagan, 1979).
12. Ibid.
13. Marley Cooling Tower Co., 71 LA 306 (Sergent, 1978).
14. Environment Elements Corp., 70 LA 912 (Milentz, 1978).
15. Clinchfield Coal Co., 85 LA 382 (Rybolt, 1985).
16. Gulf Oil Co., 57 LA 1264 (Schedler, 1972).
17. City of Sioux City, 79 LA 433, 436 (Mittelman, 1982).
18. Packaging Corp. of Am., 42 LA 606 (Sherman, 1964); *see also* Noll Mfg. Co., 69 LA 170 (Ward, 1977).
19. Vellumoid Co., 41 LA 1129 (Seitz, 1963).
20. International Harvester Co., 22 LA 138 (Platt, 1954).
21. South Bend Lathe Works, 14 LA 121 (Kelliher, 1950).
22. Lukens Steel Co., 11 LA 947 (D'Andrade, 1950); Cone Finishing Co., 12 LA 770 (Barrett, 1949).
23. The Bureau of National Affairs, Inc., *Bulletin to Management* (January 13, 1958): 3.
24. American Air Filter Co., 47 LA 129, 133 (Hilpert, 1966).
25. Charles Mundt Sons, 46 LA 982, 985 (Malkin, 1966).

26. Homer Laughlin China Co., 67 LA 1250 (Jones, 1977); Bendix Corp., 61 LA 148 (Hunter, 1973).
27. Ford Motor Co., 41 LA 609, 613 (Platt, 1963).
28. Kennecott Copper Corp., 77 LA 505, 516 (Richardson, 1981).
29. East Ohio Gas Co., 62 LA 90, 95 (Edes, 1973).

# 19

# Nontraditional Discipline

Dissatisfaction with the results of applying the traditional discipline-for-misconduct approach to absenteeism has led to growing experimentation with nontraditional discipline. Two major departures—no-fault discipline and positive discipline—are discussed in this chapter.

## NO-FAULT DISCIPLINE

Much as it had done with insurance and divorce controversies, the no-fault approach is winning favor as a means of dealing with job attendance problems.

Under the traditional disciplinary system for unexcused absences, management daily confronts a maddening melange of job attendance issues. No two cases are exactly alike, and no two supervisors handle similar cases in the same way. Valuable time is used by supervisors in attempting to verify the truthfulness of the reasons given for absences, and relationships with subordinates are strained in the process.

Employees, for their part, resent being questioned about the reasons for their absences, and they often are confused by the seemingly inconsistent practices of supervisors in deciding which absences to excuse. In addition, management at times may still find it necessary to terminate a chronically absent employee despite the acceptability of the employee's excuses for the absences.

These difficulties in applying traditional discipline to job attendance problems were summarized by Arbitrators Howard Block and Richard Mittenthal in a paper presented to the 1984 meeting

218

of the National Academy of Arbitrators. They noted that management understandably finds it hard to design and implement an attendance policy that deals effectively with the limitless variety of absentee situations and with the conflicting reactions and perceptions of supervisors and employees.

Supervisors are not lawyers, investigators, or psychologists, Block and Mittenthal noted. Their primary interest is in the quantity and quality of the company's product or service. They are not trained to make sophisticated judgments on job attendance issues.

Employees, for their part, are not likely to favor any attendance control program. What supervisors see as individually tailored responses to absenteeism will be seen by employees as disparate treatment. What management sees as a legitimate crackdown on excessive absenteeism will be seen by employees as an unduly restrictive limitation.[1]

## The No-Fault Approach

Many organizations have begun to bypass these problems by adopting a no-fault approach to employee absenteeism. A no-fault policy focuses on the frequency of the absences, not the validity of the excuses. Each absence carries a predetermined penalty, regardless of the reason, except for a few clearly defined nonchargeable absences.

Under most no-fault programs, absences are defined in terms of "occurrences." An occurrence usually is a single absence regardless of its length. Thus, a one-day absence counts the same as a three-day absence.

The rationale for equating multiple-day and one-day absences is to enable the program to zero in on the most troublesome form of absenteeism—the chronic offender who frequently misses one day. Also it is more likely that the employee who is absent for three or four days at a stretch is genuinely ill.

While any absence of a day or more will count as one occurrence, tardiness usually is assessed as a quarter- or half-occurrence, depending on how late the employee is. Early departures might receive a similar partial penalty.

But a stiffer penalty might be imposed for no-call absences. For example, an absent employee might be charged with a double occurrence for failing to call in by a specified time as required.

Although no-fault programs are designed to treat all absences the same regardless of the reason, most such programs list certain clearly defined absences as nonchargeable. This list typically includes funeral leave, military leave, jury duty, authorized union business, hospital confinement, and work-related injury.

Some no-fault programs also incorporate rewards for good attendance. Thus, an employee might be entitled to have one occurrence erased for each month of perfect attendance. Or an employee with no occurrences might be permitted to bank one or two occurrences for each month of perfect attendance.

## Enforcing No-Fault Programs

Standard progressive discipline is used to enforce no-fault attendance control programs. Absence records are maintained for a 12-month period that begins with the employee's first recorded absence occurrence. A specified number of occurrences is permitted before progressive discipline begins.

The first step in the disciplinary process may involve employee counseling by the supervisor. Additional occurrences within the 12-month period then might trigger an oral warning, written warning, suspension, and, finally, termination.[2] The following company examples describe several different styles of no-fault discipline programs currently in use.

### No-Fault Discipline

**Xerox Corp.** negotiated a stringent no-fault absenteeism program in 1983 with the Amalgamated Clothing and Textile Workers Union, which was greeted with widespread interest. This program called for terminating any employee who was absent on four "occasions" during any consecutive 12-month period.

Effective January 1, 1984, the program covers all Xerox employees in the Rochester, N.Y., area. The program was renegotiated in 1986 to run through March 1989.

An "occasion" of absence is defined as any absence of two or more workhours or of one or more consecutive workdays. Absences on days of scheduled overtime count as occasions of absence.

Nonchargeable absences are: paid holidays; regularly scheduled vacation, including single and half-days; hospitalization, including prescheduled outpatient surgery customarily done on an inpatient basis and postdischarge recovery periods; authorized leaves of absence; jury duty; appearance required by summons; death in immediate family; emergency community service; workers' compensation-related absences; maternity leave; company-declared snow days or inability to report for work due to verifiable closing of snowy roads; tardiness or early leaving for less than two hours; daily overtime; verifiable part-day absences due to emergency; and authorized dismissal for medical reasons.

An employee who has six months of perfect attendance from the last chargeable absence has that occasion purged from the record. Employees with two consecutive calendar years of perfect attendance are exempt from the plan for the next calendar year.

The employee and the union are notified when an employee incurs two occasions of absence within 12 consecutive months. A three-person review committee, consisting of representatives from the union, the company medical department, and operating management or industrial relations, reviews appeals from employees who face termination under the program but who claim they have incurred serious medical problems that require sudden repetitive short-term absences or recurring absences for medical treatment. The committee must agree unanimously that the case has merit in order to save the employee from termination.

A separate Excessive Absenteeism Counseling Program attempts to rehabilitate employees with records of excessive absenteeism, which is defined as an absenteeism rate of 10 percent or more.

Before the no-fault program took effect in 1984, the bargaining unit had annual lost-time rates of 7.0 percent for 1979–1981, 6.5 percent for 1982, and 5.2 percent for 1983. These annual lost-time rates dropped to 2.9 percent for both 1984 and 1985.

Samples of statements and forms used by Xerox in connection with its no-fault program are provided in Appendix B.

**Ford Motor Co.,** in its 1984 contract with the United

Auto Workers, instituted a no-fault progressive discipline program that starts after an employee's fourth absence in any 12-month period.

A unique feature of the Ford plan is a three-tiered disciplinary progression that aims at heading off absenteeism problems among newer, younger workers. Employees with less than five years' service incur more severe penalties than those with five to 10 years, while those with more than 10 years' service are not subject to the plan.

The Ford program took effect January 2, 1985. At that time, records of all prior disciplinary action relating to absenteeism were erased.

Penalties under the plan begin after four occurrences of absenteeism within 12 consecutive months. An occurrence is defined as either a single day or consecutive days of absence, other than for those due to holidays, vacations, personal leave, jury duty, bereavement, military duty, union leave, public office leave, economic layoffs, snow days, strikes, and disciplinary layoffs.

For the least senior workers—those with less than five years' service—the first absence in excess of the first four results in a reprimand and warning. Progressively longer suspensions are applied for each additional absence. After the eighth absence, an employee is reprimanded, warned of impending termination, and suspended for a month. Termination occurs after the ninth absence occurrence.

Workers with five to 10 years of service are afforded one additional step in the progression. Those with more than 10 years' seniority are covered by the pre-existing absenteeism control program.

**E-Systems**, a high-tech electronics manufacturer, implemented a no-fault approach to attendance control in 1985. A year later, the company had reduced absenteeism at its Greenville, Tex., division from 4.7 percent to 1.5 percent annually. In addition, fewer employees have been discharged for absenteeism, the time managers spend on employee discipline has been reduced, and required overtime is significantly less.

Under the new system, employees are rated according to steps that range from step 9, which employees can reach if they report in for 120 consecutive workdays, to step 0, which usually triggers termination. New employees begin at step 5.

For each occurrence of absence, tardiness, or early departure, the level is reduced either a whole or half step. For every 30 consecutive scheduled days worked, the level is increased to the next higher step.

Progressive discipline is used only when an employee has established an unacceptable pattern of attendance. No discipline is imposed until a worker hits step 3; at that point, documented counseling is provided. Step 2 results in a written warning. At step 1, the employee receives a three-month "in place" suspension during which the employee works and is paid but is not credited with time worked for step-increase purposes. Workers who reach step 0 are subject to termination.

Supervisors are held accountable for informing employees about the program, counseling those whose absence records exceed company standards, and positively reinforcing improved attendance through verbal praise or written notice of commendation. Other features that have helped make the program work include:

- An emphasis on attendance-tracking rather than assessment of excused or unexcused absences. Managers are required to establish departmental attendance goals, document absences and verify attendance records, and discuss absences with employees upon their return to work.

- An improved call-in policy. All employees are required to report an absence no later than 30 minutes before the start of a shift, using a specific "attendance control" number assigned by the company.

- Specific definitions and guidelines. The no-fault program defines clearly the types of absences that are chargeable offenses and sets forth the procedures that supervisors must follow before imposing discipline.

## Management's Right to Install

Management's right to install an attendance control program incorporating some no-fault features is generally recognized. "The right to control unnecessary absenteeism is the most basic and essential of management rights," one arbitrator observed. "Certainly an employer can require employees to attend upon their work," he said, since "without this requirement all other management rights would be meaningless."[3]

Another arbitrator, after reviewing reported labor arbitration decisions from 1960 through 1985, said he failed to locate a single decision denying management's inherent right to establish an absentee control policy unilaterally (unless clearly precluded by applicable past practice, specific contractual limitation, or legal restrictions).[4]

At first blush, the no-fault rules may appear arbitrary and unreasonable in their seeming rigidity. But the rebuttal is that these rules actually may eliminate the arbitrary and disparate judgments of individual supervisors.

## Test of Reasonableness

Even if a company has the right to adopt no-fault attendance requirements, the particular policy may be attacked as unreasonable. Some arbitrators, for example, have set aside no-fault plans in the belief that it is unreasonable to penalize an employee who is absent for medical reasons.[5]

Most arbitrators, however, give management reasonable latitude in the design of an attendance control plan. The following views of Arbitrator James Duff have set a frequently cited standard:

> If a plan is fair on its face and its operation in the concrete cases at hand produces just results, and other common tests of reasonableness are satisfied, a plan ought not to be declared invalid based on the mere existence of some remote probability that it could operate perversely in the indefinite future under hypothetical circumstances which have not as yet materialized. Employers should be encouraged to develop policies which can be fairly administered and which provide notice to employees of the standards to which they must adhere. This is true in the area of attendance as well as in other aspects of the employment relationship. Excessive hypertechnicality in reviewing facial challenges to such policies can only serve to discourage policy development.[6]

## Application of Just-Cause Standard

Proponents of management's right to adopt no-fault absence control plans frequently cite Arbitrator Duff's 1977 opinion. Yet in a 1985 article, Duff asserted that these plans in operation often "constitute an abdication of managerial responsibility incompatible with the just cause standard" for discipline. He commented:

> Failure to distinguish between legitimate excuses for absences and reprehensible conduct is repugnant to fundamental notions of fair play whenever it results in employees whose absences are due to valid reasons beyond their control being disciplined in the same manner as deliberate wrongdoers.[7]

Arbitrators Block and Mittenthal in their previously cited paper also noted that no-fault plans, by ignoring whether the employee's absence is misconduct and whether the penalty is reasonable, seem inconsistent with the just cause standard. Thus, they observed, both employers and arbitrators often make exceptions to the automatic operation of the plan when it produces a harsh or arbitrary result. All concerned with no-fault plans "acknowledge that a plan considered reasonable may occasionally produce unreasonable results that should be mitigated."[8]

In the 1985 article, Duff attempted a similar reconciliation between the reasonableness of no-fault plans in theory and the need to apply a just-cause standard to their operations. He commented that "the key may be to devise a hybrid system that measures absenteeism quantitatively, yet does not fail to differentiate between absences involving some culpability and ones that involve no known responsibility on the employee's part."[9]

## NO-FAULT DISCIPLINE GUIDELINES

Here are some questions management might want to ask before installing a no-fault attendance control plan:

- How many absences will trigger discipline, and what numbers should be tied to each step in the progressive discipline schedule?

- Should the slate be wiped clean of prior absence records when a no-fault plan is installed so that an employee is not penalized for prior conduct?

- Should certain absences, such as jury duty, military leave, hospitalization, or job-related injuries, be excused and not counted against the employee?

- Should an employee's record be cleansed periodically by a period of perfect attendance?

## POSITIVE DISCIPLINE

The second major departure from traditional discipline for excessive absences is the relatively new concept of "positive discipline." As noted earlier, traditional or progressive discipline imposes increasingly stiffer penalties for past poor performance. Positive discipline, in contrast, focuses on improving future performance. Its proponents claim it can significantly reduce absenteeism, turnover, and disciplinary problems.

This system replaces the progressive discipline of warnings, suspension, and discharge with these steps:

- Discussions and reminders, first oral and then written, of employee responsibility.

- Agreement by the employee to maintain certain standards of behavior and performance.

- A paid day off.

The paid suspension, known as "decision-making leave," is the linchpin of positive discipline. If initial discussions between the employee and the supervisor fail to close the gap between actual and desired performance, the employee must take a paid, one-day leave and return the next day with a decision either to solve the immediate problem and make a "total performance commitment," or to resign and find more satisfying employment elsewhere.

If the decision is to remain with the company, the employee and the supervisor together set specific goals and prepare an action plan. The supervisor should express confidence that the employee can fulfill the plan's requirements, but caution the worker that failure to meet the organization's performance expectations will lead to termination. A formal memo should document the meeting. The original should be given to the employee and a copy placed in the personnel file.

If the employee fails to live up to the agreement, he or she is terminated. Since the process has been documented, the employee presumably has little legal recourse. (See Exhibit 19.1.)

## Benefits of Positive Discipline

Proponents of positive discipline say that traditional discipline typically ignores the problems of white-collar workers until it is too late and simply punishes blue-collar workers. They also cite the following benefits of positive discipline over the traditional penalty system:

- It demonstrates to the employee the seriousness of the situation, while also affirming the organization's desire to see the worker remain with the company.

- It provides a cooling-off period for reflection by both management and the employee.

- It allows the worker to accept responsibility for current actions and future performance, instead of just "serving time."

- It eliminates the resentment and anger an unpaid suspension or other punitive action typically creates.

- It eliminates the hidden costs—overtime, inefficiency, disruption of others' work, reduced output—normally associated with unpaid suspensions and other punishment.

- It obliges poor performers to make their own career decisions, thereby reducing the number of discipline-related grievances and arbitrations. It eliminates charges of inconsistent discipline and employee attempts to reduce penalties and make other deals.

- It improves the self-confidence and managerial ability of supervisors and heightens morale by redirecting supervisors' attention to the good performance of the great majority of employees.

- Through documentation, it reduces the chances for grievances and arbitration in union-organized shops and wrongful discharge suits in nonunion operations.

## EXHIBIT 19.1

### POSITIVE DISCIPLINE

The positive discipline approach is an effective method for problem solving any type of performance discrepancy. In order for the process to operate at an optimum level, several key factors must be considered and implemented.

1. Employees must be held accountable for their behavior. Employee accountability for adult behavior must clearly be communicated to all persons from the first day of hire. Persons should be measured on their production behavior as well as their contribution toward maintaining a non-disruptive work environment.

2. Supervisors must be measured on production and managerial competencies. Often times we provide supervisors feedback solely around the meeting of production goals. The giving of feedback has to be broadened to include how positively or negatively the supervisor treats and uses his/her subordinates.

3. Develop positive employee relations policies and procedures. Policies and procedures outlining expected employee behavior are geared toward the 95 percent of the work force which regularly behaves in an adult manner. Any policies written in a negative way—for the five percenters—should be revised. Interaction with employees should be conducted in a way that clearly communicates high expectations and the belief that they can and will respond in a positive, adult manner.

4. Promptly solve problems. Begin the problem-solving process immediately after the first occurrence of unacceptable behavior. We cannot afford to be lackadaisical. When unacceptable behavior is allowed to occur several times before counseling, the chances of working a reasonable solution rapidly diminish. Prompt problem solving significantly reduces the chances of the unacceptable behavior recurring.

5. Model. Interactions with peers, subordinates, and superiors should be characterized by supportive, problem-solving adult attitudes and behavior. Lead by example. If we interact in a win-lose, conflict-oriented manner, the credibility of positive discipline is seriously threatened.

---

*Source:* These guidelines are reprinted with permission from "How To Reinforce the Process," a policy manual for supervisors, issued by Sunnen Products Co., St. Louis, Mo., as part of its Discipline Without Punishment program.

## Management's Right to Install

Since the concept is still new and unfamiliar, seeking legal counsel might be advisable before installing the system, particularly in a union-organized unit. Unions often oppose positive discipline, claiming that employees who are unfairly pushed out of the company do not fight back.

In one key case, the National Labor Relations Board ruled that a company's unilateral adoption of a positive discipline system did not violate its bargaining duty under the Taft-Hartley Act since the action was consistent with management rights and past company practices of unilateral changes in the disciplinary system.[10]

Several arbitrators also have ruled that positive discipline does not differ sufficiently from traditional disciplinary systems to violate a contract when adopted unilaterally.

## POSITIVE DISCIPLINE GUIDELINES

To produce good results, positive discipline requires careful implementation as part of a total program for managing human resources. This means management should undertake these steps:

- Review formal policies and informal day-to-day practices to determine whether the positive discipline concept fits the organization's beliefs about the way people should be treated.

- Appoint a team of supervisors and managers from different departments and levels to decide how the program will be administered, whom the program will affect, how various disciplinary problems will be ranked, what authority supervisors will have at each stage of the program, and what training will be required.

- Train and educate supervisors and managers to understand the system, its operation, and goals.

- Communicate the change by holding employee meetings at all levels to review the key elements and operation of the system, the reasons for change, and the philosophy behind the program.

## RESOURCE CENTER

For information on installing a positive discipline system, contact Performance Systems Corporation, 2925 LBJ Freeway, Suite 275, Dallas, Tex. 75234, (214) 243-8863.

For descriptions of the programs implemented by various organizations, see:

1. D. N. Campbell, R.L. Fleming, and R. C. Grote, "Discipline Without Punishment—At Last," *Harvard Business Review* (July–August 1985): 162.

2. A. W. Bryant, "Replacing Punitive Discipline With a Positive Approach," *Personnel Administrator* (February 1984): 79.

### ENDNOTES

1. H. Block and R. Mittenthal, "Arbitration and the Absent Employee," in *Arbitration 1984*, Proceedings of the Thirty-Seventh Annual Meeting, National Academy of Arbitrators, ed. W. Gershenfeld (Washington, D.C.: BNA, 1985):95.
2. For examples of company programs, see D. Olson and R. Bangs, "No-Fault Attendance Control: A Real World Application," *Personnel Administrator* (June 1984):53; F. Kuzmits, "Is Your Organization Ready for No-Fault Absenteeism?," *Personnel Administrator* (December 1984):119.
3. Celanese Corp., 62 LA 1175, 1177 (Altrock, 1973).
4. Simmons, U.S.A., 85 LA 809 (Seidman, 1985).
5. Hoover Ball & Bearing Co., 66 LA 764 (Herman, 1976).
6. Robertshaw Controls Co., 69 LA 77, 79 (Duff, 1977), cited in Coca-Cola Bottling Co., 81 LA 56, 59 (Berger, 1983) and cases cited therein.
7. J.C. Duff, "The Quantitative Monitoring of Absenteeism: Do 'No-Fault' and Just Cause Standards Conflict?," 40 *The Arbitration Journal* No. 1 (March 1985):61–62.
8. Block and Mittenthal, note 1 above, at 102; *see also* cases cited in Mueller Co., 78 LA 673, 680 (Richardson, 1982) and in Amoco Chems. Corp., 79 LA 89, 93 (Byars, 1982).
9. Duff, note 7 above, at 62.
10. Continental Tel. Co. of Cal., 274 NLRB No. 210, 118 LRRM 1598 (1985).

# Appendix A

# Sample Forms to Record Absences and Tardiness

Employee Attendance Record
(Large central bank)

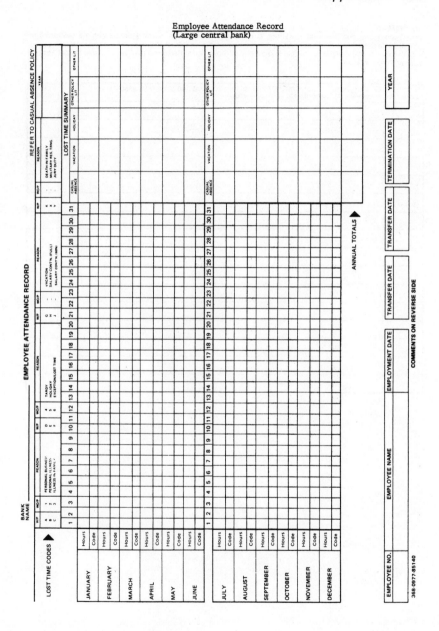

**COUNSELING**

Verbal counseling and first written warning is necessary upon 5 days casual absence within a twelve month period. Verbal **and** final written counseling necessary upon 8 days casual absence within a twelve month period. In both cases, a record of the counseling session is to be forwarded to Personnel Division. (Refer to Casual Absence Control Policy #2401.)

| DATE COUNSEL | DATE COUNSEL   RECORD ALL NOTES REGARDING COUNSELING ON EITHER ABSENTEEISM, PERFORMANCE, APPEARANCE, ATTITUDE, ETC | EMP. INITIALS |
|---|---|---|
| | | |
| | | |
| | | |
| | | |
| | | |
| | | |
| | | |
| | | |
| | | |
| | | |
| | | |
| | | |
| | | |
| | | |
| | | |

Absence & Additional Time Worked Report
(Large western state government)

**ABSENCE AND ADDITIONAL TIME WORKED REPORT**

STD. 634 (8/77)

| | PAY PERIOD | | | TIME BASE | WORK WEEK GROUP |
|---|---|---|---|---|---|

1. MONTH | YEAR | SEMIMONTHLY STATUS ONLY
☐ FIRST HALF  ☐ SECOND HALF

2. NAME (First, Middle, Last)

3. SOCIAL SECURITY NUMBER

4. POSITION NUMBER

**5. ABSENCE WITH PAY**

(s) ☐ SICK LEAVE SELF
(sf) ☐ SICK LEAVE FAMILY ILLNESS
(sd) ☐ SICK LEAVE DEATH IN FAMILY (RELATIONSHIP)
(v) ☐ VACATION

(TO) ☐ USING OVERTIME CREDITS
(TH) ☐ USING HOLIDAY CREDITS
(PH) ☐ TAKING PERSONAL HOLIDAY
(TE) ☐ USING EXCESS HOURS CREDIT
(E) ☐ PAID EDUCATIONAL LEAVE

(M) ☐ SHORT-TERM MILITARY LEAVE (CALENDAR DAYS) (ATTACH MILITARY DUTY ORDERS)
(NDI) ☐ NONINDUSTRIAL INJURY
INDUSTRIAL ILLNESS OR INJURY
(C) ☐ TEMPORARY DISABILITY
(IDL) ☐ REPORT OF INDUSTRIAL INJURY MUST BE SUBMITTED
OTHER____

(J) ☐ JURY DUTY (MAKE COPY FOR ACCOUNTING)
(SW) ☐ SUBPOENAED WITNESS  ☐ PARTY  ☐ EXPERT
COURT ____  CITY ____
☐ NO FEES RECEIVED  ☐ FEES TO BE REMITTED TO STATE
☐ FEES RETAINED
CHARGE ABSENCE TO ☐ VAC  ☐ CTO  ☐ ABSENCE WITHOUT PAY

**6. ABSENCE WITHOUT PAY**

(L) ☐ INFORMAL LEAVE GRANTED (11 WORKING DAYS OR LESS)
(L) ☐ INFORMAL LEAVE GRANTED (15 WORKING DAYS OR LESS)(CSUC)

(A) ☐ ABSENCE WITHOUT LEAVE (5 WORKING DAYS OR LESS)(AWOL)
☐ TEMPORARY LEAVE (30 CALENDAR DAYS OR LESS)

☐ ABSENCE IS WHILE SERVING A PROBATIONARY PERIOD
PAY PERIOD IS ☐ QUALIFYING  ☐ NONQUALIFYING

**7. DATES OF ABSENCES AND EXTRA TIME WORKED**
*(ENTER SYMBOL AND NUMBER OF HOURS IN DATE BLOCKS. SEE REVERSE FOR LEGENDS AND SYMBOLS NOT NOTED ABOVE. IF THE ABSENCE IS FOR A COMPENSABLE INJURY WAITING PERIOD. ADD X TO OTHER SYMBOL.)*

| REPORTING | 1 | 2 | 3 | 4 | 5 | 6 | 7 | 8 | 9 | 10 | 11 | 12 | 13 | 14 | 15 | 16 | 17 | 18 | 19 | 20 | 21 | 22 | 23 | 24 | 25 | 26 | 27 | 28 | 29 | 30 | 31 | TOTAL |
|---|---|---|---|---|---|---|---|---|---|---|---|---|---|---|---|---|---|---|---|---|---|---|---|---|---|---|---|---|---|---|---|---|
| 7A. HRLY INT/PT HRS TO BE PAID | | | | | | | | | | | | | | | | | | | | | | | | | | | | | | | | |
| 7B. SICK | | | | | | | | | | | | | | | | | | | | | | | | | | | | | | | | |
| 7C. VACATION | | | | | | | | | | | | | | | | | | | | | | | | | | | | | | | | |
| 7D. TO, TH, TE, PH, E, M, SW, J | | | | | | | | | | | | | | | | | | | | | | | | | | | | | | | | |
| 7E. L OR A | | | | | | | | | | | | | | | | | | | | | | | | | | | | | | | | |
| 7F. STRAIGHT TIME WO, P, HC, WE | | | | | | | | | | | | | | | | | | | | | | | | | | | | | | | | |
| 7G. PREMIUM TIME WO, P | | | | | | | | | | | | | | | | | | | | | | | | | | | | | | | | |

**8. REASON FOR ABSENCE OR EXTRA HOURS WORKED**  ☐ MEDICAL APPOINTMENT  ☐ DENTAL APPOINTMENT

**9. CERTIFICATE BY EMPLOYEE**
To the best of my knowledge and belief, the facts stated are accurate and in full compliance with legal requirements.

EMPLOYEE SIGNATURE ▶  DATE

**10. RECOMMENDATION AND SUBSTANTIATION OF SUPERVISOR**
☐ APPROVAL RECOMMENDED  ☐ APPROVAL NOT RECOMMENDED

SUBSTANTIATION SHALL BE REQUIRED FOR SICK LEAVE OF MORE THAN TWO CONSECUTIVE WORK DAYS. SHOW METHOD OF VERIFICATION BELOW.

SIGNATURE OF SUPERVISOR ▶  DATE

**11. STATEMENT BY PHYSICIAN** *(Not to be completed by attending physician for industrial illness or injury.)*
☐ DOCTOR STATEMENT ATTACHED
☐ AS PHYSICIAN, I EXAMINED AND TREATED OR PRESCRIBED FOR THIS PATIENT ON THESE DATES

DATE OF RETURN TO WORK | IF STILL DISABLED, GIVE ESTIMATE DATE OF RETURN TO WORK

THE ILLNESS OR INJURY CAUSING THE DISABILITY WAS

SIGNATURE OF ATTENDING PHYSICIAN ▶  DATE

| 12. PERIOD ON DISABILITY COMPENSATION | | 13. DISABILITY COMPENSATION SUPPLEMENT | | | | | 14. OFFICIAL DEPARTMENTAL ACTION | REVIEWED BY |
|---|---|---|---|---|---|---|---|---|
| FROM | TO | HOURS | SICK LEAVE | VACATION | CTO | HOLIDAY CREDIT | ☐ APPROVED____ ☐ DISAPPROVED____ | |

## INSTRUCTIONS

### GENERAL INFORMATION

1. All absences or additional hours worked by full-time or part-time employees should be reported on one Form Std. 634 for each pay period. Report all time worked for permanent intermittent and part-time employees.

2. Prepare the number of copies required by your department. Employees who want a copy for their own records, indicating supervisor's signature, may prepare an extra copy.

### INSTRUCTIONS FOR FILLING OUT FORM STD. 634 BY ITEM NUMBER *(see reverse side)*

1. Enter pay period, month and year and complete other boxes as required by your department.

2-4. Complete name, social security number and position number.

5. Absences With Pay - Check appropriate box, indicating type(s) of absence(s). Furnish all information requested in items requiring additional information. Attach Military Duty orders if applicable.

6. Absences Without Pay (Dock) - Complete all boxes, indicating type of unpaid absence and if the current pay period is qualified or nonqualified. Last box can be checked if employee is serving a probationary period to determine if employee will complete required number of working days.

   *Qualifying Pay Period* - Eleven (11) or more paid days in a monthly pay period.

   *Nonqualifying Pay Period* - Less than eleven (11) paid days in a monthly pay period.

   *Note:* If the employee is absent without pay for more than eleven (11) consecutive working days, which falls between two (2) consecutive otherwise qualifying pay periods, one (1) pay period shall be disqualifying.

7. Dates of Absences and Extra Hours Worked

   7a. Enter time to be paid for each day, including paid absence hours for intermittent or part-time employees.

   *Note:* Enter all hours to be paid in the total column.

   7b. Indicate sick leave hours and appropriate symbol on date of absence.

   Sick Leave shall be used in increments of one (1) hour and is shown on the appropriate date with a symbol "S", "SF", or "SD". If more than two (2) hours is needed for a doctor's appointment, the reason should be stated in item 8. Enter the letter symbol and the number of hours under the number(s) corresponding to the dates being reported.

   Sick Family - An employee may use up to forty (40) hours of sick leave credit for family care during any one calendar year. Unused family care sick leave cannot be carried over for use in another year.

   Sick Death - An employee may use up to five (5) days of their sick leave balance for each family death.

   7c. Vacation shall be used in increments of one (1) hour and is shown on the appropriate date with the symbol "V".

   An absence can be charged against vacation credits only when approved by the appointing power. The time at which vacation shall be taken may be specified to suit the convenience of the department. Vacation cannot be taken as an absolute right unless the appointing power does not provide a vacation for the employee for two successive years.

   7d. Post proper symbol and number of hours for type of absence being reported.

   Paid Educational Leave - Following completion of twelve (12) qualifying pay periods of continuous service, a full-time employee in State civil service employed in a position requiring teaching certification qualification shall be allowed fifteen (15) days credit or educational leave with pay. Thereafter, on the first (1st) of the pay period following each additional qualifying pay period of service, he/she shall be allowed one and one-fourth (1-1/4) days credit for educational leave with pay. The employee may earn or use educational leave credit only while in a position requiring teacher certification qualifications. The granting of paid educational leave is at the discretion of the appointing power.

   Military Leave - Attach a copy of any applicable military order. Every calendar day must be recorded, including any Saturday, Sunday or holiday.

Jury Duty or Subpoenaed Witness - An employee may be absent with pay for time actually served to perform jury duty or for time subpoenaed as a witness in a court case when the employee is neither a party nor an expert witness, providing the employee remits the fee to the State. If the fee is retained, either a charge is made against the employee's accumulated leave balance or absence is without pay. It is up to the employee to demand of the party requesting their appearance a subpoena and whatever fees and travel allowance that may be allowed by law. Witness fees for a civil trial are governed by Government Code Sections 68093 - 68096 and the fee for a criminal trial is governed by Penal Code Section 1329. The employee may keep travel allowance.

7e. Post proper symbol and number of hours for type of absence reporting, either an approved absence without pay (dock) or an unapproved absence without pay (AWOL).

   An Unapproved Absence Without Pay - Can be for any amount of time up to five (5) working days. If the AWOL exceeds five (5) consecutive working days, this constitutes an automatic resignation from State service.

7f. Enter symbols and hours to be compensated at *straight* time as indicated below:
   WO — Overtime hours worked for CTO
   P — Overtime hours worked for pay
   HC — (CSUC only) Hours worked on a holiday
   WE — Excess hours worked due to irregular work shift

7g. Enter symbols and hours to be compensated at *premium* time as indicated below (Personnel Office will convert to time and one-half (1-1/2):
   WO — Overtime hours worked for CTO
   P — Overtime hours worked for pay

   *Note:* Total column may be used for items 7b through 7g.

8. Reason for Absence or Extra Hours Worked - Employee must indicate reason for sick leave absences, including relationship of family member when reporting family sick leave.

   *Note* - This item can also be used for reporting reasons for overtime hours worked or for unpaid absences.

9. Employee's Responsibility and Signature - Employees have the responsibility to give their supervisor advance notification when they anticipate a future absence. When unanticipated emergency causes the absence, the employees are responsible for notifying supervisor as soon as possible and keeping their supervisor informed as to the possible date of return. Employees are also responsible for promptly reviewing and signing their absence report at the end of the pay period and submitting to supervisor.

10. Recommendation of Supervisor's Responsibility - Each supervisor is responsible for seeing that employees comply with the regulations governing absence from work. The supervisor is expected to recommend against approval of sick leave absences when satisfactory evidence as to need is not presented. Supervisor is then responsible for promptly reviewing and signing the employee's absence report and forwarding it to the Personnel Office.

   Before recommending approval for sick leave by an INTERMITTENT EMPLOYEE, supervisor shall certify that the employee was scheduled to work during the hours reported for sick leave.

   *Note:* Methods of verfication can include telephone, physician statement, home or hospital visit.

11. Statements By Physicians - If physician statement is attached, check first box and do not complete other information in this item.

   If supervisor has requested the physician's verification on this form, second box is checked and the doctor completes each item and signs the form.

12-13. Applicable information regarding absences due to industrial injury or illness should be recorded in this area.

14. Completed by Personnel Office only.

Report of Employee Absence or Tardiness
(Large northern utility)

## REPORT OF EMPLOYEE ABSENCE OR TARDINESS

| | | | | | | DATE OF REPORT | | TIME | AM PM |
|---|---|---|---|---|---|---|---|---|---|
| NAME_____ | | REPORTED BY_____ | | | | | | | |
| CAN BE REACHED AT_____ | | | PHONE NO._____ | | | DATE OF ABSENCE_____ | | | |
| DEPARTMENT: | | | | SCHEDULED HOURS OF WORK | | SCHEDULED DAYS OFF | | | |

| REASON AND DATA | | | | | | FOLLOW-UP | |
|---|---|---|---|---|---|---|---|
| ☐ ILL* ☐ FULL DAY ☐ PART DAY | | HOURS: | | HOSPITALIZED: ☐ YES ☐ NO | | BY | DATE |
| ☐ INJURED* | HOURS: | ☐ ON DUTY ☐ OFF DUTY | DATE INJURED: | | | COMMENT | |
| ☐ DEATH IN FAMILY | HOURS: | RELATIONSHIP: | MEMBER OF HOUSEHOLD: ☐ YES ☐ NO | | | | |
| ☐ OTHER* | HOURS: | ☐ TARDY * MINUTES: | HOURS: | | | | |
| *NATURE AND/OR REASON | | | | | | BY | DATE |
| | | | | | | COMMENT | |
| | | | | | | | |
| | | | | | | | |
| DOCTOR'S NAME | | | | | | BY | DATE |
| DOCTOR'S ADDRESS | | | | | | COMMENT | |
| PREPARED BY | | NUMBER OF ABSENCES PRIOR 12 MONTHS | | | | | |

| RECOMMENDED ACTION | | | |
|---|---|---|---|
| DOCTOR'S CERTIFICATE REQUIRED: ☐ YES ☐ NO | | **RETURNED TO WORK** | |
| INVESTIGATION: ☐ PERSONAL VISIT ☐ TELEPHONE | | DATE TIME AM PM | |
| REMARKS: | | | |
| | | APPROVED | |
| PAY: ☐ YES ☐ NO APPROVED | | | |

DD-0015 4684 3-80

Attending Physician's Statement
(Large central bank)

**ATTENDING PHYSICIAN'S STATEMENT**

| TO BE COMPLETED BY EMPLOYEE | | | |
|---|---|---|---|
| EMPLOYEE NO. | EMPLOYEE NAME | DIVISION | DEPARTMENT |
| DATE OF INJURY OR ILLNESS | NATURE OF INJURY OR ILLNESS | | |
| IF INJURY, WHERE AND HOW DID IT HAPPEN | | | |

I hereby authorize any hospital, physician, employee, insurance company, or other organization to release to _____ or its authorized representative, any and all information they may have with respect to any sickness or injury, including past and present medical history, diagnosis, consultations, treatments, operative procedures, X-Rays and pathological findings. I agree that a photostat copy of this authorization shall be considered as effective as the original.

EMPLOYEE'S SIGNATURE

DATE

| TO BE COMPLETED BY ATTENDING PHYSICIAN | | | |
|---|---|---|---|
| DATE FIRST CONSULTED BY PATIENT | DATE OF NEXT APPOINTMENT | PREGNANCY  ☐ YES  ☐ NO | IF YES, EXPECTED DELIVERY DATE |

DIAGNOSIS OR CONCURRENT CONDITION OF PATIENT

| DATE INJURED OR SYMPTOMS FIRST APPEARED | IS CONDITION RELATED TO EMPLOYMENT  ☐ YES  ☐ NO | IS PATIENT STILL UNDER YOUR CARE  ☐ YES  ☐ NO | EXPECTED TREATMENT DURATION | DATE PATIENT ABLE TO RETURN TO WORK |
|---|---|---|---|---|
| PATIENT WAS CONFINED IN HOSPITAL  FROM:  TO: | | PATIENT WAS CONFINED IN HOUSE  FROM:  TO: | | |
| PATIENT WAS TOTALLY DISABLED (UNABLE TO WORK)  FROM:  TO: | | PATIENT WAS PARTIALLY DISABLED  FROM:  TO: | | |

REMARKS: (PARTIAL DISABILITY, WORK LIMITATIONS, MEDICATIONS, COMMENTS, ETC.)

May patient continue and/or resume normal duties without any limitations:

[ ] Yes   [ ] No.   If "No", please explain:

Any other comments:

| PHYSICIAN'S NAME | BUSINESS ADDRESS | CITY | STATE | ZIP CODE |
|---|---|---|---|---|
| BUSINESS TELEPHONE | PHYSICIAN'S SIGNATURE | | DATE | |

| TO BE COMPLETED BY PERSONNEL DEPARTMENT | | | |
|---|---|---|---|
| DATE EMPLOYEE LAST WORKED | FIRST FULL WORKING DAY ABSENT | W/C CLAIM FILED | DATE RETURNED TO WORK |
| REMARKS | | | |

| CLAIM PROCESSED BY | DATE | CLAIM APPROVED BY: | DATE |
|---|---|---|---|

610-1274-85120

Attendance Reminder
(Large northern manufacturer)

### A T T E N D A N C E   R E M I N D E R

NAME_____        EMPLOYEE NUMBER_____

DATE_____        SHIFT_____ DEPARTMENT_____

You have been fully instructed in the Company Attendance Policy. This is to
remind you of the rules as set forth in that policy and to call your attention
to the following infraction:

_____

_____

_____

_____

_____

_____

This reminder is to emphasize that you must abide by the Company Attendance Policy,
and, that per the procedures of the policy, if another infraction occurs within
six (6) months, you will receive a pre-discharge warning.

It is our hope that you will be successful in your job and have a long and satisfactor
career with ———  I hope that this session will enable you to better understand
our policy and your importance to the Company.

Should there be any doubts concerning policies or procedures, I will be glad to go
over them with you now or at any other mutually agreeable time.

*Employee_____

Foreman_____

Department Manager_____

*Your signature is to signify only that this warning has been discussed with you and
is not meant to be necessarily construed as an agreement on your part.

Pre-Discharge Warning for Attendance
(Large northern manufacturer)

## P R E - D I S C H A R G E   W A R N I N G   F O R   A T T E N D A N C E

NAME_____   EMPLOYEE NUMBER_____

DATE _____   SHIFT_____   DEPARTMENT _____

    You have received a written warning for failure to comply with our Company
Attendance Policy, as instructed, on _____.
You have again failed to comply in accordance with our Company Attendance Policy
as follows:

_____

_____

_____

_____

_____

    This is a pre-discharge warning to let you know that you must abide by the
Company Attendance Policy.  If it becomes necessary to warn you again within the
next six months, you will be released from the employ of the company.

*Employee_____

Foreman _____

Department Manager _____

Personnel Manager _____

*Your signature is to signify only that this warning has been discussed with you
and is not meant to be necessarily construed as an agreement on your part. .

# Appendix B

# Xerox Corp. No-Fault Discipline Program

The following forms were reprinted with permission from Xerox Corp., Rochester, NY.

# BARGAINING UNIT LETTER

## XEROX   Internal Memo

**TO:**
ALL MONROE COUNTY BARGAINING
UNIT EMPLOYEES

**FROM:**
XEROX CORPORATION

**SUBJECT:**
XEROX ABSENTEEISM CONTROL
PROGRAM

**DATE:**
December 15 1983

On January 1, 1984, the Xerox Absenteeism Control Program begins for all
Monroe County Bargaining Unit employees:

### WHAT ARE THE RULES?

If, during any consecutive *12 month* period, you are absent on *4 Occasions*, or
if within any consecutive *24 month* period you are absent on *6 Occasions*, your
employment with the Company will be terminated.

### WHAT'S AN "OCCASION"?

An Occasion of Absence consists of 2 or more hours in any work day or a series
of working days during which you are absent from work.   This includes
absences on days when you are scheduled to work overtime.

### ARE THERE ANY EXCEPTIONS?

Occasions of Absence shall *not* include the following:
o Paid holidays (except for absence on a holiday on which you are scheduled
  to work)
o Regularly scheduled vacation
o A single day of vacation if taken with prior supervisory approval or if
  taken on account of illness
o Authorized leaves-of-absence
o Jury duty
o Death in the immediate family
o Emergency community service
o Workers Compensation injury
o Maternity leaves-of-absence
o Company declared snow closings
o Tardiness or early leaving for less than 2 hours.

### WILL I BE NOTIFIED OF ABSENCES?

The Company will notify you and your Shop Representative when you have
been absent on 2 Occasions within a consecutive 12 month period and/or
when you have been absent on 4 Occasions within a consecutive 24 month
period.

### WHAT IF I HAVE SERIOUS MEDICAL PROBLEMS?

You may have your case appealed to a Review Committee if you have a serious
medical problem (such as a heart condition or cancer) which requires sudden
repetitive short-term absences, or if you have any other condition which
requires absences for special medical treatments such as dialysis.

### MAY I GRIEVE TERMINATION UNDER THIS PROGRAM?

You may grieve your termination only where you believe that there have been
procedural violations of the provisions outlined above (for example if you
were not notified after 2 or 4 Occasions or if you were charged with an
Occasion for one of the exceptions).

XEROX ABSENTEEISM PROGRAM
(To be used as a Supervisor's Guide only: not as a
representation of the actual contractual agreement)

CONTRACTUAL AGREEMENT

Commencing January 1, 1984, when an employee is absent from
work on four (4) Occasions of Absence in any consecutive twelve
(12) month period or six (6) Occasions of Absence in any consecutive twenty-four (24) month period the employee shall be
terminated unless such termination is not upheld by the unanimous
decision of a three (3) member Medical Review Committee.

SCOPE

All Monroe County hourly paid employees.

DEFINITIONS

Occasion of Absence:

Two (2) or more hours in any work day, or a series of
consecutive working days, during which an employee is
absent from work, including absences which occur when the
employee has been scheduled to work overtime, unless
caused by any of the following reasons:

- Paid Holidays (unless the employee was scheduled to
  work on that holiday)
- Vacations
- Authorized Leaves of Absence
- Jury Duty
- Death in the Immediate Family
- Emergency Community Service
- Workers' Compensation Absence
- Maternity Absence
- Company Declared Snow-Day Closings
- Tardiness or Early Leaving for Less than Two (2) Hours

Medical Review Committee:

A committee of three (3) members, each representing one of
the following: the Union, the Company Medical Department, and either Industrial Relations or Operating Management.

Termination:

Permanent separation from Xerox Corporation.

PROCEDURE

Supervisors of hourly paid employees shall be responsible for maintaining accurate records as they relate to employee attendance, utilizing predetermined codes.

When these records reflect that an employee has accumulated two (2) Occasions of Absence, as defined above, within any consecutive twenty-four (24) month period, the Supervisor shall: Complete the Absenteeism Notification Form (attached); review the completed form with the employee informing the employee of the employee's status as relates to this program; distribute the form to the employee, Unit Industrial Relations, the appropriate Union Representative, and the employee file; and record the notification event in the employee's Travel Record. Unit Industrial Relations will, in turn, distribute copies to the General Shop Representative and the Business Agent for the Union.

This notification procedure shall be repeated immediately following each subsequent Occasion of Absence until such time as:

A) The employee is terminated, or . . .
B) The instant Occasion of Absence represents the first within the immediately preceding twenty-four (24) month period.

When the employee accrues four (4) Occasions of Absence in any consecutive twelve (12) month period or six (6) Occasions of Absence in any twenty-four (24) month period, the Supervisor shall notify the employee, the Industrial Relations Representative, and the appropriate Union Representative of the employee's termination. The employee shall have an opportunity to meet with the Union prior to surrendering the security badge and vacating Company premises. The Supervisor shall then make a termination entry in the Employee Travel Record. In no case should an employee be terminated and removed from Company premises without first having an opportunity to meet with a representative of the Union.

If the employee's inability to attend work regularly was directly associated with "serious medical problems such as heart condition or cancer, which require sudden repetitive short-term absences, or any other condition which requires recurring absences for special medical treatments such as dialysis," then the termination may be appealed by either Management or the Union to the Medical Review Committee. The employee shall not be terminated if the committee unanimously endorses exception under this program.

ABSENTEEISM NOTIFICATION FORM

EMPLOYEE NAME _____   CLOCK NUMBER _____

SUPERVISOR NAME _____   ORGANIZATION _____

On this date, _____, the above-named employee was notified of his/her status with respect to the Xerox Absenteeism Program. Specifically, he/she has accumulated the following Occasions of Absence in the past twelve (12) and/or twenty-four (24) month period:

**DATE(S) OF OCCASION**

_____   _____

_____   _____

_____   _____

_____   _____

| |
|---|
| Absences of two hours or greater for any reason other than: Paid Holidays, Vacations, Authorized Leaves of Absence, Jury Duty, Death in the Immediate Family, Emergency Community Service, Workers Compensation Absence, Maternity Absence and Company-Declared, Snow-Day closings are considered as Occasions of Absence under this plan. |
| Accumulation of four (4) Occasions of Absence in any twelve (12) month period or six (6) Occasions of Absence in any twenty-four (24) month period shall result in termination. |

Supervisor's Signature: _____   Date: _____

Distribution:
Employee
Employee File
Shop Representative
Industrial Relations Representative
Central Industrial Relations File (208-E)
- General Shop Representative
- Union Business Agent
*Statement in Travel Record

Pre-Scheduled Vacation Day Request

XEROX

---

INSTRUCTIONS:

1. Employees who are entitled to more than two (2) weeks' vacation in any calendar year may opt to use one (1) week of vacation entitlement in excess of two (2) weeks in single day increments.
2. Employees must designate one (1) week of vacation entitlement to be used in single day increments on the Hourly Vacation Request form submitted to their supervisors by December 15 preceding the calendar year of the vacation.
3. Employees and their supervisors must complete this form for all single day vacation requests <u>except</u> those used for personal illness. The completed form should be placed in the employee's file.

---

        is requesting a

_____  _____
      Employee Name          Employee Number

vacation day on _____  The request was granted/denied on
          Date to be Taken  .

_____.
    Date

The request was denied for the following reason(s):  _____

_____

_____

_____

_____


               _____
               Supervisor's Signature

               _____
               Employee's Signature

---

FORM 59407X (10/83)        Xerographic Master - Reproduce Needs

# Index

## A